Public Theology
in Cultural Engagement

Public Theology
in Cultural Engagement

Editor
STEPHEN R. HOLMES

Paternoster:
thinking faith

MILTON KEYNES • COLORADO SPRINGS • HYDERABAD

14 13 12 11 10 09 08   7 6 5 4 3 2 1

First published 2008 by Paternoster
Paternoster is an imprint of Authentic Media
9 Holdom Avenue, Bletchley, Milton Keynes, Bucks, MK1 1QR, UK
1820 Jet Stream Drive, Colorado Springs, CO 80921, USA
Medchal Road, Jeedimetla Village, Secunderabad 500 055, A.P., India
www.authenticmedia.co.uk

*Paternoster is a division of IBS-STL U.K., limited by guarantee, with its Registered Office at
Kingstown Broadway, Carlisle, Cumbria CA3 0HA. Registered in England & Wales No. 1216232.
Registered charity 270162*

British Library Cataloguing in Publication Data
A catalogue record for this book is available from the British Library

ISBN: 978–1–84227–542–9

Cover Design by James Kessell for Scratch the Sky Ltd (www.scratchthesky.com)
Print Management by Adare
Typeset by Waverley Typesetters, Fakenham
Printed and bound in Great Britain by J.H. Haynes & Co., Sparkford

Contents

Foreword

Bible Society operates on the basis that the Bible is intended to be a public text. The grounds for this are numerous: they include the fact that the biblical narrative is grounded in God's actions in creating the universe, and also in the apparently innocuous claim, 'Jesus Christ is Lord'. This, however, is no claim from some Hellenistic mystery religion. It is a full-orbed assertion that the entire world and all the culture of the Roman Empire (that is, all known culture) are subject to Jesus Christ, whose story is the focal point of the whole Bible.

This understanding of the Bible implies that Bible Society wishes to encourage the use of the Bible within the public spaces of our cultures. Whether Christ is considered to condemn, critique or create culture is, at one level, open for discussion. What is not open is that, from our perspective, all culture has some relationship to him and the Bible.

Hence, we are intentionally exploring how the Bible engages with the four key cultural areas in our society: the arts, education, the media, and politics. Equally, we wish to engage those who live and work in these areas to become more open to engaging with the Bible as a core text for informing and inspiring their work.

This book represents some of the ground-breaking and foundational thinking in this territory which Bible Society has initiated. Instrumental in sensing the importance of this issue and in constructing the early approach was Dr Colin Greene, one of whose essays is included. As you can read in more detail in Dr Stephen Holmes' introduction, the essays which form this book come from a number of symposia which we have sponsored during recent years. Of particular poignancy, but also importance, is the essay by Colin Gunton. Publishing all of them in this book is another important step in disseminating the learning we are generating, but also in seeding ongoing discussions and conversations. It is this process of grasping the value and richness of the biblical text for our culture, which we desire to see enlarged and deepened. We have already taken further steps in this direction, including an exploration within the educational field of the concept of human flourishing. This was undertaken through a conference held in Seattle with the Education School of the university there. Further, we are in partnership with St Andrews University to develop their excellent M.Litt. course, 'Bible and the Contemporary World'. This will enable professionals and practioners from the arts, education, the media, and politics to add theological competence to their range of perspectives, and so foster a community of people who take the confession 'Jesus Christ is Lord' seriously into their contexts.

We are most grateful to Dr Holmes for the lead he has taken in our Public Theology and Cultural Engagement project and we commend this book to you as a testimony to his work, but also for your careful reflection and, as appropriate, application.

DAVID SPRIGGS
Bible and Church Consultant
Bible Society

Introduction

'Public Theology in Cultural Engagement' was the title of a partnership project between the Research Institute in Systematic Theology at King's College London and the British and Foreign Bible Society. Begun under the guidance of Colin Gunton at King's and Colin Greene at Bible Society, it was wound up after Colin Gunton's death. Before that time, three conferences were held under the flag of PTCE; the papers in this volume are collected from the first two, held in 2002 and 2003.

The aims of the PTCE project were to:

- explore the possibilities of offering a theological account of the nature of human culture in general, and the characteristics of particular human cultures
- disseminate the results of such explorations by publication and other means
- create and disseminate tools to aid in the analysis of particular cultural contexts with a view to furthering Christian engagement with, and transformation of, cultures

These aims have not been forgotten, and are being carried on, particularly by Bible Society, in other ways. The papers in this book are most closely directed towards the first aim, to give a theological account of the notion of culture, and of cultural realities. This procedure itself perhaps needs defence: culture and its manifestations are, it might seem, best spoken of in sociological or anthropological terms; for a theologian to attempt to speak of culture theologically is an improper trespassing on someone else's business.

If I may be allowed a personal anecdote, such views appear to have been in place when I trained for Christian ministry. The denomination within which I was preparing to minister, and the college at which

I trained, both recognised the importance of pastors engaging with the cultural realities around them. To that end, sociology formed an important part of the curriculum, but there was no attempt to engage with the theorised critiques of sociology (and other social sciences) that have been so common in recent decades. This matters, or so I believe, because these critiques uncover the fact that socio-scientific analysis and description are not value-neutral, but rather are undertaken from a variety of committed positions, with the implicit values determining the fields of investigation and the results. As a result, there was a genuine danger that the development of the necessary skills for engaging with cultural contexts in future pastors would be, not just inattentive to any Christian theological account of the nature of those realities, but actually, if unconsciously, based on alternative accounts. It seems to me, therefore, that there is a need to develop the theoretical basis and the practical tools for a properly theological analysis of cultural contexts, with a view to equipping the church to be able to engage contemporary realities with theological truth, and to understand how to identify the relevance of biblical texts and values in their particular contexts.

All of which is to say that the PTCE project, and hence the papers in this volume, were intended to be *theological*. There is no intention here of working on the interface between theology and sociology, cultural studies, social anthropology, or any other field; what is being looked for is not a vaguely Christian form of sociology, but a thoroughly theological and biblical analysis. This is not to say that insights from other fields would not be relevant, welcome, and valuable, but it is to say that the intention behind the conferences and this publication was that the conversation and analysis that took place would be theological, rather than sociological and it is to assume and assert that theological analysis of cultural realities is possible, worthwhile and interesting. This assertion perhaps needs some defence and explication.

Christian theology necessarily claims to be able to speak truthfully about all present realities. The doctrine of creation *ex nihilo* was perhaps the first of the great patristic slogans which defended and defined Christian faith in the face of Hellenistic philosophies. A central implication of this dogma is that nothing that exists is either beyond God's control or not willed (or at least permitted) by God. The doctrine thus defends key scriptural data such as the naming of all that is as good in Genesis 1, or the insistence found throughout the Psalms and Prophets that, despite the claims of surrounding paganisms, the God of Abraham is God of all the earth, not limited in power by location, nationality, or particular function. Theology, on this account, is not locally true, for particular peoples, places, or situations, but universally

– and so publicly – true, and so publicly engaged with all created realities.

Greek philosophical notions of eternally existent matter out of which the deity shaped the world (as, for instance, in Plato's *Timaeus*), later gave rise to quasi-religious accounts, as in some varieties of Gnosticism, which insisted that the material world was evil and opposed to God. Whether eternal matter is seen as merely neutral, or as fundamentally evil, if it exists then there are aspects of current reality that are opaque to theology (as demonstrated by platonic and neo-platonic philosophies, which found little or nothing to say of the material world, other than the suggestion that it was an imperfect image of the spiritual realm – this intuition lies behind even the relatively positive estimations of the material found in Porphyry and Plotinus). Once again, the implication of the Christian doctrine of creation *ex nihilo* is that Christian theology can claim to be able to speak about every existing reality.

It is currently popular in theology to engage in conversations with other disciplines: 'theology and ...' is a common style, and even much that claims to be straightforward dogmatics, nonetheless, feels the need to listen to sociological, psychological or scientific statements with great respect. This tendency is understandable: the recent history of Western culture has seen an arrogant, and apparently irrelevant, theology deposed and derided, and so the humility to seek to come as no more than an equal conversation partner seems an appropriate mode of theological discourse. If the analysis hinted at in the previous paragraphs has any truth, however, then theology is denying its own central tenets if it seeks to approach any other discipline as an equal conversation partner. Rather, Christian theology must have the confidence to be what it is: a coherent account of all created realities in relation to God through Jesus Christ and the Holy Spirit, and of the God to whom we are thus related.

In all of this there is, of course, the possibility of an improper arrogance, but that arrogance does not lie in theologians claiming that theology makes claims about ultimate and basic realities: it necessarily does. Rather, the arrogance is found when theologians pretend that they can be expert in other fields than theology, and so seek too hastily to speak about the place of other fields, or the way theology may converse with them. The failures of eighteenth-century theology lay in the assumption that an expert theologian was competent to speak on matters of science or political philosophy, without pausing to understand these matters. (It is, incidentally, noticeable that relatively few of the 'theology and ...' proposals have been taken with any seriousness by the communities they claim to be in dialogue with.

I suspect that this is simply because they so often disregard good theology in favour of a fairly amateur practice of a different discipline by a theologian not trained in it. It may be that such projects share more than they would like to believe with the disastrous theological arrogance of an earlier age.)

An appropriately humble theology, then, will practice what John Webster has described as an ascesis: it will set its face against the fascinating and alluring paths that are on offer, the paths that seem to promise a shortcut to relevant and interesting results; instead, it will focus solely on its own subject matter: the person of Jesus Christ, as revealed in the texts of Scripture and reflected on in the doctrinal tradition of the church. It will do this with the confidence, the hope, and the prayer that in these texts will be found the key to understanding all truth and all that is truly relevant, because these texts offer the necessary insight for comprehending, and engaging with, even the present age. Of course, a part of the necessary humility of theology is the confession that, for all our efforts, we will never know fully until the day when we, and all things, are made new. But, until that day, the task of seeking to know, in humble dependence on the Spirit and as far as is possible for us, how God's all sufficient act in Christ is sufficient for our present cultural situation will remain an urgent one. In expressing the hope that the conversation of which this book is a record would be theological, it is this asceticism that was meant: many attractive possibilities were actively ignored in order to remain true to the essential nature of theology: the pursuit of deeper knowledge of Christ through the text of Scripture.

So, we intended a theological conversation. Nothing in the above denies the possibility or utility of other conversations, but it does assert the possibility and the importance of a conversation that is unashamedly theological. Inasmuch as the subject matter of the conversation is cultural realities, we tried to listen with gratitude to descriptions of those realities offered by other disciplines (whilst being alert to the necessarily theorised nature of such descriptions), but our analysis sought to be only theological, and attempted primarily to bring the biblical texts to bear on present constructions and artefacts of human culture.

I have argued that Christian theology must claim to be able to speak about all human realities; where the reality in question is cultural, however, further work needs to be done. There is a strong platonic strain in Christian theology, represented by such influential works as Augustine's *The City of God* or, rather differently, Coleridge's *On the Constitution of Church and State*. Here, an account of reality as that which is eternal, and so timeless, leads not so much to a denigration of the material as to a denigration of the temporal, and so a denial of the goodness of history. One mark of this is often as eschatology of return (contrast Irenaeus' account of the world 'growing up', where a development from creation to an eschatological vision that is different to the first perfection is precisely a part of the goodness of creation, or Edwards' thoroughly temporal account of eschatology, where progression, movement and change will not cease, because they are proper to created beings). In Augustine's estimation, there is little theologically interesting to say about the City of Man; it is an attempt, proper in itself, but ultimately of no significance, to cope with the present fallen world until it passes away. On this account, human culture is just not sufficiently theologically interesting.

The biblical data, however, is more positive about human culture than this. The protological pictures themselves suggest not a timeless resting in the garden, but a history that is to unfold under the hand of providence. Moving out from the garden, humanity is to 'fill the earth and subdue it' and to 'have dominion'; there is wilderness beyond the garden, and the garden itself is to be tended, and so God's creative work of bringing order out of chaos is to be completed, and preserved, through the priestly activity of human beings. This suggests that human history is not just a response to the fallenness of the present age, but a good intended by the Creator. More broadly, the overarching narrative of the Scriptures, moving from a garden to a city, must, I think, be taken seriously as an indication of God's intention for his creation. The products of human culture are not done away with in the end, but incorporated into the New Jerusalem.

All of this is to say that the basic biblical narrative of creation, fall, redemption, and consummation is a narrative that can explain and critique those human realities that are generally described as cultural. The further questions immediately raised by this statement are those that the PTCE project was designed to answer: most basically, how do we define 'culture' theologically? Given a definition, what can be said about culture on the basis of the basic contours of Christian dogmatics (the doctrine of God, Christology, creation, the fall, redemption, consummation, …)? If this leads to a theological account of human culture, what of human cultures? How much can we say theologically about particular human cultural realities – can we write theologically of market economics, fast food, the developments from Dixieland jazz to bebop, patterns of purchase of celebrity magazines, or whatever?

Many of the papers in this book pick up these issues. Stephen Holmes ('Can theology engage with culture?') opens up the question on a theoretical level. It is followed by a series of papers discussing the issue through the lens of particular biblical, theological, or historical data: Holmes again on the Torah; Colin Greene on Christology; Robert Jenson on election; and Colin Gunton on the Reformers. In the second part of the book, the turn is from the theoretical issue to practical examples: Greene again on the concept of religion; Luke Bretherton on drug culture and nationalism, and Brian Horne on art.

A theological account of culture is a pressing need at present: not only are cultural realities changing with great rapidity, and fragmenting, in the Western world; but the postmodern condition seeks to understand all realities in cultural terms. Just as during the Enlightenment, Christian theology was marginalised by an account of reality that assumed explanations based on the natural sciences were adequate to all things, so today it seems as if a similar situation may be arising, but now one based on social and cultural sciences.

There is a need, then, for theological engagement with cultural realities and, to work effectively, this must be public: able to take its place in the 'marketplace of ideas', because it is offering a powerful and compelling account of the nature of that 'marketplace' and all other cultural realities. As Karl Barth argued, just because theology necessarily talks about human action, no theological construction is complete until it issues in imperative address, and so a theology of culture cannot stop at analysis, but must move on to engagement and to active transformation. We thus began this project with the intention that the theological analyses of cultural realities that the project produced would involve judgements, and call for things to be different. Our intended outcome was missiological. That strand, too, is visible in the papers in this volume.

As editor, I am grateful to Bible Society for their initial sponsorship of, and continued interest in, this project; to David Spriggs for writing the foreword, and to the contributors for their patience in what has been a convoluted and protracted road to publication. I hope this final product is regarded by all as worth the work and the wait.

STEPHEN R. HOLMES
St Mary's College
St Andrews
Advent, 2006

1

Can Theology Engage with Culture?

Stephen R. Holmes

Introduction

At least a part of the reason for considering 'the theology of culture' is an intuition that the cultural sciences – sociology, anthropology, cultural studies and so on – are becoming increasingly central to intellectual debate. An analogy might be drawn with the rise of the natural sciences in the seventeenth century; this was the growth area, where serious and compelling intellectual advances were being made; any work which did not engage with it was marginalised and regarded as old-fashioned, willfully obscure or simply irrelevant.

A similar picture is increasingly true of academic discourse today; the postmodern turn that theorises and deconstructs all claims to knowledge, exposing sociological or hegemonic controls behind what were once considered straightforwardly empirical developments, is reaching the stage where it is becoming difficult for anyone to be taken seriously in the general academy without at least a nod in this direction. This tendency has reached as far as those bastions of naive empiricism, the natural sciences: even in popular level discourse, as perhaps the magazine *New Scientist*, discussions of how not just the direction, but also the results, of scientific research have been culturally driven are common.

Certain forms of theology have been at the forefront of this move: the rise of local theologies – liberationist, feminist, black, queer and the various combined versions – has alerted all theologians to the potential power claims implicit in their constructions, and a proper concern with the nature of theological language has sometimes served to intensify the suspicions, as when it is all but claimed that God-talk serves no other purpose than the legitimisation of improper hegemonies.

The project which spawned this book was a part of the Bible Society's campaign to restore the place of Scripture in public discourse, and it is, in part, this suspicion, ironically created and fuelled by theologians and biblical scholars, that makes such a task difficult: if the Bible is seen as an ancient document that has been elevated to protect patriarchal, racist or, in other ways, oppressive structures, there will be no reason for its voice to be heard in public conversations, and indeed, every reason to actively work to silence it.

There is also a style of theology that has been impatient with such moves and robust in its assertion that, without ignoring the philosophical difficulties, still language about God may be taken to accurately refer, as God has been pleased to reveal himself, or commandeer our language, and so make such accurate reference possible. In contrast to the picture outlined above, this approach insists that God speaks in Scripture, and that God speaks truth. And so the Scriptures should have not just a place, but a central place, in public discourse. This is the broad historic orthodoxy of Christian faith, upheld by the creedal confession that 'He has spoken through the prophets', and that all that happened in the life, death and resurrection of Jesus Christ was indeed 'according to the Scriptures'. This is what is witnessed to by the liturgies of our churches, whether greeting the Scripture readings with the communal affirmation 'This is the Word of the Lord' and with heartfelt praise, or standing for the entrance of the Bible at the beginning of a traditional free-church service. To believe so does not remove the problems recognised above, but it does perhaps give a hope that, with sufficient work and prayer, they may be more amenable to solution than at first sight they seemed. This paper proceeds on the basis of such a hope.

If the comparison of the postmodern rise of the cultural sciences with the modern rise of the natural sciences that I hinted at above is at all just however, the espousal of such a position carries a great risk. To ignore or refuse the challenge of the cultural sciences creates the danger of removing oneself from the mainstream of public discourse, of speaking in such a way that only those who already agree will listen, whilst others will simply laugh or mock, not quite believing that anyone can have failed so thoroughly to keep in touch with the modern questions. The term that often describes such a risk in theology is 'sectarian'.

Now, let me immediately say two things about this risk. The first is that to suggest that a position be abandoned solely because it carries a risk of being 'out of touch' is simply a failure of logic. If there ever was a period when most people were convinced that the earth was flat, that did not stop it from being round. The argument, if I may dignify it with that name, that is heard in theology from time to time, and fairly often in Christian ethics, that we must not accept such and such a position because it is 'sectarian', because it fails to connect with the current mainstream of public discourse, has no logical validity as a moment's thought will show. Second, however, this does not prevent the risk being real: Christian faith was seriously marginalised by the scientific revolution, in a whole series of ways, and we are still living with the results of that. The continually disputed place of theology in the university is only one witness to that, albeit a powerful one.

The task of theology is not merely to speak the truth; it is also to ensure that the truth can be heard. The real danger of sectarianism is not that we lose the respect of the intellectual community, or risk being excluded from certain forms of public debate. It is, rather, the danger of making the gospel of Christ something that cannot be heard or understood beyond the fenced walls of the 'Lord's Vineyard'. Hence, whilst there is an important truth in the idea that theology should simply go about its own work, untroubled by the shifting winds of fashion that surround, it must always be remembered that a part of the work of theology is to enable the hearing of the truth that it seeks to explore.

Further, it is in no way a retreat from the position I am advocating to accept that theology can, and indeed has, been misused for the establishment and maintenance of improper hegemonies. The history of the church is littered with such practices, the most lasting perhaps being the attempt to exclude certain people on grounds of their ethnic origin – clearly already a problem in the Pauline churches of the New Testament, and still a part of the dogmatic tradition of at least one mainstream church in South Africa until fairly recently. That such practices are supported only by bad theology is beside the point: it is not obvious that such theology is bad theology to those practising it, and the question of what is good and bad theology is, in any case, one that demands theological work to answer. There is, thus, a proper vigilance in theological work, alive to the possibilities of the human activity of theology becoming demonic, being used to support improper attempts to dominate and dehumanise those whom God created in his own image, and for whom he sent his Son to die. We must be constantly on our guard against such dangers, whilst insisting that theology which is true to its own calling will necessarily be liberative, in the sense of establishing the proper humanity of all people.

The present intellectual context thus offers two real and pressing tasks for theological work: on the one hand, to hear and, with due humility, accept the critique of bad theology which has been oppressive to so many – women, non-Europeans and so on – and, on the other hand, to engage with the fashionable postmodern practices of deconstruction and to deconstruct them, to insist that we have been graciously given truth, and so that language about God, and in consequence all other language, may yet adequately refer and communicate. The latter task will require epistemological work, based finally, I suspect, on a robust pneumatology; it will also, if it is indeed the social and cultural sciences that are driving the (post)modern critiques, require us to find a robustly theological way of speaking of culture. Hence, finally, the question posed by my title: can theology engage with culture?

The stages of my argument in seeking to give an affirmative answer to this question are as follows: This introduction will end with a brief definition of culture. Then I will suggest that whilst theology can speak meaningfully about most realities on the basis of a doctrine of creation, there are in fact certain clear limits. Third, I will observe that cultural realities have often been located beyond those limits, but suggest that this location is incorrect. This will be the major part of the paper. Finally, I will offer some suggestions as to how theology might engage with culture.

There is one more piece of introductory material that is necessary: a definition of 'culture'. This is a notoriously difficult task.[1] Nonetheless, we need a working definition, and so let me offer one, not my own, which at least brings out those aspects of the concept which I presently regard as most theologically interesting, 'a culture is a particular collection of socially learned ways of living found in human societies'.[2]

The key implication here is that a culture is, to use a good postmodern phrase, a constructed reality. Just as the world we inhabit is composed of physical limits, aspects of its being which just are and which we cannot escape, so each of us lives in a context in which there are certain cultural limits, ways in which we relate together and interpret the world that come to us from without and are non-negotiable. To take a trivial example, the discomfort of my train journey each morning, when I used to work in central London, was partly a result of the physical shape of that city, such that no more trains could run into Waterloo station than presently do, and partly a result of a cultural assumption

---

[1] See, for instance, Neil J. Smelser, 'Culture: Coherent or Incoherent' in *Theories of Culture (New Directions in Cultural Analysis 2)* (ed. Richard Münch and Neil J. Smelser; Oxford: University of California Press, 1992), 3–28, particularly the trends and references he lists under the title 'Vagueness' on p. 21.

[2] Marvin Harris, *Theories of Culture in Postmodern Times* (London: Altamira Press, 1999), 19.

that 9:00am is the right time to start work in the morning, leading to those trains that arrive at Waterloo just prior to nine carrying several times as many people than trains even thirty minutes later, despite significantly cheaper fares on the later trains.

These cultural givens are humanly constructed, but equally they construct us: the attitudes and assumptions we imbibe from the contexts in which we grow up are a part of who we are: they shape our relationships; determine in large part our attitudes; and so affect our lives in any number of ways. We can work to change cultural givens, but then we can work to change our physical environment as well, and the Scriptures do not encourage us to believe that telling a mountain to throw itself into the sea is any harder than calling a people to repent and believe. We inhabit cultural givens just as fully and just as necessarily as we inhabit the physical universe.

The Limits of Theological Reference

In my early, and (thankfully ...) unpublished, attempts to get at this theme, I began by asserting robustly that Christian theology must claim to be able to speak truthfully about all realities, but I now want to acknowledge that this may not be true, and certainly cannot be asserted as swiftly as once I did. My previous argument had been based on a doctrine of creation, on the assertion that if God created all things *ex nihilo*, then there was nothing that was not best understood by reference to God. It now seems to me that this argument stopped too early – before the realities described in the third chapter of Genesis, to be precise. Let me be clear what I mean by this: it is certainly the case that the fact and essence of sin can best, indeed only, be described theologically; sin is fundamentally rebellion against God, however described, and so the essence of sin is a theological reality. It may also be the case that the nature and effects of human sinfulness are best described through reference to God, but this is not immediately obvious. The division of sin into various categories, and the accounting for the various ways the world has been affected by sin, and the various human attempts to limit those effects might be considered to be straightforwardly opaque to theological description: those things that God does not will are unlikely to be illuminated by investigation into the nature of God.

A traditional way of talking about the nature of evil that has been influential in Christian history is of relevance here: the description of evil as nothing more than a negation or privation of the good has been used in considering theodicy, precisely to remove evil, and with it human sinfulness, from those things which are properly described as God's creation. The immediate aim of such a move is to remove responsibility for the existence of sin and evil from the Creator, but, as a side effect, these realities become simply opaque to any properly theological investigation. If, as was robustly asserted by medieval theology in the Latin West, rationality is a part, indeed a key part, of the good ordering of God's creation, then a consequence of this position is the fundamental absurdity of evil and sin: no rational discourse can identify anything more than the bare fact of the existence of such realities, because they are, in essence, irrational. If this is the case, then theology cannot treat in any interesting way of realities that are essentially sinful. (As an aside, given that we are talking about culture, the magnificence of Dante's vision of Satan is his ability to imagine what a being stripped of all goods might be like; Milton painted Satan as evil and treacherous, but still enjoying a form, albeit perverted, of such goods as relationship or reason. At the centre of Dante's *Inferno*, by contrast, is a figure, three-faced in horrible parody of the Triune Lord, but bereft of any relationship or rationality, and reduced solely to unconsummated hatred and unfulfilled desire. Of all the beings they meet in their travels, here is the only one to whom Virgil and Dante cannot speak: to hear and respond to the address of a fellow-creature is, in some sense, to participate in the goodness of God's world, and that is forever forfeited by the Evil One.)

Culture as Sinful?

So, I have argued that there is, or at least might be, a real limit to theological reference. If theology is to engage with culture, then we need either to demonstrate that these limits are not, in fact, actual, or to demonstrate that, actual or not, culture nonetheless lies without them. I want to take the latter option, but in doing so I am conscious that there is an argument to be had: most definitions of culture, including the one I have borrowed, refer in some way to human constructions of reality. Somewhere near the heart of a Christian doctrine of creation, however, is the assertion that the world we inhabit is God's doing and not ours. There is at least a tension here.

If we take seriously the suggestion that the early chapters of Genesis are deliberate rewritings of ancient Near Eastern creation myths, then this point is made all the more strongly.[3] A comparison of the

---

[3] On this, see Gordon Wenham, *Genesis 1 – 15* (WBC 1; Dallas: Word, 1987).

Flood narratives with the Atrahasis myth,[4] for instance, suggests both that the Genesis author(s) knew the earlier story, and that they deliberately adjusted it for reasons of theological polemic. In Atrahasis, humanity is created to resolve a dispute between the senior deities and the junior deities over who should do all the work[5] (on this account Marx was right: history is all about class conflict!); the flood comes because the gods have lost control of humanity, and need to rescue the situation;[6] and Atrahasis escapes through his own low cunning and the help of a rebel deity. In contrast, the Genesis authors urge the sheer goodness of God as the reason for creation; the sinfulness of humanity as the reason for the flood; and God's graciousness and Noah's righteousness as the reason for his escape – or, better, 'salvation'. This God never loses control, is never capricious, but is marked by omnipotence and righteousness. All of life is in his hand, and human activity, whether low cunning or devout sacrifice, can only produce results if he so wills. There is little room here for an account of humanly-constructed realities. Such an idea would seem to be the height of pride and rebellion, the sin of Babel.

If we read on in Scripture in the light of this intuition, it might appear as if culture is indeed a wholly bad thing. Salvation from sin will come, after all, only through Abram leaving Ur and going to the wilderness, and even the proto-cultures of the wilderness tribes are to be avoided: Lot's choice to dwell among the cities of the plain leads only to disaster, and Abraham's children must return to their own family to find marriage partners. Although they live for four centuries in Egypt, it is always as aliens and strangers, and when God finally gives them the promised land, they must eradicate every trace of the cultures that lived there previously, not even leaving one stone on top of another, before it is pure enough to be the dwelling place of Israel. God's people have always been aliens and strangers in this world, and any attempt to be otherwise, so often identified with the name of Constantine, will only and inevitably lead to disaster.

---

[4] See W.G. Lambert and A.R. Millard, eds, *Atrah-hasīs: The Babylonian Story of the Flood* (Winona Lake: Eisenbrauns, 1999).

[5] 'The toil of the gods was great/The work was heavy, the distress was much/The Seven great Anunnaki/Were making the Igigi suffer the work.' *Atrah-hasīs*, i.2–6 (p. 43 of edition cited). After discussion of the problem, Ea says 'Let the birth-goddess create offspring/and let man bear the toil of the gods.' (*Atrah-hasīs*, i.190–1; p. 57).

[6] See *Atrah-hasīs*, vi–vii; pp. 73–85.

Such a telling of the story is familiar enough to anyone schooled in Anabaptist or pietistic spiritualities. Somewhere there is a suggestion that the world might be good, as God's creation, but no human construction of it ever can be, and the church should exist as a counter-culture, with its own set of cultural principles and practices, utterly separate from the cultures around. To join the church is to leave the surrounding cultures behind as they are simply and straightforwardly sinful and so utterly impervious to theological analysis. Every human culture is no more than the City of Destruction from which any true Christian can and will only flee, even leaving behind wife and children if necessary, unless and until they decide to follow – because, however counter-cultural Bunyan may have been, he knew the value of writing a sequel to a bestseller.

In identifying such an attitude with pietistic spirituality, I am not intending to suggest that it is in any way intellectually inadequate: it is, indeed, represented even in central theological texts.[7] Consider, for example, Augustine's account of the progress of the earthly city in *The City of God*.[8] He acknowledges the great variety of human cultures, but considers them all to be no more than varieties of idolatry:

> ... though there are very many and great nations all over the earth, whose rites and customs, speech, arms, and dress, are distinguished by marked differences, yet there are no more than two kinds of human society, which we may justly call two cities, according to the language of Scripture. The one consists of those who wish to live after the flesh, the other of those who wish to live after the spirit; and when they severally achieve what they wish, they live in peace, each after their kind. (XIV.1)[9]

All human cultures and civilisations may be lumped together as 'the earthly city', which sets up a 'social contract' ('a kind of compromise

---

[7] Not to deny for a moment that *Pilgrim's Progress* is a theological text, of course, although it is perhaps not so 'central' theologically as it is in the fields of literature or spirituality.

[8] Quotations from Augustine, *The City of God* (trans. Henry Bettenson; Penguin Classics; Harmondsworth: Penguin, 1984).

[9] '... cum tot tantaeque gentes per tenarum orbem diuersis ritibus moribusque uiuentes multiplici linguarum armorum uestium sint uarietate distinctae, non tamen amplius quam duo quaedam genera humanae societatis existerent, quas ciuitates duas secundum scripturas nostras merito appellare possemus. Vna quippe est hominum secundum carnem, altera secundum spiritum uiuere in sui cuiusqm generis pace uolentium et, cum id quod expetunt adsequuntur, in sui cuiusque generis pace uiuentium.'

between human wills' XIX.17) to regulate the life of its citizens.[10] The fundamental end of this regulation is 'peace', the condition where all are content with the compromise. Those who engage in war, thinks Augustine, do so, not because they despise peace, but because 'they desire the present peace to be exchanged for one that suits their wishes' (XIX.12). Christians, as citizens of the eternal city, value any earthly peace that is established, however unjust (Augustine explicitly considers the question of slavery in XIX.16), because peace and quietness are better than unrest, and all injustices are passing and so of little concern to the one awaiting the peace of heaven. The only case in which Christians may oppose the 'customs, laws and institutions' – the culture – of the place in which they find themselves is where the proper worship of God is prevented (XIX.17); beyond that, such things are merely indifferent.

Culture, then, is an end in itself for the earthly city, but merely an aid to the heavenly. The citizens of the heavenly city pass through it and enjoy the good things culture brings: food, peace, order – 'the things necessary for the maintenance of this mortal life' (XIX.17) – but it is of no interest to them. On this showing, there is no possibility of thinking theologically about culture. The only room there is for human constructions of reality is the false, unstable and passing room opened up by the entrance of sin into the world. The arts and humanities matter only insofar as they contribute to the temporary stability of the temporary society in which they are created; they have no permanent value and so there is no point of reference from which to speak about them theologically. No theological aesthetic is possible: to take an example at random, Mozart's *Marriage of Figaro* mocks social structures, and so true Christians will prefer the safer music of Salieri or, indeed, Andrew Lloyd Webber.

What lies behind this account is, I think, a particular doctrine of creation. Augustine, famously, thought that it would be unworthy of God to take time over the work of creation, and so taught that God created instantly. Therefore, the days of Genesis were, variously, analogical accommodations to baser minds,[11] prophecy of the coming history of the world[12] or descriptive of the Christian life.[13] Just so,

---

[10] 'Ita etiam terrena ciuitas, quae non uiuit ex fide, terrenam pacem appetit in eoque defigit imperandi oboediendique concordiam ciuium, ut sit eis de rebus ad mortalem uitam pertinentibus humanarum quaedam compositio, voluntatum.'

[11] *De Gen. ad lit.* 7.28, 40.

[12] *c. Manichees* I.23.

[13] *Conf.* XIII.

nothing that comes after the initial creation is necessary to or proper to the perfection of creation that God brought into being in the beginning. Augustine is so committed to this idea that he posits the creation at the beginning of the *rationes seminales*, 'seeds' that contain within them what will be, and come to fruition at the appropriate time (just as the whole of humanity, according to Augustine's account of the imputation of Adam's sin, are seminally present in him). All the creatures that will ever exist have always existed, from the beginning, 'invisibly, potentially, causally, as future things which have not been made are made'.[14] There is no real change in the world, only the actualising of already present potencies; human beings can create nothing, but only bring to fruition, as second causes, that which God has already created and determined will be. In this account, there can be no place for culture, no created openness which permits the creatures genuinely to construct the world, albeit under God's good providence. Bluntly, there is no room. For Augustine, culture is a temporary, this-worldly remedy to cope with the effects of sin until Christ shall come, and sin and death and human culture shall be no more.

This is not just in Augustine, however. Even what might be the most robust assertion of genuine human construction of reality in recent theological writing, Robert Jenson's account of the eschatological role of the saints, arguably suffers from a similar flaw. Says Jenson,

> When the redeemed are ... themselves a communal agent in the triune life, they will themselves think the movements of matter and energy ... with God as he thinks and just so determines them ... we may enjoy the material universe as [God] does, because we will not merely follow along in the triune music and delight but be improvisers and instigators within it. What the saints will do with continuously generating star clusters and black holes ... will ... be to play with them.[15]

Here, in contrast to Augustine, the saints will indeed construct the world – playing billiards with black holes and so on – but notice the condition for this ability: the saints have become 'a communal agent in the triune life', 'enjoy[ing] the material universe as [God] does'. They have not, to be sure, ceased to be human, but, in Jenson's account of God's economy, they *have* become divine. Human beings, *qua* human beings, cannot construct the world still – Augustine's assumption

---

14 'Invisibiliter, potentialiter, causaliter, quomodo fiunt futura non facta' *De Gen. ad lit.* VI.6, 10.

15 Robert Jenson, *Systematic Theology* (2 vols; Oxford: OUP, 1999), 2:350–1.

remains in place – but, by our gracious incorporation into the divine life, this limitation will be transcended.

Culture within the Bounds of Creation

Is there the possibility that there may be a role for human agency in 'the movements of matter and energy' that does not depend on the people in question being 'a communal agent in the triune life'? That is, can we find a way of talking about a real human construction of reality, room for human culture, which is not either an appropriation of, or a participation in, work proper to the Creator? Let me first attempt a theological argument which will open up room for such talk, and so room for a theological engagement with human culture, before returning to the scriptural witness.

As I hinted, there is an erroneous argument implicit in those aspects of Augustine's doctrine of creation that I sketched earlier. The teaching that God did create instantaneously was based on a belief, accurate enough, that God, being omnipotent, *could* create instantaneously, and a belief that not so to do when he could would be somehow unworthy of God. However, whatever we are to make of the six days of Genesis 1, they surely suggest, as Colin Gunton has argued in connection with precisely this point about Augustine,[16] that God, in fact, chose to take his time over creating, and given that God so chose, we cannot suppose that it was unworthy of him. *Contra* Augustine, God's omnipotence, on the biblical account, is also an assertion that he is able to act in apparently limited and weak ways – a fact supremely demonstrated in the incarnation.

At the far end of the patristic development of dogmas relating to the incarnation is the monothelite controversy. I have written elsewhere about the issues and problems here;[17] suffice to say now that it seems to me that, whatever the conceptual difficulties associated with the orthodox, dyothelite position, it preserves at least one important and useful theologumenon. The monothelite argument turned on the intuitive position that there was only one will active in the life of Christ, since one person can only have one will. However, the rigours

---

[16] Colin E. Gunton, *The Triune Creator* (Edinburgh: Edinburgh University Press, 1998), 76–7.

[17] See my 'Scripture, Christology, Divine Action and Hermeneutics,' in *Christology and Scripture: Interdisciplinary Perspectives* (eds, Lincoln, Andrew T. and Angus Pattison; London: T&T Clark, 2007), 156–70.

of Chalcedonian orthodoxy then came into play: to be truly divine, *homoousios* with the Father, it is necessary that the Jewish man Jesus Christ possessed the divine will, whatever that phrase might mean; to be truly human, *homoousios* with us, it was necessary that the incarnate Son possessed a human will, whatever that might mean. For these two natures to be united 'without confusion' and so on, it was necessary that these two divine and human properties were not intermingled, or combined into a *tertium quid*. Therefore, there must be two wills operative in the one person of Christ, the divine will, and a properly human will.

Now, the caveats above were intended to indicate that I have some sympathy with the suggestion that the underlying psychology here was problematic, and that talking about 'a will' as something with discrete and actual existence is bordering on the incoherent. But what the dyothelite argument protects, or so it seems to me, is the central place of genuinely human action in the basic divine action, the mission of Jesus Christ. Revisions such as suggesting that two wills were operative, but that they were the will of the Father and the will of the Son, are in danger of conceding this important point – as, incidentally, are certain versions of the radical, Lutheran, form of the *communicatio idiomatum* which allow the human actions of the Jewish man Jesus Christ to be genuinely effective only because his human nature has been granted divine attributes. Hence the Reformed polemic which began with rather scholastic attempts to distinguish between different versions of the *communicatio,* and finally led to strong assertions of the real humanity of Christ in Owen, Edwards and Irving could be read as an attempt to defend the same point.[18]

If, then, we take seriously this christological tradition, we can, and indeed must, assert that God chooses to work through genuinely human action. Now, I am aware that thus far this argument relies only on the doctrine of the incarnation, and one could evade the claims I am making by first insisting that the incarnation is not central to God's action, but instead a 'plan B' developed to combat the entrance of sin into the world, and then offering an argument similar to Anselm's to the effect that God could only deal with sin by becoming incarnate. On this reading, God does not choose to work through human action, but rather is forced into so doing by a combination of unfortunate

---

[18] I have discussed this development in my 'Reformed Varieties of the Communicatio Idiomatum', in *The Person of Christ* (eds, Stephen R. Holmes and Murray Rae; London: T&T Clark, 2005).

circumstances. There is not room here to decide between these two positions, but I would certainly want to see the humanward orientation of the triune God that is expressed in the incarnation as basic to who God has chosen to be, and so resist this move. I would also want, I think, to align myself with the position of Irenaeus and Duns Scotus, and suggest that even had sin not entered the world, still the Son would have become incarnate, because that happening was always going to be the centre and crown of human history, the final and full revelation of all that it means to be human.

If this is the case, if at the heart of the way God is pleased to be God is his decision to act with, and not without, genuinely human action, then we may assume and assert that this is true of the work of creation as well, and so claim that there is indeed theological room for human constructions of the world. Culture is not something simply bad, and theology may engage with it.

A second necessary move can be made fairly quickly. Human action takes time, and so there must be time within God's project of creation for culture to happen. This brings me back to Gunton's point against Augustine, which I mentioned earlier: the six days of Genesis imply that God does, in fact, take time over his creation. God could have made the world in a fully-ordered state, but he did not have to, and the scriptural witness that he called Adam to name the animals and till the soil is sufficient evidence that in fact he did not. In God's good ordering of creation, there is space left for human construction of the world. Just so, history can be a good thing, under God's good providence. The perfection that God has in mind for creation can be a perfection that is to be reached, again under God's providence, by human action, through cultural activities such as tending the garden, subduing the earth or naming the creatures.

Indeed, I think we need to go further: if we take seriously the pneumatological aspects of the doctrine of creation, it is not just that God did not have to act as Augustine thought he should, but he actually could not; there is not just the possibility, but the need for this cultural aspect of creation. The Spirit is both the one who perfects creation, drawing the world forward to its eschatological fulfilment in Christ, and the one who is immanent in creation, who hovers over the face of the waters in the beginning, gives life to the beasts (Ps. 104:29–30) and blows where he wills through the earth. That these two roles are appropriated to the same divine person in the biblical tradition means that the being-moved towards perfection, the drive towards eschatological fulfilment that is a part of the world's present being will be (in part, at least) an inner drive, a result of this-worldly activity. The

Spirit does not come from without and seize the world, but acts within creation, giving life to the earth so that it may bring forth plants in Genesis 1, giving breath to the living creatures in Psalm 104 and so on. Again, the basic instance is the life of Jesus Christ. By the Spirit, the Son is made man, and Jesus acts to redeem the world precisely as the one who is filled with, and led by, the Spirit. The church, the eschatological presence and agent in the world, is brought into being by the coming of the Spirit and has life only in the Spirit.

The work of the Spirit, however, is not restricted to the church's life (as the Scriptures are eager to tell us in their stories of Job, of Ruth, and of the magi who come to worship Jesus as he is born: all of whom are from without the household of faith). If the Spirit's work is eschatological in every part, then the world's movement towards its future redemption is not restricted to the life of the church. The groaning of creation, in which the church shares, is twice explicitly linked to the presence of the Spirit in Romans 8. There is a movement within creation, under God's providence, towards the future state of the world. The creation, although good, is fallen and warped, just as the church is, and so this movement is just as ambiguous as the life of the church is, and stands just as much in need of eschatological transformation. There can be no straightforward celebration of human culture in general nor of a particular human culture, as there was in some forms of nineteenth century theology in Europe.

Nonetheless, the scriptural story starts in a garden and ends in a city, a city built of gold and precious stones, and so built – we must assume – by goldsmiths and jewellers, using their skills, the gifts that the Spirit has given them, to the praise of his glory, as did Bezalel son of Uri and Aholiab son of Ahisamach in building one of the pre-eschatological types of the holy city, the tabernacle in the wilderness.[19] Again, in the city, it seems God will be praised in the varied languages and by the varied nations which are the results of human cultural diversity. In heaven, there is no return to a lost beginning, but a celebration and affirmation of all that has been good and that has happened on the way, and a redemption of much, and perhaps all, that has not been good. We can even notice the central cultural realities one by one: music clearly has its place in heaven, and the heavenly *polis* must, no doubt, have its heavenly politics. The only cultural realities that we can be sure have no place in the city, given that it lacks a temple, and that

---

[19] Exodus 35:30–35; I owe the profound reading of the descriptions of the holy city to Jenson, *Systematic Theology,* 2:351–2.

there we shall 'know fully, even as we are fully known', are preaching and theology, which might thus be the only genuinely mundane and this-worldly activities.

Back to the Bible

What, however, of the biblical data I sketched earlier? If the arguments I have presented are correct, then there must be a better reading that does not suggest such an antipathy to human cultural constructs. Let me try an alternative reading of the Scriptures: we might see in Genesis a weaving of the need for human culture into God's good purposes in creating. Mankind is created, male and female, and the first benediction and the first command we receive is to 'fill the earth and subdue it', to 'have dominion over all' (Gen. 1:28); in the second creation narrative, this is amplified: Adam is, from the first, given work to do, tending the garden of Eden (Gen. 2:16). Then he is called to give names to the creatures (Gen. 2:19), which is a decisive action demonstrating both his authority over them[20] and, in part, his share in constructing what they are.[21] Here, in the creation narrative, there is room for a genuine human construction of the world. Finally, there is a need for companionship, and God creates Eve, and so institutes of marriage and, with it, community. All these different events are precursors of human culture, and there is no suggestion of any failure in any of them; in fact, quite the reverse. It is a part of God's good ordering of creation that aspects of it are humanly constructed, that there is room for culture.

Westermann, in his reading of Genesis 1–11,[22] sees human achievement as one of the central themes in these chapters, and finds both P and J affirming human culture, which he says is 'a section of the primeval story to which exegesis has scarcely given any attention or significance'. P, in Westermann's estimation, affirms human civilisation in the blessing and commission given to humanity in their creation in 1:26, 28. Although he has no further interest in the details, nonetheless, 'everything else has its basis and legitimation there'. J, by contrast, mentions specific human achievements, and even gives a narrative account in Genesis 11. Although there is careful interweaving of human

---

[20] So Wenham, *Genesis*, 68.
[21] So, for example, Walther Eichrodt, *Theology of the Old Testament vol. II* (trans. J.A. Baker; London: SCM, 1967), 40, 121.
[22] Claus Westermann, *Genesis 1 – 11: A Commentary* (trans. John J. Scullion, SJ; Minneapolis: Augsburg, 1984); see especially 56–62 for what follows.

cultural advances with stories of crime and punishment here and in Genesis 4, in Westermann's estimation this is not a condemnation of culture so much as a warning that culture, although good, may turn out to be dangerous. Finally, the redactor allows these sections to stand as they are, indicating his acceptance of these accounts of the goodness of culture.

If this reading is correct, and it seems to me that it is, the rest of the narrative may be read differently. Before Cain builds a city, he and his brother start a farm, and there is no suggestion that there is anything inappropriate about this cultural activity. In the account of Cain's descendants (Gen. 4:17–24), various cultural advances are mentioned (nomadic herding, music and metal-working), and these are not to be lamented. Calvin's reading of them, supported by Westermann, as examples of God's common providence, giving good things even when undeserved, is surely right,[23] and, given this, the same should be said of Cain's city.

Again, Abraham's descendants are to seek their own family because the family bears the promise, not because there is anything intrinsically evil about the surrounding cultures, as Abraham's peaceful interactions on several occasions demonstrate. God's people come out of Egypt, but with, not without, the wealth of the Egyptians, in the form of jewellery and clothes, which is to say cultural artefacts, not raw materials. Indeed, the basic instance of idolatry during the exodus is not a result of valuing these reminders of a foreign culture, but it might instead be seen as a result of not valuing them enough: the failure comes when they are treated as raw materials, melted down and formed into a golden calf. The failures of the nations the Israelites are to drive out from the promised land are spelt out and are ethical and avoidable, not necessary aspects of any human culture: trivially, it is possible for people to live together without sacrificing their children.

As the history goes on, the nation experiments with living as a theocracy, living without a culture, a construction of reality, and the experiment is a disaster. God's good providence raises up leaders from time to time to prevent the utter eradication of his people, but for long years there is anarchy, and the only epitaph fitting is 'In those days Israel had no king, and everyone did as he saw fit.' God brings salvation from a foreign culture: Ruth the Moabitess comes to live in the land, and her great-grandson David becomes Israel's second and greatest king. His reign and that of his son Solomon are seen as a golden

---

[23] Westermann, *Genesis* in loc.

age by the biblical writers, precisely because there was a flowering of culture, a culture that was not distinct from the nations around, but was clearly within the same traditions – most notably traditions of wisdom, characteristically transmitted proverbially. This wisdom tradition was the locally popular way of constructing reality, and in the Old Testament account, the greatest days of God's people were when they led the world in it.

This, it seems to me, is a reasonable reading of the Old Testament Scriptures. I think the key difference between it and the earlier reading I presented lies in the evaluation of human culture: in the first reading, culture is in itself something wrong and evil, in the second it can be, and often is, perverted and corrupted, but is not necessarily so. It seems to me that the New Testament demands that we assume the latter point.

Firstly, because, as I have indicated, it appears that the eschatological community will be with, and not without, human culture, so the biblical witness implies the existence of forms of culture that are in no way sinful. Secondly, because the Gospel narratives assert that Jesus was culturally located, and that in ways that were totally unnecessary to his mission – indicating surely that there can be nothing inherently sinful about human cultural constructions. Culture cannot, on this evidence, be in itself something bad.

How Theology Might Engage Culture

In closing, I want to suggest quickly some ways in which we might, and should, engage culture theologically. The first point to be made is that some cultural realities will be largely sinful, and so the arguments I sketched at the beginning will hold in some measure, and certain things will verge on the irrational and be more-or-less opaque to theological analysis. The various refined forms of idolatry that human cultures have developed, for example, can only be named as idolatries – to attempt to categorise or analyse them is beyond the scope of what theology can hope to do.

Second, it might seem dangerous to talk the way I have been doing, to ascribe human cultural achievement to providence and the leading of the Spirit. Eusebius of Caesarea was surely just as wrong in his uncritical celebration of human history in praise of Constantine, as Augustine was in his denial of any proper good in human history. In this century, Barth's reaction to those who saw the work of God in secular history makes the point: we may read *nothing* of God's will into wars and rumours of wars. They must come to pass, together with signs in the heavens above and on the earth below – but only the voice of the Son of Man has any meaning for theology, or the church which it serves.

There is an important distinction to be made here: to insist that we cannot trace the workings of providence in human history is not to deny their presence. Augustine was surely right to assert both that God works all things for good in his providential ordering of the world, and that this ordering is nonetheless opaque to us. As he says:

> ... we must ascribe to the true God alone the power to grant kingdoms and empires. He it is who gives happiness in the kingdom of heaven only to the good, but grants earthly kingdoms both to the good and to the evil, in accordance with his pleasure, which can never be unjust ... to examine the secrets of men's hearts and to decide with clear judgement on the varying merits of human kingdoms – this would be a heavy task for us men, a task indeed far beyond our human powers ... It is clear that God, the one true God, rules and guides these events according to his pleasure. If God's reasons are inscrutable, does that mean they are unjust?[24]

We may, without difficulty, assert the possibility of goodness within human culture, whilst, in the face of the reality of fallenness, refusing to identify any particular cultural instantiation – even the music of Mozart – as simply godly.

Third, part of theology's task in engaging with culture will thus be identifying limits beyond which human constructions are improper. There are many ways of building a city, and many things to be done in the building of it: some of each tend towards Jerusalem and others towards Babylon (like what goes on at Waterloo station in London around 8.30 every morning). Theological engagement with culture will involve a simple denial of cultural relativism: the cultural forms we develop are not merely different possible options with nothing to choose between them – trivially, it is better for people to live together without sacrificing their children. Further, it seems to me that these theological limits should not be confined to the moral sphere, although that is important; I suspect that a proper theology of creation has something to say about aesthetics, for example, as well, and will offer some sort of criteria for judging the quality of a morally neutral abstract sculpture, for example.

---

[24] Augustine, *City of God*, V.21.

Finally, if cultural realities are the result of genuine human construction of the world, there must be a contingency about them. There is no single perfection of human culture – in the heavenly city, many tongues, many tribes and many nations will share in the worship – and so there is an openness to ways in which we may chose to construct the world. This is an extension, rather than a denial, of the previous point, in that some choices are, I think, simply ethically or aesthetically neutral – the choice to write music in an octatonic or pentatonic system, for instance. I see a theological account of human culture as finally resulting in a mapping of spaces, rather than a pinpointing of perfection: sport, for example, might be seen as a good thing, but there may well be no theological reason to prefer cricket to baseball, although it pains me to express such an opinion. Theology delineates a space, but no more. This, of course, chimes well with the proper contingency that there is within the doctrine of creation as a result of the assertion of creation out of nothing, but there is no time for a full development of that particular argument.

By way of conclusion

I have sought to argue that theology can, without ceasing to be true to its proper calling, engage with culture, and to suggest some ways in which this might happen. Let me end where I began: the postmodern turn in recent Western cultures has made cultural analysis central to almost all forms of public discourse; to not be engaging with culture is to be cut off from most intellectually serious people in the West. Tertullian's rhetorical demand that theology and philosophy were different disciplines was a timely warning, but the civilisations of the ancient Mediterranean were won for Christ by theology, whilst remaining true to itself, engaging with philosophy. It seems to me that a part of the reason the civilisations of the North Atlantic were lost was a failure of theology to engage properly with natural science; and if they are to be won again then theology must engage with culture. In doing this, it must remain true to its own calling, yes, and not be seduced by the deconstructors; what has Paris to do with Jerusalem, after all? But there must be a genuinely theological engagement. Theologically, this is possible; missiologically, it is urgent. I hope the publication of these papers, like the conversations they were a part of, will be a contribution to the task.

2

Christology, Redemption and Culture

Colin J.D. Greene

Introduction

I begin with a quote from an article which, more than anything else I have read in recent years, convinced me of the pressing urgency of the subject matter we hope to address.

> If postmodernism is a philosophy of relativism, and if Einstein showed us that everything is only relative to the absolute speed of light, then that light, and postmodernism itself, declared its nervous and radioactive arrival at the roasted edges of Hiroshima's epicentre on the 6th August 1945. Its half-life ended when a different kind of Manhattan Project was completed on the 11th September 2001.[1]

The author of this article then goes on to suggest that we should be wary of the kind of selective, idealistic reading of contemporary culture that could not possible conceive of any philosophical or moral connection between those two terrible events. Why? '[B]ecause the simple etymological fact is that Harry Truman's decision was the real beginning of any modern understanding of the word *terrorism*'.[2]

No doubt any cultural engagement project worth its salt will have to discuss and debate the arrival of postmodernism both in terms of the extent of its influence and indeed whether or not it is primarily a philosophy of relativism. Hopefully we will also reflect on the extent and influence of international terrorism, whether or not we

---

[1] Read M. Schuchardt, 'The Radiation Sickness of the Soul', *The Bible in Transmission* (Summer 2002): 14–16.

[2] Schuchardt, 'Radiation Sickness of the Soul', 14.

agree that there is a persuasive logic that connects these two events and, indeed, the political significance of the various pre-emptive strikes devised by the Bush administration to eradicate the world of this pernicious evil. These are all pressing ethical and philosophical concerns, appropriate to any attempt to articulate a public theology of culture.

The more fundamental, unpalatable, yet inescapable conclusion that I drew from this particular article, however, was that it is now the domain of popular culture, however we understand it, that has become the new power broker in the endless search by humankind to answer the moral imperative, 'how then shall I live?' It is my children's generation, and therefore one that is very dear to me, who now congregate in bars and clubs and not in our churches, who search the Internet and fashion magazines and not the Scriptures, who mark, learn and inwardly digest any moral or religious titbit proffered by the contemporary film makers, and who, 'thanks to the eroded moral exoskeleton that formerly provided a common narrative to relate to or deviate from',[3] have been given the unenviable responsibility of proving their own moral righteousness. So, whatever transpires from this and other academic work on theological engagements with culture, it is the debilitating sickness of our contemporary cultural soul that I believe should be our common focus and concern. Indeed it is the search to find a remedy for that condition that makes me want to embark on the journey from Bethlehem to Jerusalem once again to see if we can locate some biblical and christological resources that might help us better understand and diagnose our present cultural predicament.

In what follows, I will begin by examining both the similarities and the distinctive emphases of the respective gospel narratives in regard to their unique christological shape and form. Secondly, I will endeavour to locate some common linkages within these narratives that could provide us with a biblically-orientated christological reading of the phenomenon of human culture. Thirdly, I will also take due note of the fact that all of the gospels are not only orientated towards different communities in their explication of the Jesus story, but do so by locating the origins of that story in different theological contexts as well. Finally, we shall look at three ways in which a christocentric reading of culture might be expedited, and also make it abundantly clear which is our preferred alternative.

---

[3] Schuchardt, 'Radiation Sickness of the Soul', 15.

The Christological Structure and Significance of the Gospel Narratives

I begin with the story that was understood to be the first, the raciest and the one used in some shape or form by both Matthew and Luke. Obviously, in the context of a paper like this, we have to be selective, but clearly Mark develops his narrative in two distinct stages; the period prior to Peter's confession that Jesus is the Messiah at Caesarea Philippi (Mark 1:14–8:30) and the period following that confession, culminating in the Roman centurion's confession that Jesus was God's Son.[4] In both periods, two christological descriptors are used to delineate Jesus' unique significance. In the first, he is the Son of God anointed by the Spirit to be the authoritative herald of God's coming kingdom. Indeed the dominant theme of Mark's Gospel is that the kingdom is already breaking in; consequently, everything that Jesus does (i.e. preach, teach, heal and exorcise demons) is a manifestation of God's eschatological rule over the whole creation.[5]

The second period is dominated by the unravelling of the messianic secret, the fact that Jesus is also the Son of Man, who must suffer an ignominious fate at the hands of the religious authorities before rising from the dead and returning again at the end of the ages (8:38; 13:26; 14:62).[6] 'Son of Man' is not strictly a confessional title, it is a descriptor used, first of all, to designate Jesus' authority to forgive sins and heal on the Sabbath (2:10, 28) and, later, to outline his distinctive destiny to suffer, die and rise again on our behalf (8:31; 9:9, 31; 10:33; 14:21, 41).

In Mark's Gospel, Jesus begins his ministry proclaiming 'the gospel of God' best understood as the good news that God's rule is at hand, but he does so only after John the Baptist has been handed over (*paradidōmi*; 1:14). The narrator deploys the same verb throughout his story to describe the fate of Jesus, the Son of Man, who will also be handed over and put to death (9:31; 10:33–34; 14:21, 41). Jesus' destiny is consequently already foreshadowed in the fate of John the Baptist. John is handed over to Herod to be put to death, and Jesus will be similarly handed over to Pilate.

Already the storm clouds of conflict and controversy are gathering. Very quickly Jesus' mighty deeds lead to further conflict with the

---

[4] In what follows I am much indebted to Frank J. Matera's fine study *New Testament Christology* (Louisville: WJKP, 1999).

[5] Matera, *Christology*, 10–13.

[6] Matera, *Christology*, 18–20.

Pharisees, the scribes and the Herodians (2:1–3:6), and the conflict settles around the issue of authority. Does Jesus have authority to forgive sins, to keep company with sinners, to heal on the Sabbath and to allow his disciples to dispense with the normal obligations of fasting, or are the religious leaders correct in their assessment that Jesus is a dangerous blasphemer and law-breaker who must be stopped in his tracks before he brings the wrath of the Roman establishment down on all their heads?

After Peter's confession at Caesarea Philippi, the conflict motif intensifies as Jesus redefines the nature of messiahship in terms of vicarious suffering, rejection and death, all of which come to fruition during his ministry in Jerusalem. The narrative reaches its climax and consummation with the centurion's confession, the only human character in the whole story to recognise that Jesus is God's Son. Paradoxically, however, the messianic secret is disclosed to him through the utter godforsakeness and desolation of Jesus' death on the cross. The earliest manuscripts of Mark's Gospel that we currently have do not possess a resurrection narrative, but the mysterious young man (which, according to tradition, could have been John Mark) echoes Jesus' own words telling the women that Jesus is risen and has gone ahead of them to Galilee. So Mark's Gospel, probably written for the more Gentile church in Rome, begins with the turbulent cultural, religious, and socio-political events surrounding the appearance of the two prophets, John the Baptist and Jesus, and ends with Jesus risen and vindicated as God's Son, returning to Galilee to be reunited with his disciples.

There are three major themes that continually infiltrate the narrative that could be appropriate to a christological account of human culture. The first is continuity with Israel's past and the significant events that constitute the beginning of the public hearing of the gospel. The second is a developing sense of conflict that hinges on the question of who Jesus is and the authority he exercises. The final is the way both themes find their resolution or consummation in the light of what transpires through Jesus' death and resurrection. So how do things fare with the other Synoptic Gospels?

The Gospel of Matthew, which was probably written for a Greek-speaking Jewish audience, stays close to the christological themes apparent in Mark's narrative. Jesus is still Israel's Messiah, the anointed Son of God whose fate and destiny is to be the rejected Son of Man. The theme of continuity with the history of Israel is intensified, however, throughout Matthew's Gospel, most notably with the inclusion of the genealogy and the birth narratives. The genealogy sweeps back to include the whole history of Israel, fourteen generations from Abraham to David, another fourteen from David to the Babylonian exile, and a further fourteen from the exile to the coming of the Messiah.[7] The birth narrative is a self-conscious re-echoing of some of the most important events in Israel's history. Like the infant Moses, a tyrannical despot threatens Jesus' life. Like the Israelites, Jesus and his family are forced to flee and live in Egypt. And, like God's chosen people, Jesus, God's chosen Son, is called out of Egypt to be the one who, unlike Israel, is obedient to his calling and vocation. The forty days in the wilderness, tempted by Satan, recalls Israel's sojourn in the wilderness, and the Sermon on the Mount presents Jesus as the teacher of righteousness and authoritative interpreter of the Torah.[8]

The theme of conflict is intensified even more dramatically. Jesus, the child born to be king of the Jews, is accepted as such by the Gentile magi, but vehemently opposed by the Herodian court. Herod's reaction foreshadows the response of Israel's leaders, and the magi that of the Gentiles, who throughout the gospel respond to Jesus' teaching (8:5–13; 15:21–28) and who are included in the scope of the Great Commission (28:19). Herod's kingship is realised through the abuse of power, violence and deception that afflicts the most vulnerable members of society. Jesus exercises his kingship as the suffering servant (12:18–21), entering Jerusalem as the king prophesied by Zechariah who, true to the meaning of his name, will save his people from their sins (20:28; 26:28). Underlying the antagonism between Jesus and the religious and political establishment is a deeper sense of conflict, that between God and Satan. Anticipated in the temptations, and culminating in Jesus' crucifixion, Satan seeks to subvert the arrival of the kingdom of heaven. The response of those to Jesus' mission determines who are 'children of the kingdom' or 'children of evil' (13:38). The consummation of this conflict takes place not in Galilee or Jerusalem, but between the time of the resurrection and the *Parousia* when the church is faithful to its calling to preach and baptise and make disciples of all nations. Only with the coming of the Son of Man in glory to gather in the elect and judge the nations will the kingdom of Satan be finally overthrown. Matthew's Gospel, accordingly, intensifies the three themes of continuity, conflict and consummation, locating the origins of Jesus' mission in the pre-history of Israel and extending the significance of his offer of salvation to encompass all nations.

---

[7] Matera, *Christology*, 28.
[8] Matera, *Christology*, 27.

Luke presents a more ordered account of things to the educated benefactor Theophilus and yet his narrative, like that of Mark, unfolds through two crucial stages. The first concerns the events surrounding Jesus' birth and his ministry in Galilee as the Spirit-anointed Messiah, and the second follows Jesus' great journey to Jerusalem, his ministry in Judea and Perea, which are understood as the fulfilment of God's plan of salvation.

Not surprisingly, the first part of the narrative underlines Jesus' continuity both with the house of Israel and indeed the whole history of humanity. Despite the intended Gentile audience, Luke's birth narratives read like an Old Testament Christology,[9] Jesus is portrayed as YHWH's Messiah from the royal house of David, who comes as the Saviour and redeemer of his people Israel. Luke's genealogy, however, reaches back beyond David and Abraham to Adam, sounding already the great theme of the universality of the gospel of salvation that will find its fulfilment in Luke's second narrative, the Acts of the Apostles.

The conflict theme reappears in Israel's mixed response to Jesus' ministry. The poor, the sick and the marginalised recognise both Jesus' power and his authority to forgive sins, to heal the sick and to preach the good news of the kingdom (4:36), and they glorify God accordingly (5:26). The scribes and the Pharisees, on the other hand, question his right to do any of these things, particularly as he associates with sinners, prostitutes and tax-collectors (7:31–35). Once again, however, underlying this conflict with the religious authorities is the deeper conflict between the kingdom of God and Satan who holds humanity in captivity. Having personally resisted and overthrown Satan in the wilderness, Jesus announces that his Jubilee ministry of salvation will ultimately dethrone Satan in the public life of his nation (4:16–21). Before that can finally happen, however, Jesus must be taken up (*analēmpseōs*) and set his face towards Jerusalem (9:51).

The second stage of Jesus' ministry not only intensifies the theme of conflict, which is true for Matthew and Mark also, but anticipates how Jesus will be taken up in his death and resurrection, and enthroned as Lord and Messiah (Acts 2:34–36). So once again the consummation of Jesus' messiahship, as he explains to his disciples after his resurrection, is the manner in which his death and resurrection are understood to be in continuity with God's plan of salvation, foreshadowed in the witness of Moses, the Prophets and the Psalms (24; 26–27; 44–47). Similarly, the

---

[9] Matera, *Christology*, 54.

resolution of the conflict between Jesus and the religious and political leaders takes place when the risen Messiah, now enthroned as exalted Lord, directs the mission of the church to proclaim the gospel to Jew and Gentile alike.

It is John's Gospel, however, where the three themes of continuity, conflict and consummation find their most complete and dramatic explication; indeed where all three are intertwined throughout the narrator's powerful and profound account of the gospel as the revelation and incarnation of the Word of God. The Prologue utilises a christological title not found in the other Gospels, and one that is never used as a confessional title throughout John's Gospel. Jesus is identified with the pre-existent Word, the Father's partner in creation who becomes incarnate to reveal the Father's glory (1:14). The theme of continuity is no longer handled solely in terms of Jesus' relationship to Israel or the history of humanity, but through his relationship to the Father in eternity before the act of creation. Indeed, in one amazingly dense christological section, Jesus is identified as the Lamb of God who takes away the sins of the world, the Son of God, the Messiah, the king of Israel, the Son of Man, the one on whom the Spirit descends and remains, and the one about whom Moses and the Prophets testified (1:29–51). So here too, in John's Gospel, the theme of continuity with the history of Israel is carefully crafted and maintained. Nevertheless, this Jesus is also the enfleshed Word of God, whose miraculous signs signify that this is the one who comes from above (3:31–36) and was sent into the world as the light of the world, not to condemn but to save all who are perishing (3:16–21).

So John's gospel message revolves around Jesus' relationship to the Father. The world dwells in darkness and can only be saved by seeing and knowing the Father. That is why Jesus, the word of life, was sent into the world, so that in seeing, hearing and knowing Jesus, the world also sees, hears and knows the Father.[10] When the Son returns to the Father, the other Comforter reminds the disciples of all that Jesus saw and heard in the Father's presence, so they can make it known to others. So the Johannine Jesus is, in some sense, equal to God because their relationship is one of mutual indwelling (10–38) and the Son reveals the Father's glory, judgement and life to the world. Nevertheless, the Father is greater than the Son, because the Son can do nothing on his own authority but only what the Father declares to him.

---

[10]   Matera, *Christology*, 236.

Not surprisingly, in John's Gospel, there is intense opposition and conflict between a Jesus who claims equality with God and the Jewish leaders who condemn him as a blasphemer (5:18; 10:13). This, however, is merely a reflection of that deeper opposition between a cosmos that dwells in darkness, sin and ignorance without even recognising this condition, and Jesus, the light of the world, who pre-exists Abraham (8:58). The denouement of the whole narrative takes place when Jesus is lifted up, exalted and returns to the Father, through his death on the cross. Simultaneously, Satan is cast down, the victory has been won, the Son is glorified in the Father's presence and his work is finished (19:30). Probably written in a context where opposition to the Jesus movement from other Jews was reaching a climax, John's Gospel dramatically portrays a Jesus continually at odds with his own people, the world and the devil, yet also continually at one with the Father whose mission to the world he embodies and fulfils.

The Continuity of Jesus' Relationship with his own *Sitz em Leben*

Still Searching for the Historical Jesus

We noted that all the Gospels begin their story concerning the saving significance and import of Jesus at different locations. Mark's Gospel presents a Jesus who comes announcing a radical message of the impending arrival of God's kingdom, in the context of other religious and political reform movements that reactivated ancient hopes and aspirations in the midst of the poverty and grinding hardship of first-century Palestine. As Tom Wright notes:

> God's kingdom, to the Jew-in-the-village in the first half of the first century, meant the coming vindication of Israel, victory over the pagans, the eventual gift of peace, justice and prosperity. It is scarcely surprising that, when a prophet appeared announcing that this kingdom was dawning, and that Israel's god was at last becoming king, he found an eager audience.[11]

It could be possible, therefore, claim the biblical scholars, to trace the continuity and discontinuity between Jesus and other such

---

[11] N.T. Wright, *Jesus and the Victory of God* (London: SPCK, 1996), 204.

prophets and religious leaders of the day. If we can use historical and sociological methods to look behind the gospel records and relocate Jesus within his own particular cultural and political context, it may also be possible to discover a Jesus who can once again radically address the cultural, religious and political context of our own day.[12] It is this form of historical scholarship that has initiated in our time yet another quest to find the historical Jesus. The first quest, Wright claims, began with Reimarus and ended with Albert Schweitzer; the second quest began with Ernst Käsemann and ended with Schillebeeckx; the third quest was dominated by E.P. Sanders and Geza Vermes; and the 'renewed new quest', as Wright labels it, is probably best represented by Dominic Crossan and the Jesus Seminar.[13]

A 'quest' it inevitably is, because it is this elusive figure, it is contended, that lies behind the different and diverse christological titles we find scattered around the New Testament. Rarely, therefore, does any scholar nowadays commence christological investigation with a simple lexicographical method that seeks to delineate the implicit meaning of the various christological titles. Rather, it is assumed that the christological titles, such as Logos, Wisdom, Messiah, Son of God, Son of Man, and the New Adam, actually amount to post-resurrection, public professions of faith that tell us as much about the social, cultural and religious context of the early Christian communities as they do about the person of Jesus.

So a different route to the one we have been following, particularly by many now involved in this latest episode of Jesus research, is to draw a firm line between the historical and the theological, and to contend that what the New Testament scholar can legitimately concern him- or herself with is the former and not the latter. We will briefly look at some of the results of this investigation, because at its source is the notion of discovering some sense of continuity between Jesus and other discernible contemporary religious types or figures that might help us in our task of making Jesus more amenable to the cultured despisers of religion in our own day.

---

[12] The present article was written before the publication of my *Christology in Cultural Perspective* (Carlisle: Paternoster, 2003; Grand Rapids: Eerdmans, 2004) but paradoxically it has ended up being published later! Accordingly the next two sections can be found in fuller form in *Christology*, 6–15; 110–32.

[13] Wright, *Victory of God*, 13–121; cf. also M. Goodacre, 'The Quest to Digest Jesus: Recent Books on the Historical Jesus', *Reviews in Religion and Theology* 7.2 (2000), 156–61.

1. Jesus the Cynic

One of the more fashionable trends proffered by representatives of this burgeoning industry is the notion of 'Jesus the Cynic', a thesis intriguingly ventured by Dominic Crossan, Burton Mach and Gerald Downing.[14] Bold and, at times, overtly historicist and unsubstantiated claims are made that with Jesus we find another variety of the popular philosophers who roamed the Greco-Roman world, offering their own brand of cynical withdrawal from a corrupt and decadent society. The difficulty here, however, is that Jesus' worldview and his own preaching appear to be permeated with an essentially Jewish eschatological expectation concerning the impending judgement brought about by the proximity of the kingdom of God, a theme which is almost wholly absent from the message of the Cynics. Many involved in the Jesus Seminar, however, avoid this apparent conundrum by translating eschatology into social and political ethics. So, it is asserted, although Jesus' ministry and message appear to be housed within an apocalyptic worldview, his real intention was to offer a less bombastic, cynically debunking, amusingly fun-poking form of radical and social critique, aimed at generating a new egalitarian reform movement that would dislodge the hierarchy of the elite from their pedestals of money, power and domination.

2. Jesus the Spirit-filled Mystic or Spirit-possessed healer

Outside the rarefied atmosphere of the Jesus Seminar, we discover a more restrained thesis offered by Marcus Borg, Vermes and Graham Stanton, that in Jesus we find a charismatic prophet with unusual healing gifts. Borg claims that the Spirit-filled person is a well-known religious type with two distinguishing characteristics: frequent and vivid experiences of God of a mystical or visionary nature, which would correspond to Jesus' acknowledgement of God in intimate terms as *Abba*; and, similarly, such a person easily becomes a conduit, or a living

---

[14] Cf. John Dominic Crossan, *The Historical Jesus: The Life of a Mediterranean Jewish Peasant* (New York: HarperCollins, 1992); also B. Mach, *A Myth of Innocence: Mark and Christian Origins* (Philadelphia: Fortress Press, 1991); M. Borg, *Conflict, Holiness and Politics in the Teachings of Jesus* (Lampeter: Edwin Mellen, 1984) and *Jesus: A New Vision: Spirit, Culture, and the Life of Discipleship* (San Francisco: HarperSanFrancisco, 1991); also F. Gerald Downing, *Cynics and Christian Origins* (Edinburgh: T&T Clark, 1992).

embodiment of the Spirit's power, manifested in healings, miracles and exorcisms.[15] Steven Davies, although constructed from very different historical premises, offers a similar argument.[16] Building on the earlier work of James Dunn and Geoffrey Lampe,[17] he concludes that Jesus was a spirit-possessed charismatic healer, and that this is the link between the Jesus of the Gospels and the Christ of the NT communities, i.e. 'Christology grew out of Pneumatology'.[18]

---

[15] Borg, *Jesus, A New Vision*, 28–32.

[16] Steven L. Davies, *Jesus the Healer: Possession, Trance and the Origins of Christianity* (New York: Continuum, 1995).

[17] J.D.G. Dunn, *Jesus and the Spirit: A Study of the Religious and Charismatic Experience of Jesus and the First Christians as Reflected in the New Testament* (London: SCM, 1975); cf. also G.W.H. Lampe, *God as Spirit* (Oxford: Clarendon, 1977).

[18] Davies, *Jesus the Healer*, 187. To a certain extent, and some might add, inevitably so, all these attempts to identify the historical Jesus with other recognisable religious itinerants of the time – be that a Cynic or a Galilean charismatic holy man, a spirit-filled mystic or indeed a wisdom teacher – suffer from similar flaws and weaknesses.

At worst, they demonstrate a tendency to manipulate, or at best show an un-warranted preference for, certain dubious historical sources. For instance, in the case of Crossan and those involved in the Jesus Seminar, the denigration of Marcan priority in favour of an exaggerated over-reliance on extra-canonical sources such as the Gospels of Peter and James, despite the latter's obvious Gnostic influences; and an equally imaginative reconstruction of a source referred to as Q (the material common to Matthew and Luke, but not Mark). Witherington quotes David P. Meier's amusing comment concerning the status of this hypothetical document, 'I cannot help thinking that biblical scholarship would be greatly advanced if every morning all exegetes would repeat as a mantra: "Q is a hypothetical document whose exact extension, wording, originating community, strata, and stages of redaction cannot be known."' See B. Witherington, *The Jesus Quest: The Third Search for the Jew of Nazareth* (Carlisle: Paternoster, 1995), 163.

The use of arguably questionable standards of historical verification – such as multiple attestations – to, supposedly, get back to the earliest layers of the sapiential tradition, itself a questionable hypothesis. As Witherington notes:

[M]ethodology is not an indifferent net – it catches what it intends to catch. Just so, and Funk, Crossan and their kin have engaged in a method that casts a net with large holes into the canonical ocean, while casting and recasting a net of fine mesh into the apocryphal sea. The result is they have caught what they were looking for – a radical, counter-cultural Jesus, a magician with little or no Jewish flavour but more like a wandering Cynic, espousing the modern politically correct notions of radical egalitarianism and a world with few if any boundaries between sinner and saint, good and bad, in and out, believer and infidel. It is appropriate to ask whether this portrait is accurate characterisation or inaccurate caricature. (Witherington, *Jesus Quest*, 79)

Further, such attempts suffer because of the dissolution of the old eschatological consensus dominant in NT studies since Schweitzer, and the consequent

3. Jesus the Hasid

Geza Vermes seeks to reconfigure Jesus as essentially a charismatic Galilean holy man in the tradition of the *hasids*, especially Honi the Circle Drawer and Hanina ben Dosa, despite the fact that the Gospels supply us with very little evidence of Jesus as a prayer warrior and an abstemious observer of the law which was typical of the *hasids*.[19] According to Vermes, there was a distinctive trend of charismatic Judaism that existed during the later part of Second Temple period. Similarly;

> These holy men were treated as the willing or unsophisticated heirs to an ancient prophetic tradition. Their supernatural powers were

---

virtual abandonment of any apocalyptic or eschatological context to Jesus life and ministry, or the translation of eschatology into ethics. They also display an inability to take seriously or examine rigorously the passion and resurrection traditions, despite the fact that Kahler once referred to Mark's Gospel as an extended passion narrative:

> For my part, I do not for a minute believe that the Gospel writers were badly mistaken when they concentrated half or more of their Gospels on the last week of Jesus' life. Nor do I doubt that most if not all that Jesus said or did prior to Passover week would have been long forgotten if it had not been for the events of that week. Nor do I doubt that Acts has it right when it insists that the early Christian preachers focused on the death and resurrection of Jesus and, like Paul, rarely quoted Jesus' parables of aphorisms so far as we can tell. (Witherington, *Jesus Quest*, 92)

In this regard, NT scholarship may well change as the outstanding scholarship of R.E. Brown's two volume work *The Death of the Messiah: From Gethsemane to the Grave: A Commentary on the Passion Narratives in the Four Gospels* (London: Geoffrey Chapman, 1994) is fully absorbed and sifted by those presently engrossed in Jesus research.

Not surprisingly such portrayals of Jesus as largely an egalitarian itinerant reformist or 'Galilean Camelot … disregarding societal structures, defying hierarchical patterns, irritating elites and confounding the powerful' (Witherington, *Jesus Quest*, 92), 'denude the Synoptic of all christologically focused passages or nuances, declaring them later accretions to the Jesus tradition' (Witherington, *Jesus Quest*, 103).

We should pay due regard to the cultural, and some would say ideological, context of much contemporary North American NT scholarship with its inevitable antipathy toward fundamentalism, and its corresponding tendency to construct a Jesus who reflects the emaciated individualism of that particular egalitarian consumerist ethic. This thesis does, however, depend on one major presupposition that we will shortly have to make explicit.

19 G. Vermes, *Jesus the Jew: A Historian's Reading of the Gospels* (London: Collins, 1973).

attributed to their immediate relation to God. They were venerated as a link between heaven and earth independent of any institutional mediation.[20]

In his latest rendition on this theme, Vermes has modified his former notions only in so far as Jesus is now seen as a prophet-like holy man and charismatic leader-cum-exorcist whose character and charm exceeds by far the normal credentials of the *hasidim*. Vermes, however, still holds on to the old development thesis, that Jesus the holy man was gradually elevated to the status of incarnate Lord largely due to the influence of Paul and John.[21]

4. Jesus the Jew: Prophet or Reformer

Not surprisingly, there has been a counter-trend in the third quest to firmly situate the historical Jesus within a first-century Jewish context, and here the work of Sanders has been highly influential. Sanders seeks to underscore the link between the historical Jesus and the early Christian communities, by portraying Jesus as essentially an eschatological prophet, preaching and expecting the imminent arrival of the kingdom of God. In Sanders' case, a restoration eschatology, rather than any particular social or political reform, takes central stage as Jesus, like the Qumran community, waited for the judgement of God upon a corrupt temple, and the restoration of Israel as the covenant people of God; concerns that are still clearly discernible in the early Christian church. 'Jesus looked for the imminent direct intervention of God in history, the elimination of evil and evildoers, the building of the new and glorious temple, and the reassembly of Israel with himself and his disciples as leading figures in it.'[22]

In a rather different vein, Gerd Theissen, Richard A. Horsley and R. David Kaylor[23] have sought to depict Jesus as a radical social prophet,

---

[20] Vermes, *Jesus the Jew*, 79.

[21] G. Vermes, *The Changing Faces of Jesus* (London: Allen Lane, 2000).

[22] E.P. Sanders, *Jesus and Judaism* (London: SCM, 1985), 153.

[23] G. Theissen, *Sociology of Early Palestinian Christianity* (Philadelphia: Fortress, 1978); G. Theissen *The Shadow of the Galilean: The Quest of the Historical Jesus in Narrative Form* (London: SCM, 1987); R.A. Horsley, *Sociology and the Jesus Movement* (New York: Crossroad, 1989); R.A. Horsley and J.S. Hanson, *Bandits, Prophets and Messiahs: Popular Movements at the Time of Jesus* (Minneapolis: Winston, 1985); R.A. Horsley, *Jesus and the Spiral of Violence: Popular Jewish Resistance in Roman Palestine* (San Francisco: Harper & Row, 1987); R.D. Kaylor, *Jesus the Prophet: His Vision of the Kingdom on Earth* (Louisville: WJKP, 1994).

initiating a renewal and reform movement within contemporary Galilean Judaism. Concentrating their corporate efforts on exploring and detailing the religious, economic and socio-political setting of first-century Galilee and Judea, they draw comparisons between Jesus and his disciples and the Jewish reform movements of the time. Theissen maintains the Schweitzerian consensus that Jesus expected the imminent arrival of the kingdom, whereas Horsley prefers a Jesus with a radical social agenda who sought to challenge the power structures of his native land, particularly patriarchy, and reorder Galilean society along essentially egalitarian lines. Maintaining the egalitarian theme, Kaylor discovers a Jesus who sought to return to pre-monarchical covenant theology based on peace and justice for all.

A purely reformist Jesus, and indeed even a Jesus with an acute eschatological expectation, does not necessarily maintain a strong connection between Jesus of Nazareth and the later full-blooded christological affirmations of the NT. Indeed, many NT scholars are still inherently suspicious of any such connections, so it is refreshing to find other scholars who actually acknowledge the crucially important nature of this question, because to leave it as a mere historical lacuna is to effectively barter away some of the essential capital of early Christianity.

5. Jesus the Sage

In line with these comments, it is perhaps more profitable to look at the efforts of those scholars who are unafraid to investigate what some have referred to as the 'Christology of Jesus'.[24] Here again we can refer to two recent works, both of which have different emphasis, but put Jesus firmly within the hinterland of first-century Jewish expectation. Ben Witherington and Elisabeth Schussler Fiorenza view Jesus as essentially a prophetic Jewish sage, 'standing at the confluence of prophetic, apocalyptic and wisdom traditions'[25] and so offering a counter-wisdom to the Judaism of his day.[26] Fiorenza has been a highly influential figure in the feminist reconstruction of the Jesus tradition. She prefers a Jesus who is a radical prophetic figure, standing in the

---

[24] B. Witherington, *The Christology of Jesus* (Minneapolis: Fortress, 1990).

[25] Witherington, *Jesus Quest*, 163.

[26] B. Witherington, *Jesus the Sage: The Pilgrimage of Wisdom* (Minneapolis: Fortress, 2000).

line of the more egalitarian tradition of Judaism and so opposed to both the hierarchical and patriarchal structures of contemporary Judaism. In the name of the Sophia God, Jesus created a 'discipleship of equals', an essentially reformist movement within Judaism that connects with the equally anti-patriarchal Christian movement of the early church, situated as it was within Greco-Roman structures of domination.[27] In this way, Fiorenza endeavours to overturn what she and other feminists concur is a baleful history of 'androcentric' bias in biblical scholarship, and so valorise a Jesus who is a liberator of women and other marginalised and oppressed groups within his native Judaism.

6. Jesus: Personified Wisdom

Witherington goes further than Fiorenza and unearths a very important strand for modern Christology. His investigation of the wisdom tradition found in the Old Testament and other apocryphal sources concludes that wisdom was already personified in this tradition as an attribute of divine agency distinct from God. Relying heavily on the material referred to as Q, Witherington suggests that Jesus understood himself, not simply as a prophetic sage, but as the very personification of God's wisdom on earth, and that this helps to explain 'some of the key elements in Jesus' teaching: his emphasis on the kingdom, Son of Man, God as Father, creation theology, the lack of *halakic* material, the absence of any "thus says the Lord" formulas and the stress on justice and the reversal of fortunes'.[28] Similarly, it is precisely such convictions that are taken up in the christological hymns of the Epistles (Phil. 2:6–11; Col. 1:15–20; 1 Tim. 3:16; Heb. 1:2b–4), brokering a transition from the sapiential messianology of the teachings of Jesus to the high Christology of the later Christian church.[29]

7. Jesus the Messiah

In terms of those who want to develop what Wright refers to as a pincer movement in NT studies, both moving forward from an analysis of early Judaism and backwards from the Gospels and the

---

[27] E.S. Fiorenza, *In Memory of Her: A Feminist Theological Reconstruction of Christian Origins* (New York: Crossroad, 1983), 99–159.

[28] Witherington, *Jesus Quest*, 244.

[29] Witherington, *Jesus Quest*, 270.

witness of the early church, a number have somewhat surprisingly happened on a Jesus who is only understandable as, in some sense, a Messianic figure.[30] Here special mention should be made of the meticulous and painstaking scholarship of John P. Meier.[31] Meier demonstrates that, even in the postmodern world of hermeneutical pluralism, a scholarly application of the historical critical method to the canonical material can reap surprising dividends.[32] Meier cautiously, but deliberately, constructs a basic life of Jesus that offers few surprises, but establishes Jesus as both a marginal Jew, and so a mere blip on the radar screen as far as the larger Greco-Roman world was concerned, yet, nevertheless, a Messianic figure in the line of Moses, Elijah and Elisha.

> Whatever his precise relationship to the Elijah of old, Jesus the eschatological prophet was acting out the role of the eschatological Elijah as he both proclaimed the imminent coming of God's rule and made the rule a reality even now by his miracles. It was this convergence and configuration of different traits in the one man Jesus … that gave Jesus his distinctiveness or 'uniqueness' within the Palestinian Judaism in the early first century AD.[33]

Meier creatively explores the similarities and the differences between the respective persons and ministries of John the Baptist and Jesus, concluding that Jesus was initially a disciple of John; consequently,

---

[30] See, for instance, P. Stuhlmacher, *Jesus of Nazareth – Christ of Faith* (Peabody: Hendrickson, 1993); J.D.G. Dunn, *Christology in the Making: A New Testament Inquiry into the Origins of the Doctrine of the Incarnation* (London: SCM, 1980), and 'Messianic Ideas and Their Influence on the Jesus of History', in *The Messiah: Developments in Earliest Judaism and Christianity* (ed. J.H. Charlesworth; Minneapolis: Fortress, 1992); M. Bockmuehl, *This Jesus: Martyr, Lord, Messiah* (Edinburgh: T&T Clark, 1994); I.H. Marshall, *The Origins of New Testament Christology* (Leicester: IVP, 1976); P. Pokorny, *The Genesis of Christology: Foundations for a Theology of the New Testament* (New York: Continuum, 1997); M. de Jonge, *Jesus, the Servant-Messiah* (New Haven: Yale, 1991); Witherington, *Christology*; Wright, *Victory of God*; Wright, *Who Was Jesus?* (London: SPCK, 1992). This surprising consensus moves us beyond the previous impasse on this matter that dominated the older quests for the Historical Jesus.

[31] J.P. Meier, *A Marginal Jew: Rethinking the Historical Jesus* (2 vols; London: Doubleday, 1991).

[32] The same could be said of another work in progress: that of N.T. Wright, as he seeks to exercise his particular methodology of critical realism in regard to historical scholarship.

[33] Meier, *Marginal Jew*, 1045, quoted in Witherington, *Jesus Quest*, 205.

it would be highly unlikely if he abandoned, or radically altered, the eschatological tone of John's message.

One of the most helpful aspects of Meier's work for our purposes is his rigorous and detailed examination of Jesus' teaching concerning the kingdom of God. It is helpful and judicious, because it demonstrates just what historical critical scholarship can establish and what it cannot. In this regard, he concludes that kingdom of God, an expression that was sparsely used in early Jewish literature, formed the centre of Jesus' teaching and was not a metaphor for socio-political reform, but referred to the coming of God in person to reverse the tide of injustice, suffering and poverty in favour of God's just and inclusive reign and rule. Less helpful is Meier's tendency to return to the old 'Jesus of history – Christ of faith' distinction that once again drives a wedge between history and theology, and creates a bifurcation that, as we shall see, leaves Christology outflanked as far as its biblical basis is concerned.

Even though Meier and other scholars quite rightly want to take seriously the fact that Jesus was crucified under the epithet 'King of the Jews', it is as well to keep in mind James H. Charlesworth's comment that we should distinguish Christology, the affirmation that Jesus was the Christ, the anointed viceroy of God, from messianology, the disparate notions concerning various messianic figures we find in post-exilic Jewish literature.[34,35] Similarly, the phrase 'the Messiah' rarely occurs in the Old Testament, and only very rarely in early Jewish literature generally, so not surprisingly the origins of messianology are extremely fluid, going back to the Son of Man figure we find in Daniel 7 and 1 Enoch, as well as the expectations of another king in the Davidic lineage.

7. Jesus the Eschatological Prophet

In rather different, but nonetheless equally important, vein, Wright claims that both the symbolic import and practical impact of Jesus' ministry was directed at changing Israel's whole worldview. Such narratival worldviews represented by Jesus, the Qumran community,

---

[34] J.H. Charlesworth, 'From Messianology to Christology: Problems and Prospects', in *The Messiah: Developments in Earliest Judaism and Christianity* (ed. J.H. Charlesworth; Minneapolis: Fortress, 1992), 3–35. Although it is interesting that N.T. Wright takes issue with Charlesworth on precisely this point, cf. *Victory of God*, 486, n. 30.

[35] See, for instance, J. Neusner, W.S. Green and E. Frerichs, eds, *Judaisms and their Messiahs at the Turn of the Christian Era* (Cambridge: CUP, 1987).

the Pharisees, the Zealots and the Sadducees, revolved around certain central questions, although they all differed in how to effect the necessary change. These fundamental questions and typical responses were:

1. *Who are we?* – The normal and almost universal answer was, 'We are Israel, the chosen people of the Creator God.'
2. *Where are we?* – 'We are in the Holy Land focused on the temple, but, paradoxically, we are in a sense in exile.'
3. *What is wrong?* – 'We have the wrong rulers; pagans on the one hand, compromised Jews on the other, or halfway between, Herod and his family. We are all involved in a less-than-ideal situation.'
4. *What is the solution?* – 'Our God must act again to give us the true sort of rule, that is, his own kingship exercised through properly appointed officials (a true priesthood, possibly a king) and, in the meantime, Israel must be faithful to God's covenant charter.'[36]

Consequently, it was not for nothing that Jesus was likened to Elijah, John the Baptist and Jeremiah. That is because the Gospels provide us with a profile of Jesus as essentially a prophet, whose message and praxis intertwined in 'a new way the prophetic styles of oracular prophets on the one hand and leaders of renewal movements on the other'.[37] In Jesus' message and revolutionary praxis, Wright discerns four interrelated themes.

1. Jesus' invitation to Israel to embrace eschatological repentance and faith at the expense of Zealot revolutionary zeal and insurrection.
2. The unconditional message of forgiveness expressed in the welcome of sinners to table fellowship that symbolically expressed the return from exile predicted by the prophets.
3. The challenge to live as the new covenant people of God with a particular lifestyle epitomised in the Jubilee principle.
4. Jesus' redefinition of messiahship according to his kingdom praxis.

---

[36] N.T. Wright, *The New Testament and the People of God* (London: SPCK, 1992), 268; see also Witherington, *Jesus Quest*, 221.
[37] Wright, *Victory of God*, 169.

Jesus' journey to Jerusalem, climaxing in his actions in the Temple and the upper room, and undertaken in full recognition of the likely consequences, was intended to function like Ezekiel lying on his side or Jeremiah smashing his pot. The prophet's action *embodied* the reality. Jesus went to Jerusalem in order to embody the third and last element of the coming of the kingdom. He was not content to *announce* that YHWH was returning to Zion. He intended to enact, symbolise and personify that climactic event.[38]

In a manner reminiscent of Schweitzer, Wright claims Jesus went to Jerusalem intending to force the issue. He sought to take upon himself the testing that preceded the coming of the kingdom of God, defeat the Satan by letting it rent its fury on him and allow YHWH to act redemptively through him. Not everyone would agree with Wright's interpretation of the eschatological dimensions of Jesus' message and ministry. Similarly, there is a hint that it is the Lucan Jesus that Wright actually prefers, and some would quarrel with his basis thesis that Jesus personified and symbolised in his teaching and actions the long awaited return of YHWH to Zion. However, enough has been said to indicate that located here could be fruitful foundations for a full-blown Christology.

There are a number of critical factors that this brief review of some of the main strands of recent Jesus research demonstrates. The first is that, with the notable exceptions of Wright, Borg, Horsley and Meier, the conflict motif that is central to the gospel accounts of Jesus' relationship to the religious establishment and the deeper realities of sin and evil in the world is all but absent. Sander's consistently minimises the significance of Jesus' conflict with the Pharisees, because he wants to stress the continuity between Jesus and his contemporary Jewish context. Similarly, with Jesus the wandering Cynic, mystic, charismatic wonderworker or *hasid*, one has a hard time coming up with a good reason why this person was unfortunate enough to get himself crucified! Indeed, for many involved in this kind of scholarship, the passion narratives and the christological claims and counter-claims that are at the centre of this particular controversy are deliberately excluded from the plot. Furthermore, one can legitimately ask why it is that the historical and the theological have to be separated in the name of so-called objective historical research. The NT eschews any such distinction, because both are inextricably intertwined and form what we might refer to as the basic

---

[38] Wright, *Victory of God*, 615.

ecology of salvation.[39] Jesus only becomes accessible to us not when we try and detach him from the witness of the early church, which is precisely what much modern critical scholarship from Reimarus to Adolf von Harnack and Johannis Weiss; and now of course, the Jesus Seminar, has endeavoured to do, but when we apprehend him through this particular context. The light that shines forth from Jesus, as it is refracted through this particular lens, offers a much more multidimensional image than the often rather bland stereotypes that emerge from historical-critical reconstruction of the original Jesus.[40] Finally, the Jesus that does emerge from these sociological and historical continuity studies often appears tailor-made to appeal to the emaciated individualism that typifies the consumer ethos of our own cultural situation. So would it be more profitable, therefore, to start where Luke and, to a certain extent, Matthew begin their accounts, i.e. with Jesus and his relationship to the history of humanity. This was the route taken by one of the few modern theologians who did actually endeavour to give a theological account of the reality of human culture, Paul Tillich.

The Continuity of Jesus' Relationship with the History of Humanity

Searching For a Philosophy of Religion

It is important to realise however, that Tillich's attempt to delineate a theology of culture is based almost exclusively on categories borrowed from the philosophy of religion, rather than any christological or biblical account of the same. More particularly, Tillich's theology of culture revolves around his understanding of the relationship between religion and culture. In his early lecture, 'On the Idea of a Theology of Culture' (April 16, 1919), Tillich defines religion as 'experience or directedness toward the Unconditional':

> Religion is the experience of the unconditioned, and this means the experience of absolute reality founded on the experience of absolute nothingness. One experiences the nothingness of entities, the nothingness of values, the nothingness of the personal life. Wherever this experience

---

[39] In this regard, see Wright, *Victory of God*, 8–9.
[40] So, for instance, G. Bornkamm, *Jesus of Nazareth* (London: Hodder & Stoughton, 1960).

has brought one to the nothingness of an absolute radical 'No', there it is transformed into an experience, no less absolute, of reality, into a radical 'Yes'.[41]

It is very difficult to avoid the conclusion that Tillich's conception of religion is but a twentieth century equivalent to that of Schleiermacher. In place of idealist concepts borrowed from Fichte and Hegel, we have existential equivalents borrowed from Schelling, Kierkegaard and Heidegger, and, noticeably, there is the same evolution of thought that moves from the more objective grounding of religion in a concept of the infinite to the subjective dimension of religion located in the self-awareness of the human person.

Like Schleiermacher, Tillich views our experience of the Ultimate as that which is mediated through our experience of finite reality. However, this time it is not a sense of the groundedness of the totality of finite things in the infinite which mediates this relation to the divine, but an experience of the fracturedness, the nothingness, the essential estrangement of finite reality from its eternal source. The difference comes from Tillich's conception of the relationship between essence and existence that he ultimately derived from Schelling. The human situation, according to Tillich, is one characterised by the estrangement of existence from essence. In true platonic fashion, Tillich views the essence of being as an ontological reality but not actual existence. Rather, it is the 'potential, unactualised perfection of things'.[42] When that essence is actualised, it becomes existence, but because existence is both finite and fallen, it is imperfect and, therefore, estranged from its perfect essence. Existence is disrupted and distorted due to this fracture from true essence. This, of course, applies to every form of the manifestation of being including, of course, human culture. The nature of religion is, consequently, to make this disruption and distortion evident, by relating everything to its infinite origin in the 'unconditioned'. This disallows any conflict between religion and culture, because religion is not something over and against culture; it is the theonomous substance of which culture is the autonomous form.

In his later essay on the 'Basic Principles of Religious Socialism' (1920), Tillich clarified his thought considerably. He claimed that religion

---

[41] P. Tillich, 'On the Idea of a Theology of Culture', in *Paul Tillich: Theologian of the Boundaries* (ed. M.K. Taylor; New York: Collins, 1987), 40. See the note providing a more accurate translation by Victor Nuovo, 40–1.

[42] Grenz and Olson, *20th Century Theology* (Downers Grove: IVP, 1997), 122.

always exercises a dual role in relation to culture: 'It contains within itself a "No", a *reservatum religiosum,* and a "Yes", an *obligatum religiosum.'*[43] The 'no' occurs when the prophetic element in religion discerns 'the demonically distorted and conditioned forms of an epoch'.[44] Here there is an inevitable withdrawal, as religion falls back upon its own sacred communities and prophetic figures, examples being: the attitude of early Christianity to its pagan environment, the mysticism of the late medieval period, and Reformation Lutheranism. However, because religion expresses its relationship to the 'unconditioned' in cultural forms, any complete withdrawal contributes to the demonisation of culture and society. The opposite extreme, the naïve identification of culture and religion, results in exactly the same consequences. And here, Tillich clearly endeavours to distance himself from his liberal forebearers, and also issues a warning to his contemporaries:

> [C]ulture is right in renouncing culture–Protestantism, and religion is right in rejecting the identification of religion and socialism. The only proper attitude toward culture and also toward socialism is that characterised by the double demand of *reservatum* and *obligatum religiosum.*[45]

(Tillich later claims that he endeavoured to exhibit the same dialectical relationship towards the influence of Marx on religious socialism. There was a 'yes' to Marx's realistic and humanistic analysis of the abuses of capitalism, but a firm 'no' to the propaganda and calculating materialism of Marx's rejection of religion.)[46]

In his *Systematics* which, as is well known, was dominated by his infamous method of correlation, Tillich develops his thought further. His cartography of cultural evolution bears witness to three crucial stages of cultural form, 'autonomy', 'heteronomy' and 'theonomy'.[47] In the early and high Middle Ages, Tillich discerns a partially theonomous form of culture, a culture where the ultimate meaning of life becomes transparent in the various finite structures of thought and action. On the other hand, Tillich defines the later Middle Ages as heteronomous, because of the attempt by ecclesiastical institutionalised power to curb

---

[43] P. Tillich, 'Basic Principles of Religious Socialism', in *Paul Tillich: Theologian of the Boundaries* (ed. M.K. Taylor; New York: Collins, 1987), 59.

[44] Tillich, 'Basic Principles', 59.

[45] Tillich, 'Basic Principles', 60.

[46] P. Tillich, 'Autobiographical Reflections', in *Theology of Paul Tillich* (ed. Charles W. Kegley and Robert W. Bretall; New York: Macmillan, 1952), 13.

[47] Cf. P. Tillich, *The Protestant Era* (University of Chicago Press, 1948), xvi ff.

and dominate theological self-expression. Not surprisingly, then, the Renaissance leads to another form of autonomy as the human spirit triumphs once again over ecclesiastical control. In the dialectical mysticism of Luther and the emergence of the great Protestant principle of justification by grace alone, we find another flowering of theonomy. This, however, was soon to dissolve into another form of heteronomy with the emergence of Enlightenment scientific rationalism, which obscured our relationship to the ultimate ground of reality, in favour of a manipulative, technological mastery of nature and a competitive individualism. The domination of 'technical' reason, in turn, gives way to that of 'planning reason'. Exploitative bourgeois capitalism creates its counter-ego totalitarian oppression, the tyranny of absolutist states. Western culture has accordingly encountered three 'faces' of the Leviathan. The ecclesiastical face of the late Middle Ages, the technological face of the age of the machine and the political face of totalitarian ideology (Fascist, Nazi and Communist). If such an analysis is accurate, what, asks Tillich, might be the cultural situation of the modern person?

> The man of today . . . is aware of the confusion of his inner life, the cleavage of his behaviour, the demonic forces in his psychic and social existence. And he senses that not only his being but also his knowing is thrown into confusion, that he lacks ultimate truth, and that he faces, especially in the social life of our day, a conscious, almost demonic distortion of truth. In this situation in which most of the traditional values and forms of life are disintegrating, he often is driven to the abyss of complete meaninglessness, which is full of both horror and fascination.[48]

If it is true, as indeed Tillich concluded, that the immediate post-war years constituted a new spiritual wasteland, European civilisation caught in the throws of a vast cultural disintegration, then the positive side of such an apparent abyss is the possibility of a 'sacred void'. It might transpire that, out of the depths of our existential despair, irrationality and meaninglessness, we cry out for manna from heaven, and that a new theonomous culture could in fact emerge. Theonomy is the answer to the question implied in autonomy, not the subjugation of the human spirit under some rule of terror, be that ecclesiastical or political, but the acknowledgement that at the heart of our quest for existential meaning and significance is a proclivity for religion. There is a need for a new self-transcending realism that will relocate nature

---

48   Tillich, *Protestant Era*, 202.

and history in the context of what is the true character of our 'ultimate concern'.

The fundamental question that needs to be asked at this juncture is this. Are we attending to a successful correlation of terms drawn from the philosophy of religion with equally realistic biblical and christological alternatives? Personally, I think not. The concept of theonomy acts as a mediating principle between autonomy and heteronomy. None of these terms, however, can encompass the dramatic realism of the gospel account that moves from continuity (which is not equivalent to autonomy) to conflict (which similarly can not be equated with heteronomy) to consummation (which is not the same as theonomy). Neither is there the sense in Tillich's account of the matter: that human culture needs to hear and respond to the gospel, if it is to witness to the triumph of the Son of God over sin, the flesh and the devil. So then, if we are not to begin with Mark and the New Questers and develop a theology of culture out of the continuity that might exist between the Jesus phenomena and other religious reform movements of the time; or if we are not to begin with Luke, Matthew and Tillich and locate the origins of a theology of culture in Jesus' continuity with the whole history of humanity; where are we to begin? There is, of course, only one alternative.

The Continuity of Jesus' Relationship to the Father

Searching for the Pre-existent Logos

I begin with a quote from Wolfhart Pannenberg, simply because he acknowledges that the crucial issue in the Gospels is Jesus' relationship to the God whose coming kingdom he proclaims. In John's Gospel, this is understood in terms of the continuity of relationship that exists between Jesus and the Father, expressed in Jesus' earthly ministry which is also a reflection of that which has existed from all eternity. Consequently, it is John's Gospel that most insistently raises the question of the pre-existence of the Son, or *Logos*. Similarly, it is here where we will find the essential clue to developing a christological account of the reality of human culture:

> If the relation to the historical person of Jesus of Nazareth in eternity characterises the identity of God as Father, then we must speak of a pre-existence of the Son, who was to be historically manifested in Jesus of Nazareth, even before his earthly birth. Then we also must view the

earthly existence of Jesus as the event of the incarnation of the pre-existent Son. Certainly we may not think of this Son in isolation from the historical filial relation of Jesus to the Father if the affirmation of his pre-existence is grounded on this alone. Theologically the eternal relation of the Father to the Son may not be detached from the incarnation of the Son in the historical existence and work of Jesus. Nevertheless, we are to understand this relation as part of the eternal identity of the Father. We can thus speak of a state of pre-existence of the Son of God, who was manifested in the history of Jesus, even before his earthly birth, just as for the same reason we may speak of an abiding relation of the Crucified and risen Lord to the Father in consequence of his exaltation to fellowship with the Father and to participation in his lordship.[49]

Pannenberg constantly affirms that the relationship of the Son to the Father implies a relationship of differentiation and subordination. This is not to be derived from some general metaphysical principles concerning the eternal generation of the Son from the Father, but from the actual relationship of Jesus of Nazareth to his God. Jesus did not make himself equal with God, but clearly differentiated himself from him as the one God to whose coming rule and reign he subordinated all other concerns. In so doing, Jesus recognised that his own identity and vocation were determined by this primary relationship. 'I tell you the truth, the Son can do nothing by himself; he can only do what he sees his Father doing, because whatever the Father does the Son also does' (John 5:19). This also constitutes the nature of the intra-trinitarian relationships because, as Athanasius recognised, the Father's identity is also bound up with his relationship to the Son. Jesus' Sonship, however, also reveals a relationship of subordination which, unless we are to lapse into adoptionism, entails that this is also a relationship that belongs to the eternal God.

> The relation of the Son to the Father is characterised in eternity by the subordination to the Father, by the self-distinction from the majesty of Father, which took historical form in the human relation of Jesus to God.[50]

This self-distinction of the Son, or *Logos*, from the Father, and here is the nub of the matter, is also the basis of the distinction of all creaturely existence from God and so also of Jesus' human existence.

---

[49] Wolfhart Pannenberg, *Systematic Theology* (2 vols; Edinburgh: T&T Clark, 1994), 2:368.

[50] Pannenberg, *Theology*, 2:377.

Karl Barth worked out these relationships in terms of the doctrine of election. When the Father elects the Son as his covenant partner, the whole creation, and therefore our existence as creatures, is included within that covenant relationship. Karl Rahner, in somewhat Hegelian fashion, views the *Logos* as the person who is brought forth from the *kenosis*, or self-emptying, of the Father. This relationship also forms the basis of God's unity in distinction with his creation. Pannenberg, on the other hand, views the relationship of the Father to the Son in terms of a voluntary differentiation and subordination that also includes within it the freedom of the creation and, therefore, also the realm of human culture. Indeed, in the differentiation of the Son from the Father, there is a moving out of the Son from the divine life that comes to partial realisation in the independence of the creation and the election of Israel. The Son was always on his way towards his manifestation as the promised Messiah. 'He was in the world, and though the world was made through him, the world did not recognize him' (John 1:10). The incarnation means that this relationship, which formed the basis of the differentiation of the creation from the Creator, comes to actual human and historical embodiment in the person, Jesus of Nazareth: 'He came to that which was his own, but his own did not receive him' (John 1:11).

> By distinguishing the Father from himself as the one God, the Son certainly moved out of the unity of the deity and became man. But in so doing he actively expressed his divine essence as the Son. The self-emptying of the pre-existent is not a surrender or negation of his deity as the Son. It is its activation.[51]

Similarly, if the *Logos* is already the generative principle of life, the basis of all creaturely independence in relation to the Creator, then the incarnation of the *Logos* does not need to be viewed as the entry of something alien or foreign into the human sphere. Rather, as both Rahner and Pannenberg affirm, and indeed the cosmic christology of the later Pauline corpus (Eph. 1:1–14; Col. 1:15–23), human nature was ordained for the incarnation of the eternal Son.[52] Human nature, which includes its articulation in cultural forms, is already orientated towards the *Logos* as its source of origin in the self-distinction of the Son from the Father. Consequently, the life history of Jesus can be viewed as the historical manifestation of that which had been taking shape since the moment of

---

[51] Pannenberg, *Theology*, 2:377.
[52] Pannenberg, *Theology*, 2:385–6.

creation and throughout the long history of Israel's election. This process was brought to completion in the resurrection of Jesus from the dead, which is the eschatological fulfilment of human life in fellowship with the eternal God.

As we have maintained throughout our analysis of the basic conflict that is common to the story told by all four Gospels, in his ministry, Jesus claimed authority as the one who represented and realised the rule of God amongst his people. This led to the ambivalence that surrounded his identity as the Son of God. For the religious authorities, he was a blasphemer who made himself equal with God. The charge resulted in his execution:

> The upshot was that on account of the supposed arrogance of making himself equal with God, he was put to death. Death exposed his finitude as distinct from his alleged equality with God (Mt. 27:40–43 par.) It was a punishment for the sinner and his delusion of being God's equal. It showed his finitude. The light of his resurrection revealed, however, that he had not deserved this sinner's death. This means, then, that in truth he suffered in our place as sinners. In the light of the Easter event the transgressors are those who rejected his message and ministry and contributed to his death.[53]

Again, as the four Gospels maintain, the Easter event, the cross and resurrection of Jesus, reveals the true extremity of Jesus' continuity and suffering identification with the whole history of humanity: humanity set at odds with the Father because of the continual attempt to ignore our finitude and mortality and make ourselves equal to God. So both Jesus' essential unity and continuity with sinful humanity, and the conflict that lies at the heart of our relationship to the Creator, are consummated through Jesus' death and resurrection. What are the implications of all this for a christological account of the significance and importance of human culture?

First of all, the beginning with John's Gospel with the eternal pre-existence of the Son subsumes humanity and therefore its self-expression in cultural forms within the trinitarian life and history of the eternal God. Contrary to Tillich, therefore, there is no autonomous realm of human culture, or indeed a historical manifestation of human culture, that assumes or acquires autonomy over and against its essential origin and intention in the differentiation of the Son from the Father. To use the Barthian terminology, humanity, human nature

---

[53] Pannenberg, *Theology*, 2:374.

and, therefore also, the various forms of human culture, find their true ontological significance, intrinsic worth and dignity, because they are eternally elected to participate in the shared life of the Father, Son and Holy Spirit.

Human culture is, consequently, always that which exists in some sense in continuity with its origins in the eternal differentiation and subordination of the Son form the Father. Human culture is but another manifestation of the freedom and fecundity of the creation, whose true purpose, however, is to reflect the eternal fellowship and unity of the Son and the Father mediated through the Spirit. A mediation and consummation that is as true for the internal differentiation of the Trinitarian persons as it is for the expression of that community in human relationships and cultural forms.

Secondly, the differentiation and freedom of the created order is the gift of life and the promise of human flourishing that comes forth from the eternal plenitude of the differentiation of the Father and the Son. Its fundamental *telos* is to exist in subordination to the Father's will and purpose to go forth and multiply and subdue the earth. Human culture, like all forms of human existence, enters into conflict with both its essential *logos* and *telos* when it ignores this primary relationship. Then human culture, similar to all forms of human existence, can lurch into the demonic, as it seeks its own internal legitimisation in arrogant and ultimately blasphemous isolation from the Creator God. This may not mean that culture fails to acknowledge its finitude, but it does mean that certain forms of human culture can fail to acknowledge its divine source of derivation, and so is unable to glorify the Creator. As the book of Daniel, the Apocalypse and Tillich suggest, the figure of the Leviathan has appeared in numerous forms throughout human history, and its' very distortions, internal conflicts and demonic manifestations are a deeper expression of the good gift, which has lost its soul.

So thirdly and finally, in such situations, human culture, as is true of humanity in general, needs to hear again the good news of the gospel, that God was in Christ reconciling all things to himself, that, through the Easter event, human culture has been ontologically reconstituted and reinstated as that which can once again glorify the triune God. In so doing, we recognise with gratitude and wonder that every good gift comes from the one who created us in his image and designed us to reflect his glory.

3

Election and Culture:
from Babylon to Jerusalem

Robert W. Jenson

The organisers of the symposium behind this book have given this essay a clever title. And I see what they mean. It might, however, suggest there is *culture,* represented by Babylon, from which one is *elected* into another kind of thing, Jerusalem. If it does suggest that, I have a problem with it. For the first thing I am going to argue is that 'culture' is not a single something, outside the elect community, and another thing I am going to argue is that the call into Zion is a call into a specific culture. Thus, there is not a general problem about the relation of the elect community to culture, a problem of how the elect community, which is not a culture, should regard and relate to this other thing, culture, around it. The title of the most famous book in the vicinity of my assignment, *Christ and Culture,* evokes a pseudo-problem with the conjunction, so that it is no accident that while everyone reads, and most praise, the book, no one seems to be much enlightened by it.[1]

I suspect each paper in this symposium will suppose or develop a slightly different use for the word 'culture'. For the topic assigned me, I will use the word as it is used within some kinds of social theory. Culture in this use is all that part of a human group's mutual or cooperative behaviour, whose diachronic community is achieved by teaching and not by biological inheritance – and if some animals, other than humans, have cultures in this sense, that does not seem to me to make a problem with the definition. A second classic definition, of a different sort but compatible with the first, is that culture is the whole of a human group's mutual or cooperative behaviour insofar as this can be abstracted from those doing the behaving, and can then

---

[1] N. Richard Niebuhr, *Christ and Culture* (New York: Harpers, 1951).

be understood for itself as a mutually determining system of signs – the relationship of this definition to structuralism in semiotics is, of course, obvious. I will rely on both definitions, though mostly on the first, since the second abstracts from what seems to me culture's very reality, its historical embodiment.

With nothing more than these vague definitions before us, it is already apparent: the community we call the church *has* a culture, or indeed and equivalently, the church *is* a culture. No anthropologist, coming across the church as a new discovery, would delay the judgement for a moment. Eucharist, baptism, the ceaseless repetition of certain texts and forms of words, the ten commandments and the creeds, the idiosyncratic structure and legitimation of her leadership, the shape of her buildings, the eschewing of infanticide and euthanasia – all these, and a thousand things more, are the very sorts of doings and artefacts which persist only by teaching and, in their systematic relationship to each other, constitute a culture. Culture simply as such can be no problem for the elect community, in that this community is itself a culture.

It cannot count against this observation that the church also manifests cultural diversity within herself, as for major example the great cultural divergence between the Eastern and Western churches – or between Anglicans and dissenters still. This is simply an instance of a general phenomenon of exclusion and overlap between cultures. Those who share the *business culture* of General Motors will belong to diverse religious or geographical or ethnic cultures. And likewise those who belong to, e.g. the church in Greece mostly belong also to Greek culture and not to Italian culture. Of course, that the Greek church and Greek ethnicity so much overlap, while it is Italian ethnicity which dominates the headquarters of Roman Catholicism, may well cause problems between the two churches. Having noted this aspect of the matter, I will not make much of it later, not because it is unimportant but because space is limited.

There is a parallel, indeed perhaps identical, point about *religion*, the recalling of which may be clarifying: Is there such a thing as 'religion' absolutely? In my view, Schleiermacher got it right: what is *universal* is simply that humans are religious beings, that is, hung up on the infinite; there is no one set of practices or ideas or actualised feelings that would be 'religion' absolutely. If there is a set of religious practices or convictions which in fact all humans share, this is contingent – I would say it is a God-determined contingency – but that does not alter the principle. Religion is actual only as the many different religions. So also the word 'culture' can meaningfully refer either to the mere fact that humans do indeed transmit much of their behaviour by teaching or to some particular culture (or indeed to all cultures at once), but not to anything in between.

Now the human propensity itself can hardly be a problem for the elect community – in any other sense, anyway, than that in which being *human* is a problem for the elect community. A particular culture, on the other hand, may of course very well be such a problem – or even *all* particular cultures other than the church itself.

A specific problem which the organisers of the conference had in mind, when they assigned this topic to me, was the relation between the culture out of which someone is called into the elect community, and that person's subsequent life in the elect community. When we think of this question, we are of course thinking of the *church* as the elect community. Again, if this problem is conceived as a general problem, so that one is thought to be called out of 'culture' into something else, or even out of 'the culture of this world' into the church's culture, this is, in my judgement, a pseudo-problem. But a call from a *particular* culture into the culture of the elect community can be quite another matter. Indeed, we will eventually ask whether there *could* be a culture from which one could be called into the elect community without the sort of wrench with which moral and spiritual catechesis is intended to deal.

Reference to the call of individuals leads – after all this throat-clearing – to a first material and fundamental consideration: that we must *not* take the call of individuals as the paradigm case of election. In Scripture, God's election is initially and foundationally his election of the people Israel. I think the Deuteronomistic Theology can, in this matter, be taken as a definitive witness. So Deuteronomy 7:6, 'For you are a people holy to the LORD your God. The LORD your God has chosen you out of all the peoples on earth to be his people.' And this is presupposed also in the New Testament: Romans 11:28, 'As far as the gospel is concerned, [the unbelieving Jews] are [God's] enemies on your account; but as far as election is concerned, they are loved on account of the patriarchs.'

God does not assemble his people by calling one person at a time. In the case of canonical Israel, the election of individuals is not election into the people, but to exercise roles in the people's life: so the Levites, the judges, David and his house, some, at least, of the prophets, etc. Also in the case of the church, God elects the church with me in it, not the other way around – I cannot take time to argue this here, and will simply refer you to Karl Barth's arguments, which we need not accept entirely to be convinced of this point.[2] In considering our problem, or rather in considering what our problem might be, we should not begin with the called individual and his or her antecedent culture.

Thus, the first substantive question with which we must deal concerns the relation between Israel's election and her culture. And at first it may seem that this will be a short paper. For did not the Lord choose Israel independently of her achievements or other qualifications, that is, independently of her culture? Could he not, indeed, have chosen some other nation altogether with its *other* culture? We are told that the Lord gave up Egypt and Ethiopia (Isa. 43:3) to have Israel, though she was the least of the nations – a rebuke which might seem to have no bite unless he could just as well have given up *Israel* to have Egypt or Ethiopia. As for the church, the Corinthians are told to consider their calling, which is characteristically from among those displaced from what would have been their culture or at least, as we would now say, marginalised in it.

It is thus sometimes argued that election is, with respect to culture, simply random. The church, it is argued, could be or have any culture at all; the gospel can be as well 'inculturated' in the form of a Hindu sect as in the culture named by the phrase 'one ... catholic church'. The director of the Center of Theological Inquiry and I were once one side of a fairly vigorous argument with Miroslav Volf, when he was one of the Center's residents; Volf took great offense at the very notion that the church might have a culture that is her own. One can understand his reasons: in his ancestral part of the world, the culture wars had become murderous, and he wanted the church simply to be above all that.

The Creator became the God of Israel just because he loved her, indeed because he fell in love with her, and love notoriously gives no reasons. So, for example, Deuteronomy 7:7–8, 'The LORD did not set his affection on you and choose you because you were more numerous than other peoples, for you were the fewest of all peoples. But it was because the LORD loved you and kept the oath he swore to your forefathers that he brought you out with a mighty hand.' So could the Creator not just as well, with the same lack of reasons, have fallen in love elsewhere?

The answer to that question, however, cannot be straightforward. It is surely in one way true that love gives no reasons. And yet, when Blanche Rockne and I met, had I given stupid answers to her theological

---

2   See Karl Barth, *Church Dogmatics* II:2 (trans. by A.T. Mackay and others; Edinburgh: T&T Clark, 1961), particularly §34, 'On the Election of the Community'.

probes, like other seminarians she knew, or had I indeed been *positively* ugly, I doubt that her considering eye would have lingered as she tells me it did. On our first encounter, she was wearing jeans, and it was not yet the era when designers had paid much attention to this garment; and I paid no particular attention to its wearer. On a second, she was in a quite different sort of garment, and I did pay attention. What if she had always worn jeans?

The proposition, 'God could have chosen the Egyptians' is true, but it is also logically odd. For had *this* God chosen the Egyptians, they wouldn't have been the Egyptians: that is to say, they could not, as people of *this* God, have been the people with tombs for standards, the people pinned to their specific ground as was no other of the generally location-bound ancient world. Or we may even put the question the other way around: Had God chosen the Egyptians, would he then have been the *same God* as the one who called a wandering Aramaean and led his descendents through a wilderness? If the Lord were not the God of an intrinsically wandering God-people, would he have had the name revealed to Moses?

God's election is doubtless unmerited. But had the Lord compelled the Egyptians into the desert, and then behaved as he sometimes did there with Israel, the Egyptians would not just have threatened to go back, as the Israelites did, they would assuredly have killed Moses or sat down and died themselves, rather than go a-wandering without any clear route or timetable, and with, of all preposterous things, a portable temple. A fiery or cloudy will-o'-the-wisp may have been an impressive standard for Moses' ragtag, but not if you were used to pyramids. It is almost a merely rhetorical question: Could the Egyptians have been the people of the God whom the Lord, in fact, chooses to be?

The logical oddity is that there is no nation of Israel for God to elect, prior to his electing her – Israel, in the classic christological terminology was anhypostatic and enhypostatic. For the Lord to have chosen Egypt, he would have had to choose not an antecedently existing Egypt, but would have had to choose that there *be* this nation – and then would not Egypt have come out looking just like Israel? If it walks like a duck and quacks like a duck, is it not a duck? If it wanders like Israel and obeys and disobeys like Israel, is it not indeed Israel?

The final root of our problem is, I think, a theological conundrum that has long divided the theological schools: Does God choose the good because it is the good, or is the good good because God chooses it? Let me suggest a solution of a pseudo-Barthian sort. The good is the good because God chooses it, but God's choice of what is good is identical with his choice to be the God that he is; so that had he chosen, say, mendacity to be virtue, he would not be the God he is – which is, of course, impossible, but again only in a very odd way.

There is an impenetrable and final contingency that is the ground of all things: the sheer fact that there is the God there is, with the will that he is. Indeed, even this is too general a proposition. The final contingency is simply the utterly underivable fact of the *Father* as *person*, of the *monarchos* before which there is not even nothingness. For our topic, this means that the sheer rebuke to Israel, that God could have fallen in love with the Egyptians, cannot function as the premise of any other argument. It cannot in *any* way trump the fact that it was those descendents of a wandering Aramaean with whom in fact he fell in love. For the fact that God fell in love with this people *instead* of some other is a decision, and the act of that decision is, as both those who read Barth and others will teach, identical with the fact of God's existence.

God creates his people by electing them, and they would be that people if they instantiated a radically different culture than that with which they are created. Thus Scripture does not just *propound* the proposition that Israel is eternally elected, it *narrates* the election of Israel, and the tale it tells is a classic tale of the instigation and perpetuation of a culture. The Lord *teaches* Israel at the Sea and at Sinai – and indeed throughout his history with her – what it is to be his people; and his teaching extends to the whole range of her culture.

Thus, at Sinai, the Lord gave the ten words. It is regularly observed that he would hardly have needed to do all that stone-cutting, since the prohibited crimes are, in any case, universally recognised as crimes – Israel did not first find out that stealing is a bad thing when gathered around Sinai, any who tried it on the Egyptian brick-contractors would quickly have been instructed in the matter. Nevertheless, the Lord wanted to teach these people even what they already knew, and, as the Book of Deuteronomy endlessly insists, he wanted those same words to be taught again, to be handed on in the archetypical cultural process.

At Sinai – to continue with some other random examples – he taught Israel architecture. He ordained the tabernacle – and so eventually the temple – in painful detail. It may be that the culture of Israel was more determined by the features of this structure than by any other one thing; at Sinai *the very act of election itself includes detailed instruction* in those features, right down to the kinds of fabrics to be used. Then, life with the tabernacle teaches, vice versa, who it is that laid down that law. As for dietary laws, banking practices, leisure-time provisions and restrictions, etc. we need only ask any observant Jew to tell us about it.

We are compelled, I suggest, to say that not only is God's elect people in fact a culture; this culture is an *elect culture*. The particular culture of Israel is the culture the Lord chooses to occur, within the welter of cultures, as the culture of *his* particular people.

There could, one supposes, have been a descent from Abraham and Sarah without God's election of that group – though consideration of the exceptional nature of Sarah's pregnancy would modify that proposition – and this people would have had a culture. Moreover, the phenomenon of cultural overlap with other cultures appears with Israel also: so the temple shared a basic floor plan with most other ancient temples – Solomon, in fact, hired a foreign contractor. Israel-as-culture is in these formalities like other national cultures, even though every defining feature of that culture is specified by the Lord's electing call. Of course, that Israel and we *believe* that the defining features of her culture were ordained by God is itself a fact of Israel's culture and could be explained without positing the truth of the belief. All of which needed to be noted, but once noted may be forgotten.

If we now turn to the church, her structure as an elect culture is more complicated than that of Israel, owing to the church's situation between the times, to her being what I have elsewhere called a 'detour' on God's path to fulfilling his election. There is, however, what seems to me a first and fundamental circumstance: the church claims to continue the community of canonical Israel, she claims to *be* Israel, to be in true descent from Abraham.

Therefore, if Israel is elect to, and as, its culture, then the church must, in this respect, claim that continuous teaching maintains within her systematically decisive behaviour and artefacts of the culture that is Israel. Of course, all cultures change, including the elect culture, and if Israel and the church are indeed elect of God, also the changes belong to his election, to his 'providence'. Specifying, for any culture, what cannot change without producing simply a new community, is tricky. Still, that specifying something is difficult does not mean there is nothing to specify. The church's claim to be Israel is a claim to have the elect *culture* of Israel.

Thus the church has, to be sure, no building as its temple, but neither does Judaism. Each deals with the absence of the Jerusalem temple in similar fashion, the church by devotion to a portable temple, the body of Christ, which the Johannine Christ identifies with the Jerusalem temple; and the synagogue by devotion to the Torah and the sages who embody it. And, what is most important for the present point, according to remarkable research done at my own place of work, the Center of Theological Inquiry, by Robin Darling Young, such identifications were prepared *before* the destruction of the Jerusalem temple, within Second Temple Judaism, by identification of the martyr with the temple sacrifice and, indeed, with the temple itself.

Or again, antinomianism in the church, the feeling that we have gone beyond those 'Jewish' commandments, has ever been accompanied by a loss of the gospel also. A church that does not share the sages' love of God's commandments is at best well underway to being no church – all those seventeenth-century churches with the commandments on the wall of the apse had a right idea. Or yet again, even the purity and ceremonial of Leviticus may have more relevance to the church than modernity thought. Can Gentile Christians eat pork? According to Paul they can, but only and precisely as *Gentiles*, grafted into a tree whose trunk is constituted by those who do not eat pork. Was not Michael Wyschogrod perhaps right, when he told the Jewish archbishop of Paris that his being a Christian was perhaps according to God's will, but that he should keep mitzvoth?

Yet, of course, the church is, precisely with respect to election and culture, in one way very different from Israel. Israel was, after all, continuous through time, not only by teaching but also by biological descent – as is Ukrainian culture, Norwegian culture, or whatever. One can be adopted into the descent of Abraham and Sarah, but this is indeed *adoption*. The Lord loved Israel because he loved her *and* – I have now to acknowledge the rest of that passage – because the persons he made into Israel by falling in love with them were descended from the patriarchs to whom he had promised it. In this, Israel was like other cultures of the sort we call ethnic: the group's culture is identified by abstracting from biological continuity, but the group's existence cannot be. And indeed, the cultures of other sorts of commonalities also, say, that of General Motors, are abstracted from antecedent pre-cultural group formations, of another kind than biological descent.

One cannot, however, be born into the *church*, one must be reborn into her, by baptism. Are we then to say that the church's continuity through time is not at all determined by descent? Not quite. For the church would not be the church were she not the church of Jews *and* Gentiles, were there no descendents of Sarah and Abraham among her members. Grafting branches onto an olive tree depends on the continuing existence of the tree.

For the last part of this essay, we thus lay up two questions. In what ways must the church be Jewish to be herself? And how are we to understand Gentile conversion into the church?

So far, I have proceeded more or less descriptively. There is, in fact, a culture which God created by electing it, and therefore God's act of electing is, vice versa, an act of *teaching*, as this determines the specific reality of culture. We cannot get much further by this method. We have to ask: How are we to understand the phenomenon of an elect culture systematic-theologically? Crudely put: Why does God do this?

We must, I think, first remind ourselves that both the human propensity to teach and learn, and the various human cultures and subcultures are *creatures*. Like everything else other than God, they exist because, and only because, the triune God does that peculiar thing called 'creating'. This is, of course, a theologically obvious point, but it is one easy to forget also in the course of theological discourse. We are all, however clearly we now think we see the Enlightenment's disadvantages, deeply shaped by it. And one result is that, as soon as we begin to think about 'culture', we tend to think like atheists: thus I took my definition of culture from sociology, whose definitions are shaped strictly to a purely human artefact. But if the book that made John Milbank famous is even approximately right, then not only is modern sociology, with the other forms of modern social theory, methodologically atheistic – which has always been understood – but it was created by atheistic impulse and to further atheism.[3] The program has been successful: that, for example, modern European culture is a creature of God hardly controls even Christians' daily discourse about it, or for that matter the first half of this paper.

It accords with this circumstance that, although sophisticated theology of creation has been fully Trinitarian from Paul on, in contexts like the present one, we tend to wield the notion of creation as if the Creator were a monotheos. Also those who know better regularly handle '... God the Father ..., Creator of heaven and earth', as if the appellation were a simple identification of the Father as the doer of Creation, leaving the Son and the Spirit to take care of other matters. The theological task is to interpret the *specificity* of one aspect of God's creating, his creating of cultures, the *triunity* of that work, and how and why the creating of cultures involves the calling of an *elect* culture.

In my *Systematic Theology*, I inadequately explored the differences between sorts of creatures, particularly with respect to the mutual action of the divine persons; I considered humankind as one sort of creature, rocks, galaxies and pussy cats as all another sort, and the angels under another rubric. All creatures, I said, exist in that God

---

[3] John Milbank, *Theology and Social Theory* (Oxford: Blackwell, 1990).

speaks of them, and humans exist *as* humans in that God speaks also *to* them. And that, I continue to think, is the first distinction to be made. But in a variety of contexts, it has been brought home to me that as there are ontological differences between galaxies and cats, so different aspects of human existence are subjects for differentiated analysis of their creatureliness.

One way to do that is to note that within human existence, it is endlessly possible to distinguish paired realms of freedom and necessity. Thus, with the Greeks, we can distinguish the polity as a realm of freedom from the economy as a realm of necessity, art as a realm of freedom from manufacture as a realm of necessity, etc. In the present context, I have been all along surreptitiously distinguishing culture as a realm of freedom from biological inheritance as a realm of necessity – we can of course repeat the distinction within either.

Now wherever there is freedom, the Spirit is doing the liberating. As in God the Spirit is the freedom in which the Father and the Son can love one another, so in creation, the *Spiritus Creator* is the *liberator* of all the contingency-laden dynamic processes which finally compose creation. The chief feature of the universe is spontaneity, which can be interpreted either as chance or as freedom; faith knows it is freedom. Within creation, relative realms of determinacy can multifariously be distinguished from paired realms of freedom, but faith knows that this is always a matter of distinctions within freedom. Creation, theology must maintain, is enveloped in an ultimate freedom. This is, among other things, the reason there can be *chosen* creatures.

Since teaching is always interpretation, the diachronic reality of a culture is a tissue of choices that could have been made otherwise: a culture is a particular realm of creaturely freedom. But that is only to say, it is the *Spirit* who agitates every culture, luring it towards the kingdom. Just here, of course, there is a complication. The creation which the Spirit agitates is fallen. The heart of a culture is its religion, and our religions are the chief loci of our fallenness. The word for fallen religion is idolatry, the attempt to use God for our own purposes, or what is exactly the same thing, the attempt to be God.

In a piece for *The International Journal of Systematic Theology*,[4] I argued that God establishes creation as *creation*, as the bringing forth of what is truly other than himself, by taking action to defend that otherness, action to block the attempt –*celebrated* by non-biblical religion – so to return into God as to be God. God has made us for himself, and just so

---

4   Robert W. Jenson, 'Creator and Creature', *IJST* 4.2 (2002), 216–21.

our *fallen* hearts are restless until they appropriate his position. Only as we are prevented from divinising ourselves, and so come to know God as God, can Augustine's great saying be rescued from the parody I just committed, can we say that rest in the true God was all along the goal of our unease?

It is only, I argued, in that God intrudes the incarnation that his bringing forth a reality other than himself is an act of *creating*. Thus this intrusion is not a single punctual event on some timeline exterior to it; but is foundational to all that on the created time line would be said to precede or follow it. According to John, the Word that is Jesus was the Word spoken at the beginning, and that identity works both ways. The Word spoken at the beginning is the Word that is Jesus; 'God said, "Let there be . . .", and there was . . ., and God saw that it was good.' Good for what? Good for Israel, and Israel's Christ, Jesus our Lord, and his body the church, and finally for the kingdom. That is to say, as the Spirit draws every creature on in some mode of freedom, it is just and only as the Spirit is the spirit *of* the incarnate Son, that their freedom is not freedom not to be creatures – which is freedom not to be at all.

All this holds true, let me now suggest, also for that aspect of God's creating that is the Spirit's drawing out of the cultures. All cultures tend towards God, but as fallen cultures the way they tend towards him is that they seek to master and replace him; analogically, one can indeed say that every culture of the fallen world is Babylon. Insofar as a culture is a polity, it will be shaped and moved by the political form of self-worship, which Augustine called the *libido dominandi*; insofar as it makes artefacts, it makes graven images, projecting its own lusted-after divinity; insofar as it builds, it builds ziggurats, etc.

That is why, if the creation is in this of its aspects to be *creation*, God's creating cultures involves a correlated aspect of the incarnation's pre-emption of its own past: the Spirit's drawing of a certain evolutionary strain into communities diachronically constituted in freedom, that is, his creation of cultures necessarily involves creation of a particular culture that is the culture of the Son's communal body. Without this, the cultures would not be creatures, but indeed only ghostly Babylons. From the beginning, the creation of cultures requires a specific christological culture, for which the Spirit takes what is Christ's as the content of his culture-constituting teaching. Without this, humankind's entire cultural enterprise would become a rush back into God, to possess him.

Here too we engage an anciently controversial point of theology: the relation of nature and grace. Surely the calling of an elect community is the very paradigm of *grace*, but I have just argued that it is constitutive in that drawing forward by which the Spirit *creates*. Solutions to this matter range from Catholic neo-Scholasticism's strict separation of 'nature' and 'supernature' – intended to meet Reformation critique – to Karl Barth's doctrine that the covenant, the actual covenant with sinners that is identical with the existence of Jesus Christ, is the inner ground of creation. It will be seen that here I follow Barth.

It is an established item of ecumenical theology: the eternal difference and relation between the Son and the Father is the ground of God's creating what is other than God. The question is: Who is this Son? It is possible, I think, to elide the problem about whether there ever 'was' a *logos asarkos,* and stay strictly with the *who* with the question of *identity.* And then I think we must say, the Son whose relation to the Father enables creation is the incarnate Christ.

At long last we can ask, about all of the above, 'So what?' The church is Israel opening to the Gentiles, a specific detour on God's way to fulfilling his promise to Abraham. Thus, this elect community is culturally determined in two directions.

In the one, the church's cultural identity simply is Israel; to see what is our culture as church, we can only read the Old Testament. If the church loses her cultural identity as Israel, she is no longer church. Of course, as we have noted, the teaching by which a culture is maintained is always interpretation and so is not itself mere repetition. Moreover, the church is Israel only by way of a great *continuity*: the crucifixion, the destruction of the temple and the opening to the Gentiles. Thus, the church's identity as Israel is at all times threatened and, indeed, is in principle problematic. It is, therefore, an abiding task of the church to *cultivate* her Israelite culture, by teaching that is interpretation. This means at least the following.

Even as the church's reading of the Old Testament is always an interpretation by the crucifixion and resurrection, it remains the case that to know what is appropriate to her culture she has no place else to look. So, for example, there is a specific rhetoric and diction appropriate to her discourse, whether verbal or literate: the diction and rhetoric of the Psalms, the Prophets and the Wisdom literature. So the church has a style of meditation, which is not the emptying of consciousness, but rather is the meditation of the Jewish sages, the filling of consciousness with the commandments of God. So the fundamental question about the architecture of her gathering places must be: There is a most holy place here with a wall around it, like that of the temple; but is this the wall of the church building or an enclosure *within* that enclosure? We could go on to fill a book.

The church's Gentile members eat shrimp – if they afford it – and can do so without breaking fellowship with Jewish members. The body of Christ does not *look* like a temple. The continuation of Israel as the church of Jews and Gentiles in the time between the times shows and must show discontinuities with canonical Israel. But, I propose, the burden of proof always lies with argument for discontinuity. It requires to be *shown* that Gentile converts may continue on their dietary ways – and it may even be that Paul proceeded in such matters rather too apodictically. Eucharist should be recognisable as Passover, if indeed as Passover on the other side of crucifixion and resurrection. Christian ministers are a sort of blend of rabbi and temple priest, and should occupy and conduct themselves accordingly. There are, in short, limits on 'inculturation'.

The church, I said, is culturally determined in two directions. The second direction is to the cultures from which Gentile converts come and which they bring with them. The conversion of a Gentile into the church is her entry into a culture, membership of which is not otherwise established, by ethnicity or class or whatever. This sets a question and a task. First, the question. The Gentile convert will not cease to be Zulu or Norwegian-American or whatever, and middle-class or working-class or whatever, etc. Thus, wherever the mission carries the church, she will have an immediate relation to other cultures. How is the church to regard and deal with this?

The Spirit creates all cultures by drawing them into the freedom of the kingdom. I think it unlikely that God would allow any culture so to resist the Spirit as to be Babylon the Great; but if any do, so be it. The expectation of the church must anyway be to seek and find the ways in which a culture, any culture, is a creature of the Spirit of her Lord. The church does not even need to 'despoil the Egyptians', only to receive what she can from the Egyptians, as a gift of the Spirit. So the church should simply rejoice when African communal solidarity or Roman basilicas so wonderfully enable her life.

But of course all these cultures are also fallen. If no actual culture can achieve the goal of being altogether Babylon the Great, neither can any be the kingdom. The church, therefore, must also expect, as a regular feature of her cultural history, life-and-death conflict between her culture and those from which her converts come. As the *Didache* had it, those on our 'way' do not abort their children, the ways followed by most around us do, and between these practices there is hardly an accommodation. My oft-cited model here is Cyril of Alexandria. In his big book against 'the Greeks', he spends chapter after chapter berating them for their idolatry. Then suddenly he says, 'But we do not altogether despair of you. There are some with whom conversation is possible.' He then embarks on a calm and irenic discussion of a nice point in Plato. What he must combat, he does, what he can take up, he appreciates.

The culture that is the church can, in my judgement, only play catch-as-catch can with the other cultures. What of, for example, American culture can be received by the church, or even promoted in the society when the church has the power to do so, and what must be rejected, and even combated in the society when the church has the power to do so, is a matter of case-by-case discernment. We will have to trust the Spirit, having no other controls at our disposal.

Finally, at the very end, what about that convert? Two features of what happens to her stand out.

Firstly, in moving to the new culture, she has *nothing* to support her but teaching. Secondly, the convert brings her old culture along, so that the church's situation, as just considered, cuts right through. The convert knows both the Spirit-worked harmony between his previous culture and the church's culture, and their deadly conflicts, in her own life. In short, nothing can save the Gentile convert except serious catechesis. The ancient church was aware of that. She knew that the shock of entry into a culture at some points so at odds with the convert's antecedent cultures, could be spiritually fatal, unless the converts were carefully prepared, unless the church sat her converts down at the base of Sinai and taught them about those commandments, and about not consorting with temple prostitutes, and about not breaking up indentured families, and about the Christian Passover, and about all the rest of it. And just so, was the sacrament of their election. Then in the centuries during which the church's culture was in a sort of – stormy – marriage with the chiefly present other culture, sloth found excuse to evade such labours. Those days are gone, and unless catechesis can be renewed, large branches of the church with them.

4

Torah, Christ and Culture

Stephen R. Holmes

I

Let me start with a proposition that I hope will be obvious once stated. The first five books of the Bible, in their final redaction, and taken as a literary whole,[1] describe God's activity in bringing into being a particular cultural reality – Israel. One significant feature of these books is narrative sections which describe God's choice of and faithfulness to a particular family, who become a people separated from other peoples. A second feature is parenetic sections that describe the culture this people will adopt when given a land of their own to live in. The piece as a whole ends with Israel poised on the boundary of this promised land, ready to enter and establish the culture that God has instructed them in.

A recent study notes that Torah is a 'central biblical concept', but also 'an issue which Christian theology has only recently begun to address'.[2] Given this, that Israel, or the ideal Israel described in prospect and narrated in these books, is best understood as a culture may need some defence. Israel is perhaps usually thought of as a nation – a polity. There is, however, much more than politics in the Mosaic law: eating habits; story-telling practices; family structures; purity standards, and so on. It may be that there are good arguments as to why some or all of these things are properly matters for political deliberation, but they are outside the definition of the word 'politics' as we currently

---

[1] For some good reasons to continue to regard the Pentateuch as a literary unit, see Brevard S. Childs *Introduction to the Old Testament as Scripture* (London: SCM, 1979), 128–32.

[2] Frank Crüsemann, *The Torah: Theology and Social History of Old Testament Law* (trans. A.W. Mankhe; Edinburgh: T&T Clark, 1996), 1.

understand it. Thus, to claim that what is envisaged by Torah is merely a polity is inadequate.

Equally, Israel is not merely a religious entity. Whilst regulation of belief, patterns of sacrifice and holiness codes are all part of what we would now understand by the term 'religion', the situation is less clear when we consider that the Torah offers, for instance, patterns of allocation of farm land and regulations concerning admissible evidence in murder trials. Thus, as with politics, there are religious elements to the entity the Torah describes, but that entity is more than merely a religion. To quote again, 'Torah demonstrates an astonishing breadth of content. It comprises legal, moral, cultic, religious, theological and historical statements.'[3] To this list we might add familial, economic, political, educational and even culinary. The word 'culture', although its definition is difficult and contested, seems to be the only available English word that adequately conveys what is being created in Genesis to Deuteronomy.

This recognition does not seem widespread in OT studies, although I write as a layman in that field, and it might be that there is a rich literature which I have failed to uncover. Of the various designations commonly given to Israel, perhaps the one that comes closest to appreciating its specifically cultural nature is the discussion of Israel as 'the people of God'. This itself has been a patchy theme within studies of the OT,[4] but even when fully recognised and embraced does not adequately capture the cultural specificity of what the Torah describes as being brought into being, at least to my mind. The fact that the Christian church, which is endlessly reinculturated,[5] can still easily be described as the 'people of God' is perhaps sufficient evidence.

So, the calling of Abraham, the gift of Isaac, the providential guiding of Joseph, the theophany to Moses, the plagues sent on Pharaoh, the wanderings in the wilderness, and all the other events of the books of Torah are not about salvation, considered in some narrow spiritual sense, or about liberation, conceived in some narrow political sense.

---

[3] Crüsemann, *The Torah*, 9.

[4] John Goldingay suggests that this was particularly true within the biblical theology movement, citing the difference between the editions of Vriezen's *Outline of Old Testament Theology* as a telling example: the theme of the people of God was 'virtually absent' from the original edition, but the later edition is 'largely structured' by it. John Goldingay, *Theological Diversity and the Authority of the Old Testament* (Grand Rapids: Eerdmans, 1987), 59, n. 2.

[5] This is discussed and argued for below.

God does not merely set out to gain worshippers for himself, or to set an oppressed nation free. He sets out to create a culture, and that culture is called Israel. If this is the case, it is not unreasonable to ask about its relevance for a theological account of culture in our own times, and so for the matter of this book. This paper, then, is an attempt at a theologically-serious reading of the Old Testament material with the question of culture in mind.

One immediate answer suggests itself, before some more careful investigations become necessary: this recognition demands that human culture, and indeed the variety of human cultures, is not irrelevant theologically. This position is not merely obvious, as it is possible to conceive of a religious system that considers culture to be no more than an irrelevance. Whilst ancient Judaism, and indeed medieval and modern Islam, saw the progressive instantiation of particular cultural realities as central to their mission, one can imagine a system which regards culture as something to be transcended, and so something fundamentally unimportant. Such a system might treat human cultures in ways similar to those in which the various Gnostic systems treated the physical realm; as something utterly irrelevant to truth and salvation, there may be a striving for escape from all forms of culture, or a licentious indulgence in any form that appears momentarily attractive.

Having said this, I am not going to offer any detailed exegesis of the particular texts in the Pentateuch that describe the particular forms of culture that God demands of Israel. This is for two reasons: firstly, because this culture is in some important sense contingent, in that its purity laws reflect the peculiar forms of idolatry prevalent in the surrounding cultures; secondly, because it has often been assumed, explicitly or implicitly, that the details of the Old Testament law are not relevant data for Christian theology, and unless and until I can demonstrate otherwise, there is no point in offering such exegesis. This paper then is preparatory to such exegetical work, establishing and announcing the possibility of it.

Before turning to other responses, a critical issue must be addressed. In arguing that the Pentateuch, as a whole, describes an act of cultural creation on God's part, the most interesting text is perhaps the Genesis pre-history. I have argued before[6] that this account of creation allows human culture to be understood as something created and intended by God. The issue now is whether these chapters should

---

[6] In my other contribution to this volume.

been seen as something separate, a prologue that merely sets the scene for the story of Abraham and his children which is to follow, or whether they are an intrinsic part of that later story. Very bluntly, when God said 'Let there be light', was it only so he would be able to see Israel?

In the final redaction of the text, I think the answer must be yes. Although the stories of the first eleven chapters of Genesis are rather different in feel from those that fill the remainder of the book, there are also structural features which bind them together into a unity. Most notable of these is the repeated use of the phrase 'These are the generations of ...' or 'This is the history of ...' – the Hebrew word *tôldôt* can carry both senses. These historical lists introduce each new character in the book: Adam, Noah, Abraham, Isaac, and so on, each time giving a wider context for the coming historical material. Not only does this structural feature link the prologue with the main narratives, but the first of these lists concerns the history of 'heaven and earth' (Gen. 2:4) – so the family history of Abraham is not only identified as God's particular interest within the human family, but is also traceable back to being of central interest in the creation of the heavens and the earth. On this reading, only the poetic or liturgical text of the seven days can be seen as a prologue. From the beginnings of the story of Eden, the rest is an integral part of the story that culminates with Moses, on the banks of the Jordan before his death, describing the culture that is to be.

It would be possible to overplay this point: the created order is more than merely a canvas on which to display cultural images; the genuinely prolegomenic nature of the first chapter of Genesis, with its ascription of goodness – moral worth – to each part of creation as it comes into being ensures this. It is important to recognise this, as those elements of the cultural sciences that have learnt most from postmodern theorising can occasionally give the impression that culture is more basic than the physical world; and, whilst there are ways in which this observation is not wholly untrue, a theological account of culture will want to resist it and stress the givenness and goodness of our physical surroundings. 'Let them be left, the wildness and wet/Long live the weeds and the wilderness yet!' as a Jesuit poet, who knew much of the goodness of the physical, had it.[7]

---

[7] Gerald Manley Hopkins, 'Inversnaid'. It is worthy of notice that Hopkins's stress on the particular and complex beauty of a given place, the 'inscape', was not merely a Romantic celebration of wilderness; the inscape of 'Duns Scotus's

That said, the force of my first proposition should not be minimised: from the creation and naming of the animals – a cultural act, surely – and the creation of communal culture in Genesis 2, the end in view in the narrative is that Israel shall be. Other nations exist, and are not outside God's care (the Lord is known by Ishmael's mother to be the 'God who really sees'), but they pass in and out of view in an fleeting and partial way, like perhaps the minor characters in Joyce's *Portrait of the Artist*, or the mere impressions of background figures in a Renoir crowd scene. The narrative is not interested in them, except insofar as they tend towards the existence of the Israel that God desires to be, and the same is in part true of the created order. The genealogy of this cultural instantiation goes back not just to Adam, but to the creation of heaven and earth.

II

A second proposition: both in the narrative world of the canon and, as far as we can tell, in history this blueprint for a culture was never actually lived out. The text that we have is utopian; despite God's action, the culture that he created the world in order to see has never actually been seen. Historically, we might point to the common observation that there is good reason to believe that Jubilee was never celebrated, and to many other variations between the culture that is narrated and the historical record, as far as we can read it. It seems to me, however, that the canonical part of this proposition might be the more interesting part. As the narrative moves on beyond the death of Moses, the Deuteronomic History makes clear that the culture was not shaped according to the strictures of the Torah: sometimes because the people refused to obey God, but also because God's own action was not always in accord with the pentateuchal instructions.

The commands concerning racial purity offer an obvious example of both points. It is clear that the culture that God set out to create was to be utterly pure. There was a demand that it be hospitable to aliens and strangers, but equally a demand that it refuse to assimilate them. In the most extreme case, described in Deuteronomy 23:2–8, descendants of mixed marriages involving Moabites and Ammonites were excluded to the tenth generation. In that text, even the descendants of inhabitants

---

Oxford', whilst it has been ruined by its 'base and brickish skirt' of suburbs, is 'towery' as well as 'branchy between towers'.

of favoured nations, Edom, described as 'your brother', and Egypt, where Israel had lived, were to be excluded to the third generation. The demand for purity is severe.[8]

Even on the canonical telling, however, it never came to pass: on the one hand, the failure of Joshua to carry through his divinely mandated programme of genocide led to the inclusion of others within the community, albeit only as 'hewers of wood and drawers of water' (Josh. 9:21). On the canonical telling, whilst this is in part due to the cleverness of the Gibeonites in playing a trick on the leaders of Israel, it is also due to Israel's failure; the decisive text in the story records that 'the men of Israel sampled their provisions but did not enquire of the LORD'. On the other hand, the story of Ruth tells us that God chose David, son of Jesse, a third-generation immigrant, and a descendant of hated Moab, to be Israel's greatest king.

This seems to me to be interesting. It is clearly true canonically; it seems to me likely that it is also true historically, in that the final redactor(s) of the pentateuchal text must have been aware of this history, even as they put together the cultural narration which it contradicts. The book of Ruth is notoriously difficult to date,[9] but it is surely inconceivable that, even if of late date, it would have achieved the status it did within Israel if its central claim concerning David was novel.[10] No doubt the traditions of racial purity enshrined in the Pentateuch were also of ancient origin;[11] nonetheless the decision to preserve, indeed to emphasise, a fundamental contradiction between God's narrated desire for the culture and God's actions in establishing the culture is worthy of reflection.

---

[8] The commentators find the relatively light prohibitions directed against Edom and Egypt, not traditional allies of Israel, to be significant in terms of dating, whilst recognising that there is older material underlying the current form of the text.

[9] For a recent survey of some of the arguments concerning linguistic features, resulting in a cautious ascription of a date in the early post-exilic period, see Frederic W. Bush, *Ruth/Esther* (WBC 9; Waco: Word, 1996), 18–30. For a contrary view, relying on arguments concerning the purpose of the book, see Kirsten Nielsen, *Ruth: A Commentary* (OTL; Louisville, WJKP, 1997).

[10] This novelty does seem to be regularly assumed by the commentators, but I have yet to read any attempt to describe how it might have been introduced in a way that would have made it even momentarily plausible after David had attained the heroic status he did and, in that absence, I take it that the genealogical claims, whether true or not, must be more-or-less contemporaneous with David's rise. Such contemporaneity, if accepted, is in turn an argument for the truth of the genealogy, of course.

[11] So Gerhard von Rad, *Deuteronomy* (trans. Dorothea Barton; OTL; London: SCM, 1966), 145.

Many commentators suggest that these texts point to a division amongst the theologians of Israel. The discussion is often couched in terms of the relationship of the book to the Davidic monarchy: some commentators take the view that the book is written to defend David's claim to the throne;[12] others that the reference to David is a way of legitimating the moral point made by the story,[13] an interpretation which can be traced back to at least the Rabbis. There is then dispute about the moral point of the story: an older tradition of critical scholarship sees Ruth as part of the polemical response to Ezra's demands for purity; a more recent tradition sees it as a more general demand that the ethical virtues of hospitality and generosity should not be limited by ethnic, religious or indeed cultural barriers. Identifying such disputes in the background to one or another Biblical writing is exegetically helpful, of course, at least to the extent that we can reach clear conclusions, which currently seems doubtful in the case of Ruth.[14] However, from a theological point of view, there is a need to make sense of the texts of Scripture in their canonical context as well. If there is a contradictory witness, we must struggle to make sense of it.

That the events of the book of Ruth are ascribed to providence by the author(s) of that book is, I think, beyond doubt. The particular form of providence here narrated is unusual in Old Testament literature: there is no suggestion of a miraculous and decisive intervention by God, but rather the bringing about of the divine purpose through the confused and messy events of human relationships and business affairs.[15] God brings Naomi's sorrow to an end, and then the great-grandson of Ruth the Moabitess becomes Israel's second and greatest king. This is not, first, a case of God making the best of a bad situation, or some similar escape clause. I confess to having little time for accounts of providence which picture God as having to rather desperately compromise in order

---

12 So, for instance, Nielsen, *Ruth*. This view requires her early dating of the book: there is little evidence that David's claim to the throne was in dispute around the time of the exile. The earliest suggested date of which I am aware, within the reign of Solomon, is advanced for similar theological reasons by Ronald M. Hals in *The Theology of the Book of Ruth* (Philadelphia: Fortress, 1969), 65–75.

13 So, for instance, Katherine Doob Sakenfield, *Ruth* (Interpretation Series; Louisville, WJKP, 1999), 3–5.

14 I find the suggestion that the book is a 'subtle and complex literary creation', which thus has 'many possible levels of meaning', more convincing than any particular theory. See the brief discussion in Bush, *Ruth/Esther*, 48 (whence the quotations), which draws on fuller discussions by Clines and Rauber.

15 Hals, *Theology*, suggests that the book aims to emphasise not just providence *simpliciter*, but the hiddenness of God's actions.

to recoup something from the mess we have made of his plans, but, in any case, here we are faced with a simple act of individual election, not a compromise solution to a problem. God chooses David to be king; there is no suggestion anywhere in the text that this is because no one else in Israel worthy of the role could be found; indeed, such indications as there are in the account in Samuel point entirely the other way. In contrast to Saul, who stands a head above his fellows and seems marked for kingship, the ordinariness of David is emphasised, even comically, through the stories of his anointing by Samuel. The youngest son, left tending the sheep whilst his father and brothers go about the serious business of religious devotion, is the Lord's chosen.

One could understand the writer of the historical material emphasising David's dubious racial history for polemical purposes: not only an ordinary shepherd, but of unclean birth, but because his heart is right with God he becomes central to what Israel is and is to be. The question is, however, why the other way around? Why, given the history of David's place in Israel, do redactions of the law codes that are generally held to post-date his reign continue to stress commands of which his very existence is a violation?

III

A historical answer, at least, might be found in a third proposition: the generally accepted date for the final redactions of the pentateuchal texts suggests that they have a contemporary purpose in describing God's historical intentions to create a culture. The literature seems to have reached two significant points of consensus on this question. One is that the Pentateuch in its canonical form is post-exilic, probably reaching its final form in the fifth or fourth century BC, although the latest strata of additions was relatively minor, comprising mostly some isolated narratives and some smoothing of the law codes. The second, resulting from the study of tradition-history, is that the complex of source documents that lie behind the final form began to be collated very early – perhaps as early as the twelfth century, in oral traditions – and that they were, in some important senses, public documents for most of this time.[16] These texts are coming together, then, around the

---

[16] Alexander Rofé, *Introduction to the Composition of the Pentateuch* (Sheffield: SAP, 1999) is an introductory text, but as such offers a useful survey of the current state of scholarship, on which I am drawing. An interesting account of the coming-to-be of the Pentateuch, which reflects some of the concerns I am discussing here, can be found in Crüsemann, *Torah*.

time of the refounding of Israel after the exile, and so the narration of the way God originally shaped the people of Israel might be assumed to be told with the intention of reshaping the people in their second colonisation of the promised land. On this basis, it is not unreasonable to suggest that the commands to racial purity are necessary and important, not primarily for their historical reference, but because they legitimise events such as Ezra's programme of reformation.

This indicates an important theological use to which these texts have been put: the narration of Israel's journey into the wilderness to become in every detail the people – the culture – that God wants them to be has become a powerful story of reformation within Christian history. Whether it be the monastic retreat to the desert in protest at the worldliness of the Constantinian church, or the puritan 'errand into the wilderness' of New England, the story of the exodus from Egypt and the formation of God's people in the desert has been powerfully resonant for groups despairing of the cultural failures or accommodations of the church of their own day, and desirous of a new dawn of true godliness.

There is an important difference, however, inasmuch as Ezra's reformation was based on Torah more than history. The people coming back from Babylon were to live out the culture described in the pentateuchal books in every detail. Obviously, this is not true of Christian renewal movements that dwell on these texts. The narrative structure – of God forming his people in the wilderness, of the demand for obedience and the lengthening of the wanderings through failure – this is what is endlessly recalled and retold by Christian groups; the details of the culture that was to be formed in the desert are incidental and ignored. The detailed sacrificial regulations of the early chapters of Leviticus have not, generally, been regarded as of particular significance for Christian cultural renewal.

IV

The reason for this is obvious, but let me identify it formally in a fourth proposition: the coming of Jesus is seen by his followers as the fulfilment of this cultural project. The details of the relationships of the various New Testament texts to the Torah are complex and much-disputed, of course – not least in different reconstructions of the 'historical Jesus' on the one hand, and the cluster of debates that tend to be lumped together as 'the new perspective on Paul' on the other. It is clear, however, that even within the apostolic period, some

Gentile churches, at least, felt no need to conform at all to the cultural distinctives that were to have marked God's people, with (if the evidence of Acts 15 is to be believed)[17] circumcision being thrown out at an early date, and even that council's stipulations concerning (what we would now call) kosher meat seemingly set aside fairly quickly – Paul clearly teaches the Corinthians not to be bound by them, and there is little historical evidence of Gentile believers following such regulations in the immediately sub-apostolic period.[18]

If, as is now widely accepted, the Jerusalem council's list of prohibitions is a conscious recalling of the regulations of Leviticus 17 and 18, concerning Gentiles residing amongst the community of Israel,[19] then the rapid widespread setting-aside of the tradition is striking: the council's decision was, in effect, the suggestion that the coming of Christ did not set aside the cultural distinctiveness of God's people, but merely opened the possibility of others living as aliens within that culture. Its rejection was the insistence that the cultural imperatives of the Torah had, for Christians, come to a decisive end.

Nor, I think, is there anything comparable which replaces this cultural experiment. Christianity cannot be shown to be a specific culture in the way that the Israel, described by the Torah, is, either historically in its original foundation, or aspirationally in its foundational texts. The very possibility of talking of 'Jewish Christianity' and 'Gentile Christianity' in the apostolic period, or later of Greek, Latin and Syrian forms of the faith, suggests the point strongly. The qualifiers

---

[17] Which even Gerd Lüdemann suggests it should be. Gerd Lüdemann, *Early Christianity according to the Traditions in Acts: A Commentary* (trans. John Bowden; London: SCM, 1989), 170.

[18] On the particular issue of idol sacrifices, there is a little evidence that Paul's view did not completely carry the day. Justin Martyr's *Dialogue with Trypho the Jew* has Justin arguing that Christians should not eat meat sacrificed to idols, although he is forced to concede Trypho's point that many in fact do. For a few more examples, see J.C. Brunt, 'Rejected, Ignored or Misunderstood? The Fate of Paul's Approach to the Problem of Food Offered to Idols in Early Christianity.' *NTS* 31 (1985), 113–24. The fact that Brunt can only find three references within the first three centuries of the patristic period, suggests (contra to his own argument) that the point is not general. See also Anthony C. Thiselton, *The First Epistle to the Corinthians: A Commentary on the Greek Text* (NIGTC; Carlisle: Paternoster, 2000), 660–1 for convincing reasons to suggest that even those references Brunt does find are softened if understood in context.

[19] See C.K. Barrett, *Acts XV–XVIII: A Critical and Exegetical Commentary on the Acts of the Apostles* (ICC; Edinburgh: T&T Clark, 1998), 734 for this view, and some indication of its popularity, although the author finally rejects it.

are cultural, and so point to the possibility of the church existing in different cultural forms.

Further, within the Gospels there are many hints that Jewish exclusivity is being challenged. From God's first revelation of the nativity to pagan astrologers and the Baptist's announcement that God can raise up children of Abraham from stones, through Jesus' dealings with Samaritans and Syro-Phonecians, to the many multi-cultural features of the passion narratives, these stories subvert the distinctively Jewish cultural-religious complex in which they are set.

Thirdly, within the book of Acts, one could point not just to the decision of the council of Jerusalem, and Peter's vision there narrated, but also to the event of Pentecost: the table of nations there listed is surely intended to represent the whole world, and there is a surprising refusal to reverse the curse of Babel: the miracle of Pentecost, still being fulfilled, is not the (re-)uniting of human languages, and so of human cultures, but the effective infiltration of the gospel into every language and culture. God's word can be effectively spoken in every human language, and faithfully lived out in every human culture. It is no longer culturally specific to the people of Israel, or confined to the language of Hebrew. Given Bible Society's involvement in the project behind this book, it is not inappropriate to note that the drive to translate the Bible into every human tongue, however minor, is a distinctively and faithfully Christian understanding of the way God's word relates to human cultures; the comparison with the Islamic demand that the Qur'an be read only in Arabic is telling.[20]

Fourthly, in the Pauline (and deuteropauline) letters, my own (admittedly amateur) take on the issue of covenant nomism includes a suspicion that the polemics about circumcision are, at least in part, to do with this issue of inculturation. Paul sees faith in Christ as possible in any and every cultural milieu.

Finally, the pictures of final salvation in Revelation are avowedly and surprisingly multicultural: notice particularly chapter 7, where John listens to the number who are sealed, counted out carefully in the tribes of Israel, and then looks, and instead of the neat ranks of the twelve tribes, sees 'a great multitude that no one could count, from every nation, tribe, people and language, standing before the throne'.

---

[20] The promotion of the Vulgate, whilst not (to my mind) wholly defensible, was not predicated on any suggestion that Latin is particularly appropriate to the speaking forth of God's word, but questions about shared and authorised translations of the Scriptures.

The church, then, is not a cultural project in the way that the Israel of the Torah is. Instead, it is an entity that is capable of various – possibly endlessly various – inculturations. There are four obvious things that were central to the communal identity of the early church: the confession of belief in Christ, fairly rapidly coalescing into the *regula fidei* in its various forms; a commitment to a particular canon, originally of Jewish Scriptures, expanding fairly quickly to include a (slightly ill-defined, initially) set of early Christian writings; the practice of certain particular religious rites, notably baptism and Eucharist; and the maintenance of particular ethical positions.

There is some evidence to suggest that these distinctives were not dissimilar to those that formed the basis of the distinctiveness of the various mystery religions of the early imperial period, and so that, within the Roman Empire at least, there was a comprehensible cultural niche into which Christianity could fit. The conscious adoption of the habits, and indeed apparel, of the philosophers by apologists such as Justin Martyr, modelled no doubt on the Paul's activities in Athens, and his borrowings from the Stoic household codes, might be seen as a similar, although alternative, attempt to locate the practice of Christianity within existing cultural forms. Equally, there is evidence that Christians were regarded as occupying the same cultural niche as the Jews within the Empire early on. These different attempts to find a home within already existing cultural spaces failed, perhaps mainly because the refusal to burn incense to idols, coupled with the refusal to become a subculture like the Jews had done, ensured that Christianity did not quite fit in any of the available spaces, but the attempts are, I think, significant, in that they suggest that there was no attempt to found a Christian subculture; instead the energies were directed towards finding a home in various already available cultural locations.

I suspect that this history is paradigmatic of the relationship the church will have to its host cultures: there will be no basic conflict, but equally no easy co-existence. The first, because, unlike the Israel of the Torah or indeed Islam in its classical formulations, the church is not a cultural project. The second, because the church carries the inheritance of Torah, however transformed or fulfilled, and so will not and cannot be simply uninterested in cultural questions. Instead, to use an image from Torah that itself is taken up, reapplied, and transformed in the New Testament literature, Christian people will find themselves 'aliens and strangers', with 'no abiding city'.

This is the evidence for describing the coming of the Messiah as the ending of the cultural project described in the Torah, at least for those who believe he is the Messiah;[21] what of describing Jesus as the fulfilment of that same project? The significant texts, of course, are Romans 10:4 and the early part of the Sermon on the Mount. In Romans 10:4, Christ is described as the *telos nomou*, the 'end of the Law'. Whilst there seems to be some sort of consensus that *nomos* here should be understood as essentially the Torah, whatever qualifications concerning the meaning of Torah in first-century diaspora Judaism need to be added, there is a fundamental divergence of opinion over the meaning of *telos*: is this 'end' in the sense of the passing of,[22] or 'end' in the sense of completing of [23] (as in 'teleology')? I have not the knowledge, nor (thankfully) the need, to solve one of the more hotly-disputed questions in New Testament studies, but two features of the current debate may be helpful for my purposes. The first is the seemingly increasing popularity of the suggestion that Paul's usage was deliberately ambiguous, which I find unlikely, but suggestive.[24] The second is the increasing recognition on all sides of the debate that, whatever the correct exegesis of Romans 10:4, both the idea that Christ brought the Torah to an end, and that he was its goal, are positions that are congruent with the wider sweep of Pauline theology. That, after all, is all I am seeking to argue under this head.

The Sermon on the Mount, by contrast, is unambiguous, at least on this basic question. Jesus announces that he did not come to abolish (*kataluō*) the Law (and the Prophets) but to fulfil (*plēroō*) it. Nonetheless, Davies and Allison, with customary exhaustiveness, find no less than nine possible interpretations of what this means, and then opt themselves for a combinational view which is effectively a tenth.[25] In essence, however, the options are three: Jesus fulfils the law by living it out, the only Israelite ever to do so; Jesus fulfils the law by exposing its inner meaning, and so replacing the long lists of commands with

---

21. I make no claim in this paper in either direction about the appropriateness, post-Jesus, of continuing to live by Torah, and so about Christian supercessionism.

22. So, to give just one example, Stephen Westerholm, 'Paul and the Law in Romans 9–11', in *Paul and the Mosaic Law* (ed. James D.G. Dunn; Grand Rapids: Eerdmans, 2001), 215–37.

23. So Robert Badenas, *Christ the End of the Law: Romans 10:4 in Pauline Perspective* (JSNT Supp. Series 10; Sheffield: JSOT Press, 1985).

24. As Heikki Räisänen comments, 'Even if we cannot make up our mind between two linguistically possible options, it is suspect methodology to conclude that Paul could not either.' Heikki Räisänen, *Paul and the Law* (Philadelphia: Fortress, 1986), 53.

25. W.D. Davies and Dale C. Allison, *A Critical and Exegetical Commentary on the Gospel According to St Matthew, Vol. 1* (ICC; Edinburgh: T&T Clark, 1988), 485–6.

the law of love; or Jesus fulfils the law eschatologically, in that he is the promised Messiah, who is the *telos* of the law.

Notice, however, that these suggestions implicitly assume that Torah is something fundamentally religious or ethical, rather than political or cultural. One person cannot live out a political or cultural programme – if that is not already obvious, I will argue it later. Whilst a political theory might be reducible to inner core principles, political reality, and cultural even more, are notoriously resistant to such reductionist explanations – the whole programme of anthropology and, more recently, cultural studies has been a testimony to that fact. Finally, whilst it is conceivable that a cultural project might be created with the intention of forming a particular individual, this seems a difficult interpretation of the verses.

In any case, the point is more general, or so I believe. The New Testament texts and the early church alike simply assume that Israel's Scriptures, and so the books of the Pentateuch, point clearly, unambiguously, and possibly even only, towards Jesus Christ. He is consistently presented as the fulfilment of all that is talked about in these books. The only possible way that the respect for the holy books of Israel that is evident in the NT and the early church can be coherently held alongside the refusal to seek to instantiate the cultural project outlined in these books is to offer a theological account of the way the economy of salvation has been changed so radically by the life, death and resurrection of Jesus Christ that what stands written can no longer be read in the same way by those who follow this Jesus.

This is hardly an original point, of course; that God's purposes for Israel are somehow gathered up and fulfilled in the person of Jesus is a standard Christian theme.[26] It seems to me a more difficult theme, however, if God's purposes as described in Torah are recognised as irreducibly cultural. Once again, whilst one person can offer true obedience to God, for instance, I am not sure that one person can successfully instantiate a culture. I recall once talking to an expert on the ancient Cornish form of the Gaelic language, which did, in fact, die out around 1800 before being resurrected from grammars and dictionaries; he raised the question of whether a language dies with its last speaker, or with its penultimate one, since then the language will

---

[26] Generally, of course, asserted in a supercessionist mode. I do not want to rule out the possibility that for Israel to continue to live as Israel may be a faithful response to God, even after the coming of Christ, but nor do I want to regard that possibility as decisive for our understanding of what faithful Christian following after Christ might look like.

never be spoken again.[27] A culture, far more than a language, would seem to demand shared systems of meaning and so on, which cannot exist in one person alone. Cultural realities are, I submit, irreducibly communal. Just so, it is far from trivial to work out what it means to speak of Jesus as 'the fulfilment of the law'.

For what it is worth, my suspicion is that Davies and Allison's multiple witness, and the confusion over the meaning of Paul's words in Romans 10:4, are the key indicators. If the Torah is best understood as cultural, then it is a complex and multivalent reality. Just so, there are necessarily many aspects to its fulfilment; to 'fulfil the Torah' is a significant cultural activity, and so, necessarily, one that is not reducible to any simple action, whether religious, ethical, political or whatever. The fulfilment and transformation of Torah is complex, multivalent and irreducible.

As a result, reading the Old Testament, and particularly the Torah, is not a trivial task for the church; the literal sense speaks of a set of duties and realities – of a cultural project – that is no longer ours. The response to this has been a variety of reading practices which seek to take the text seriously as Christian Scripture by discovering a *sensus plenior*, a fuller truth, that is contained within the text but is not immediately obvious or available to the unskilled reader. The most basic form of such reading, typology, was precisely a way to take the now seemingly irrelevant cultural texts and make them apply to Jesus. More interestingly, perhaps, in the fully developed fourfold exegesis of the medieval schools was the anagogical sense, which applied the text eschatologically, and so potentially to a new cultural situation.

The fourfold interpretation of Scripture was a development of typology, and so everything was seen refracted through the lens of Jesus Christ. In Christ, God's blueprint for a human cultural experiment in Torah could be reinterpreted as a description of the way God's people will live together in the heavenly Jerusalem. Now, I have neither the space nor the desire to defend or criticise the fourfold exegesis and, in any case, I am trying here to offer a theological account of human culture, not a christological hermeneutic of the Old Testament. So let me simply note that if anagogy is an appropriate reading strategy, then it might be useful in developing a theological account of culture, and leave the point there.

---

[27] Cornish was a rather special case, he informed me, since its last speaker was survived by her parrot!

The example of the fourfold exegesis, however, might suggest a way forward. Its origins, as a hermeneutical strategy, lie in the way in which the meanings of Old Testament texts and concepts get re-envisioned by the writers of the New Testament books, precisely through reflecting on them in the light of Christ, and reappear in radically new forms. Whether this procedure is best seen as a form of midrash, or as typology, or various other things is not my concern; in each case the decisive point is the gospel history of Jesus Christ, which forces and shapes the recasting of the concepts. If we are to make sense – Christian theological sense – of the cultural programme set out in the first five books of the Bible, then it will be by understanding the grammar of these translations and applying that same grammar with care and sensitivity to every cultural demand of Torah – from the land reform programme of Jubilee to the refusal to boil a kid in its mother's milk.

The grammar, however, is complex – one thing, at least, that the medieval exegetes understood. Let me close with just two examples to demonstrate that point, both phrases regularly used to describe the culture that God is calling into being in the Old Testament texts, and both taken up in different ways in the New Testament and later theology. God set out to create a cultural reality that is described as both his child, or son, and his betrothed, beloved, or bride. How do these images translate across the life of Christ that divides the testaments, and what is their cultural significance?

To describe Israel as God's Son is (theologically) necessarily to stress the fulfilment of all that Israel is in Jesus Christ. There is a focusing down, a concentration of all that Israel is called to be, in the one true Israelite who walks his lonely road to the cross, and rises triumphant from the grave. That much is standard, but the same problem raises its head: how is the cultural reality that is Israel focused down into the one man? We might respond with some form of the doctrine of the *totus Christus*, of the corporate fullness of Christ, which is the church. I am not sure, however, that this is a helpful solution here, as it is precisely the time of the incarnation in which this question is at its sharpest, and that time is the hardest in which to speak about the *totus Christus* in any meaningful way. If this problem is put aside for a moment, however, the renewal of the image in the New Testament is rather interesting: the church is nowhere, I think, described as God's child; rather Christians are described as God's children. Jesus the Son is the firstborn among many. And so the images pile up. Israel, the child, has come to an end, at least for Christians, in Jesus. Others, Jews and Gentiles, now take their places as adopted children alongside God's only-begotten in the family. Alongside the one Son, God is bringing many children, from every tongue, tribe and nation – every human culture – to glory. The cultural aspects of this image appear to be set aside or transcended in the fulfilment of the Torah by Christ.

By contrast, the description of Israel as the espoused of God remains in the New Testament. Christ is not the bride, but the bridegroom, and the transformation is from Israel as the bride of God to the church as the bride of Christ. On this showing, the fulfilment of the image is the people of God as an eschatological unity, still each bringing their particular cultural riches, but bringing them in a united whole, a heavenly *polis*, that is united with the Son. These recognitions are not original, of course, but they do perhaps illustrate the point: if Torah describes a cultural reality, then it is not reducible to particular themes and principles; instead, it can only be comprehended using what social scientists call 'thick description', and so its fulfilment in Christ is complex and multivalent.

V

What, then, are the themes for a theological account of culture that grow out of this recognition that Torah is a cultural description? Firstly, that culture matters: it is not irrelevant to the ways and works of God. Secondly, however, I have suggested that the particular cultural blueprint given in the Pentateuch is not decisive in straightforward ways, partly because it is clearly contextual in a whole host of ways, partly because it is fulfilled in the coming of the Messiah in complex and not easily predictable ways. Thirdly, I noted, although without exploring the point, that cultural renewal within the church has tended to appeal to the narratives of cultural formation, rather than the details of the culture there described. Fourthly, I suggested that, whilst the church does not instantiate a particular culture, because of this cultural heritage, it will not fit easily into existing cultures, and it will necessarily transform any culture in which it takes root. Finally, I have given a brief indication of ways in which the cultural descriptions and stipulations of Torah may be read through the lens of Christ. This last point, at least, is programmatic if accepted, although it was developed far too briefly. There is, as ever, more work to be done.

5

Reformation Accounts of the Church's Response to Human Culture

Colin Gunton

I To Set the Scene: a Search for Criteria

Culture is all those things which human beings make of the created order, what we call the material created order, including those only apparently non-material dimensions like words and music. (If everything but God is created, then words and music too are constituted of the same kind of stuff as sticks and stones.) There is a case for claiming that culture is one of the activities implicit in the doctrine of the image of God; that is to say, Genesis 1:28, 'fill the earth and subdue it', can be called a cultural mandate. To be sure, we must beware of turning that verse into a general principle.[1] It does not follow that, because in the beginning the first human inhabitants were commanded to fill the earth, unlimited expansion is called for; nor that 'subdue' should be taken in a post-Enlightenment sense of mechanistic domination. Nor must the verse be understood outside its broader Old and New Testament context, and here we can appeal to the explicit celebration of the Spirit's gifts in the work of the craftsmen of the tabernacle in Exodus 31, a chapter whose words deliberately echo those of Genesis 1. Yet despite the qualification, there is to be found in Genesis 1, I believe, a mandate of a kind which should be taken eschatologically and pneumatologically.

An eschatology of creation is one according to which creation is to be understood as project. That which is made in the beginning is very good, yet remains to be perfected: perfect and to be perfected. It is not yet subdued, all things not yet brought together under one head, even Christ (Eph. 1:10). Eschatologically speaking, even 'in the beginning',

---

[1] So Barth.

before the fall, things are not yet as they are created to be, because there is a task laid upon those created in the image of God and it involves both the moral and the cultural, insofar as they can be separated. The agent of this perfecting is to be man, male and female together, who are placed there as God's representatives – I think we should say, sacramental representatives – in order, as part of the created order, to superintend that perfecting. In this context, culture, we might say, is that set of activities in which those made in the image of God share in the divine perfecting of that which was made in the beginning. This should not be understood in a Pelagian sense. Perhaps we should not use the word 'agent' in connection with man and woman – though we are indeed agents – but sub-agents, just as Tolkien rightly warned that we should not speak of ourselves as co-creators but sub-creators in the cultural task. That attempt to perfect the world apart from God's prevenient agency is almost a definition of sin, to which we shall come, but it does not follow that there is no proper human action empowered by God.

That brings us to our pneumatology and to Basil's otherwise un-developed principle that the Holy Spirit is the perfecting cause of the creation. There is a certain amount of tautology in that sentence, for 'holy' means perfect and to be the *holy* Spirit therefore means to be the one who perfects the created order (through the Son, of course, as we shall see). This means that he perfects the *material* creation, and here two gnosticising tendencies which have vitiated much of the tradition must be identified. The first is to construe the Spirit's action merely, or largely, anthropologically, in terms of perfecting human beings in the moral or religious life. That 'spiritualising' which limits redeemed human action to the 'religious', or non-worldly, dimension makes the word 'holy' applicable only to the world of human piety. Whatever we are to make of Leviticus' teaching on holiness, there seems little doubt that it is concerned with material – bodily and social – and not 'spiritual' perfection in a narrow sense. We shall come to that later. But the point to be made here is that an adequate account of the Spirit's perfecting action will embrace the human, the non-human, and the two in relation. It is with the latter, with culture, that we are here concerned: with the way in which the Spirit enables human action to interact with the creation in such a way as to enable it to be perfected.

The second gnostic tendency is to take 'spiritual' to mean 'non-material'. To say that God is spirit is to say, I believe, not that he is non-material – though, of course, that does not have to be denied – but, positively, that he is able to transcend the ontological divide between the Creator and the created, in order to transform and perfect the *material* world. More attention to Ezekiel 37 in the development of the doctrine of the Spirit , and less to the development of what Gibbon and Hume – and later Nietzsche – rightly saw to be world-denying 'monkish virtues', would have avoided a great deal of distortion. Romans 8 is not just nice rhetoric for when we want to feel ecologically pious, but intrinsic to a sustained pneumatology, in which Paul moves from Christ, through the community of redemption, to the way in which the human creature is not to be perfected apart from the liberation of the world in which it is set.

That means that on this – our – side of the ontological divide, 'spiritual' most definitely does not mean 'non-material', but must refer to the Spirit's enabling of the perfecting of the material world: both via human agency and independently of it.[2] We, therefore, need to eschew without qualification the deep-seated tendency in our culture, theological and secular alike, to construe spiritual as 'non-material'. Here I cite Douglas Knight, who is speaking of aspects of idealism, but need not be:

> The least spiritual is the least material, the least enduring, the most badly-executed and provisional, that cannot hold any form it is given. Spiritual does not mean ethereal and fleeting. Material does not mean thicker, or more durable.[3]

Our model here must be the resurrection body of Christ and the 'spiritual' body of the resurrection which it presents: a body or, perhaps better, whole person perfected by the Spirit, the first fruits of the perfecting of all the creation, the form for which all human beings have been created.

There is, however, as that illustration suggests, no Spirit without the Son, and any general pneumatology without Christology is doomed to the very spiritualising which we must avoid, at all costs, if we are to develop an adequate theology of culture. There are two reasons for this, and they are both to be kept in mind if we are to understand Genesis 1:28 in the broad context of the divine economy. The first is the fall. However we are to understand that, it reminds us that the project of creation can be achieved only through redemption, and that means the life, death, resurrection and ascension of Jesus of Nazareth understood as divine action. As things are, the human race fails in its cultural

---

[2] The latter, to be sure, is not culture, but must not be left out of account. How difficult is it to do theology without distortion!

[3] Douglas Knight, e-mail to the author, 25 July 2002.

mandate and, *consequently*, the remainder of the creation fails to be offered in praise to its Maker. The purpose of the cross is, accordingly, the bearing of the power of evil, so that the creation, first the human and then its environment, should be returned to its proper course. The project of creation is achieved only through its redemption, not simply through its perfecting; or rather by its perfecting through redemption – by its release from its bondage to decay. The biblical expression of this fallenness, this bondage to decay rather than orientation to perfection, is to be found in the cursing of the earth in Genesis 3. Work with this curse is no longer simply work, but laborious and unpleasant. The disruptive effects of sin upon culture are seen especially in Genesis 11, to whose treatment in the Reformers we shall come. On the other side, Ephesians 1:1–10 seems to imply a close link between the death of Christ ('redemption through his blood') and the reconciliation of all things in the fullness of time. How does the Spirit operate in this context? The short answer is, by the resurrection of Jesus from the dead, the eschatological perfection of this sample of the material creation in anticipation of the summing up of all things. And who raises Jesus from the tomb? The Father, through his perfecting Spirit.

The second christological locus is the incarnation, and that means the life, etc. of the eternal Son, understood as human action in the materiality of human flesh. This takes the form of a Jewish man's involvement in Jewish culture, and it is to be noted that, outside the Gospels, the chief extended treatment of this is to be found against the background of a sustained engagement with the Old Testament in the Letter to the Hebrews. In this context, to borrow the title of Robert Jenson's Maurice Lectures, we have to understand Christ as culture. It is a material human body which is offered perfect to God the Father through the eternal Spirit in the context of a particular ministry (that of Israel's prophet, priest and king) in a particular religio–political context. How does the Spirit operate in this context? The short answer is by enabling the Son's humanity to be an authentic humanity, *who*, in the words of our letter, 'through the eternal Spirit' offered his perfect sacrifice of obedience and praise. It is the perfecting Spirit's action which becomes the means of the re-constitution of the cultural mandate in its God-given form in this particular instance.

Our next step must take us into the present. How does the Spirit operate in this context? The answer, without which any theology of culture remains abstract, is by the forming of a particular kind of culture, the church, around the one truly perfected life. We gain a cumulative picture of some of the things this might mean, if we look at some of the ways in which the New Testament writers speak of the church. To refer to Romans 8 again, we can see that, there, life in the Spirit in the church provides a link: 'the first fruits of the Spirit' leads to expectation, in the context of the creation's groaning, of 'the redemption of our bodies' (Rom. 8:23). While the Thessalonian letters, Ephesians, 1 Peter and especially Revelation might offer some insight into the church's relation to political culture,[4] 1 Corinthians especially provides a series of insights into Paul's view of the church as a form of culture: as communion and cult, but those as they take shape in relation to the moral, legal and religious institutions of the city. What shapes the culture which the church is should not be the institutions of the old world, which is due to pass away, but the proclaiming and living of Christ crucified in the hope of the resurrection. As Irenaeus almost alone among the church's theologians came to teach, the Lord's Supper is not an act of individual religious piety whose meaning is found in the *inward* – the spiritual in the bad sense – but in part an offering of the world, human and non-human, to God in the light of its coming perfection.

II Mainly on the Reformers

It is in such a light that we must view the developments in the era known as Christendom which provide the background to the Reformation. We must insist here that it is the material world that is to be perfected as material, and that is why forms of Platonism and Gnosticism, which either downgrade to semi-reality or actively despise the material world, are to be rejected *a limine*, as Barth liked to say. They should be, but often have not been. In contrast to this, there is a tendency in Christendom to view material culture as the result of the fall, just as in the theologies of Origen, and less explicitly of Augustine, materiality and fallenness are close bedfellows. It is one of the marks of the Augustinian aesthetic that has ruled even until now, that mere material beauty is, or should be, the ladder to a higher, non-material and heavenly beauty: 'Heard melodies are sweet, but those unheard are sweeter.'[5] There is a tendency, which we shall meet, to treat material culture as inferior to the so-called spiritual, and it is found in conflict with other more biblical pressures in the Reformation, as we shall see. Let me risk some one-sided generalisations about the nature of what can be called the theology of culture in Christendom.

---

[4] To the principalities and powers, Ephesians 3:9–10 in relation to 1:1–10.
[5] John Keats, 'Ode on a Grecian Urn', ll.11–12.

The Reformation was partly the result, and partly the cause, of a breakdown in a European culture whose roots reach down to the earliest centuries of the Christian era. It is arguable that this change, which could almost justify the overused expression cultural revolution, is receiving its finishing touches in the convolutions of the so-called postmodernity. It is also arguable, almost incontestable, that Christian theology has, as yet, failed to come fully to terms with it. The essence of that culture is that it represented some kind of fusion of biblical and pagan culture, which was all-embracing in its reach. Some symptoms can be isolated. One is Constantine the Great, that more than merely symbolic figure, of whom Gibbon, whose sardonic observation of the social advance of Christianity should be taken with the greatest seriousness, observed:

> He artfully advanced the hopes and fears of his subjects, by publishing in the same year two edicts; the first of which enjoined the solemn observance of Sunday, and the second the regular consultation of the Aruspices.[6]

Teste David et Sybilla: those words, institutionalised in Christendom's Requiem Mass, are a symptom of paganism's partial displacement of the Old Testament, with all its dreadful consequences. Another symptom is the institutionalising into mainstream Christian theology of the barely-christianised pagan theology of the pseudo-Dionysius, whose claim to Christian antiquity puts him almost in the same class as the donation of Constantine. Christendom is a sometimes unequal marriage of biblical affirmation of the created order and a semi-gnostic spiritualising.

The point here is that the problem goes far deeper than the political. The use of the label 'Constantinian' – for example, in the tradition of Yoder – as a portmanteau word for all that is wrong with the eras which succeeded him is in danger of narrowing and oversimplification. It is often contended that the Reformers were still essentially Constantinian in their view of church and state, and that may be true to the extent that they assumed that society was expected to be Christian (though even Stanley Hauerwas has admitted that this is not necessarily in every way a bad thing). This approach, however, tends to conceive the drawbacks of the era too narrowly in terms of the political realm, and so to lead to dangerously over-moralistic accounts of the situation in

---

[6] Edward Gibbon, *Decline and Fall of the Roman Empire* (ed. David Wormersley; Harmondsworth: Penguin, 1996), 2.311.

representatives of what has been called the Radical Reformation. To really reach the heart of things, however, we have to find more truly theological concepts, for what is at stake are rival conceptions of the relation of God to the world. Here again much hangs on the different meanings of the word 'spiritual' and, in particular, on the construction of the being and action of the third person of the Trinity.

The rock on which the medieval synthesis was wrecked was a false conception of the Spirit, according to which the spiritual and the material are conceived of as, in some sense, opposites. The most dangerous manifestation of this was among the first to be picked up by Luther: the division of culture into two realms, the spiritual and temporal, turning as it did the biblical two-era, apocalyptic view of the world into a version of the platonic, non-eschatological, two-world conception. Luther put the axe to the root of this tree in what may seem to be his very Constantinian *Appeal to the German nobility*. In the following brief exposition, I shall refer to two spheres of culture and concentrate on those aspects of this writing which use the words 'spirit' or 'spiritual'.

The first is the ecclesiological.

> It is pure invention that pope, bishop, priests and monks are called the spiritual estate while princes, lords, artisans and farmers are called the temporal estate ... Yet ... all Christians are truly of the spiritual estate, and there is no difference between them except of office. Paul says in 1 Corinthians 12 that all are one body, yet every member has his own work by which it serves the others.[7]

Similar is the christological principle underlying the reference to 1 Corinthians.

> We are all one body of Christ the Head, and all members one of another. Christ does not have two different bodies, one temporal, the other spiritual. There is but one Head and one body.[8]

Secondly, Luther's attack on Aristotle is of a piece with this, for it implies a recognition that, in Christendom's hybrid culture, the human mind has displaced the Holy Spirit as the source of the knowledge of God. 'What are they [the universities] but places where loose living is practised, where little is taught of the Holy Scriptures and Christian

---

[7] Luther, *Works*, 44 (ed. James Atkinson; Philadelphia: Fortress, 1966), 127.
[8] Luther, *Works*, 44, 130.

faith, and where only the blind heathen teacher Aristotle rules far more than Christ?' The problem with the most influential of Aristotle's books is that they 'boast about nature, although nothing can be learned from them either about nature or the Spirit'.[9] Luther saw a direct link between the philosophy of Aristotle and the corruption of the church, because it attributes to the unredeemed human mind powers which ought to be attributed to God the Spirit.

When it comes to his treatment of culture in general, Luther, despite his continuing and sometimes lyrical appreciation of music, speaks in sometimes rather bleak tones. His exegesis of what I have called the cultural mandate of Genesis 1 stresses rather what has been lost at the fall. There remains 'some appearance of dominion'[10] but 'Our faculties today are leprous, indeed dull and utterly dead.' To be sure, much of this pessimism can be attributed to the dark days in which Luther believed he was living, something he shared with Calvin. Yet there is a difference of emphasis in the latter, which makes his view of human culture sometimes strikingly different, and it is because he has a different pneumatology. Let us compare the differences in their exposition of Genesis. In some respects, they are remarkably similar, for example on Babel, where in both cases the sin is not in the culture, in building the city, but in the self-regard and aggrandisement with which they did it. Luther comments that the saints also built cities,[11] Calvin that 'To erect a citadel was not in itself so great a crime; but to raise an eternal monument to themselves, which might endure throughout all ages, was a proof of headstrong pride, joined with contempt of God.'[12] Yet even here the differences between the two begin to emerge. Luther tends to stress the absolute difference between the era of Babel and that of the Spirit. The difference of languages is for him the seedbed of all evils, leading to political and economic confusion, only overcome by the gift of the Spirit as it is recorded in Acts 2, which Luther recognises as referring to an overcoming of Babel.[13] Calvin's account of the differences between the eras is more subtle, and, although he does not here mention the Spirit, we shall see later that pneumatology is behind the differences of emphasis. He writes that, after Babel:

---

[9] Luther, *Works*, 44, 200.

[10] Luther, *Works*, 1 (ed. Jaroslav Pelikan; St Louis: Concordia, 1958) 67.

[11] Luther, *Works*, 2 (ed. Jaroslav Pelikan; St Louis: Concordia, 1960), 211, 214.

[12] Calvin, *Commentary on Genesis* (tr. John King, Edinburgh: Calvin Translation Society, 1843), 324. He might be speaking of Constantine.

[13] Luther, *Works*, 2 (ed. Jaroslav Pelikan; St Louis: Concordia, 1960), 214f.

Now, although the world bears this curse to the present day; yet in the midst of punishment, and of the most dreadful proofs of Divine anger against the pride of men, the admirable goodness of God is rendered conspicuous, because the nations hold mutual communication among themselves, though in different languages; but especially because He has proclaimed one gospel, in all languages, through the whole world, and has endued the apostles with the gift of tongues.[14]

The difference between the two Reformers emerges in their account of culture 'after Cain'. On Genesis 4:22, Luther comments that Jewish interpreters are wrong to suggest that, because the earth was cursed, Cain's descendants were forced to engage in other activities. Culture itself comes rather from a false desire for mastery.

The fact that they invented music and devoted their efforts to developing other arts is proof that they had a plentiful supply of everything they needed for sustenance. They had turned to these endeavours and were not satisfied with their simple manner of life, as were the children of Adam, because they wanted to be masters and were trying to win high praise and honour as clever men.[15]

Luther sometimes sounds rather like a modern eco-fundamentalist. By contrast, Calvin's account of the same material is less gloomy. I cite him at length because it is so entirely contradictory to popular expectation. What is, above all, clear from this passage is that the Spirit is the universal perfecting cause not simply the source of piety, important though the latter is for Calvin.

Moses ... expressly celebrates the remaining benediction on that race, which otherwise would have been deemed void and barren of all good. Let us then know, that the sons of Cain, though deprived of the Spirit of regeneration, were yet endued with gifts of no despicable kind; just as the experience of all ages teaches us how widely the rays of divine light have shone on unbelieving nations, for the benefit of the present life; and we see, at the present time, that *the excellent gifts of the Spirit are diffused through the whole human race*. Moreover, the liberal arts and sciences have descended to us from the heathen. We are, indeed, compelled to acknowledge that we have received astronomy, and the other parts of philosophy, medicine, and the order of civil government, from them.[16]

---

[14] Calvin, *Genesis*, 331.

[15] Calvin, *Genesis*, 318. 'Nevertheless' he adds, 'I believe that there were some among them who went over to the true church and adopted Adam's faith.'

[16] Calvin, *Genesis*, 218. He nevertheless adds, 'let us still value far more highly that grace of regeneration with which he peculiarly sanctifies his elect unto himself.'

Although, however, there is a stronger pneumatology, it is evident from other things that he says that, like Luther, Calvin still belongs in two worlds. (We should not expect anything different: what is interesting about any thinker is the way in which he transcends his world while continuing to be part of it. There is an analogy, though, of course only an analogy, with the incarnation there: the particular Jewish Jesus is the universal truth.) Calvin's two-worldedness comes out in his celebration of the goodness of 'secular' culture in Book 2 of the *Institutes*. Here it must be said that, although this passage is partly pneumatologically determined, Calvin sails far too close for safety to the medieval nature-grace theology, and the semi-gnostic divine spark anthropology which characterised it. He sets the scene by a treatment of reason which, because it 'is a natural gift, it could not be completely wiped out'. He thus still operates with the doctrine that the image of God is to be found in reason, and the term he used is surely significant: 'some sparks still gleam. These show him [man] to be a rational being'.[17]

Calvin's view of human reason, we might say, is a pessimistic version of that which Luther so roundly rejected. But the pessimism is mitigated by two features which are not, it seems to me, ultimately compatible. The dominant one, as we have already seen, is the Spirit. 'If we regard the Spirit of God as the sole fountain of truth, we shall neither reject the truth itself, nor despise it wherever it shall appear, unless we wish to dishonour the Spirit of God'.[18] Calvin is here speaking of human political skills and, in the next section, says similar things about science and art. '[I]f the Lord has willed that we be helped in physics, dialectic, mathematics, and other like disciplines, by the work and ministry of the ungodly, let us use this assistance.'[19] The second mitigating factor is a continuing appeal to natural endowments, traces of which are left even after the fall. '[S]ome seed of political order has been implanted in all men. And this is ample proof that, in the arrangement of this life, no man is without the light of reason.'[20] '[T]his evidence clearly testifies to a universal apprehension of reason and understanding by nature implanted in men.'[21] Now, it may be contended that there is no great difference between the two features: the gift of reason implanted in all

---

[17] John Calvin, *Institutes of the Christian Religion*, II.2.12 (ed. J.T. McNeill; trans. F.L. Battles; Library of Christian Classics 20; Philadelphia: Westminster, 1960), 270–7.

[18] Calvin, *Institutes*, II.2.15, 274.

[19] Calvin, *Institutes*, II.2.16, 275.

[20] Calvin, *Institutes*, II.2.13, 273.

[21] Calvin, *Institutes*, II.2.14, 273.

may simply be another way of speaking of the gifts of the Spirit, and that is indeed the way Calvin takes it. And it has a measure of biblical justification: the Spirit is the one who both moves over the face of the waters in the beginning and brings eschatological life to the body of Jesus in the tomb. But, before coming to this and other general problems left behind by the Reformers, let us review our progress so far.

Luther's insistence that the gifts of the Spirit are universal among Christians, and Calvin's attribution of secular culture to the gift of the Spirit have together done much to shape the modern world. Enough has been made in the literature of the way in which the former has shaped the development of modern science, and I content myself with alluding to Hooykaas's claim in his book on the origins of modern science that the biblical insistence on the goodness of the work of the hands alongside the opening of true discipleship to the laity were among the causes of the development of natural science.[22] Less widely known is the influence of Reformation theology on the development of music. It was, for example, a mark of the Puritans not to be hostile to culture, as they are widely thought to have been, but to have concentrated their efforts on the reformation of those forms of culture used in worship. Section 3, of the entry on 'Puritans and Music', in the *Oxford Companion to Music,* is entitled 'The Complete Acceptance of Music other than in Church.'

> When Bach was in the service of Prince Leopold of Anhalt-Cöthen … his compositions were not of the nature of organ music or church music of any kind, but of chamber music. This was because the Prince was a Calvinist …; no music beyond simple chorales was required in the church service, and Bach's musical energies … were … employed in the provision of music for the court's entertainments.

> This was much the position in the English Puritanism of the previous century. There was no objection to music; indeed, secular music flourished as never before. But there *was* an objection to elaborate church music.[23]

This much then should be clear. The Reformation tradition was the seedbed of science and culture alike, quite apart from the modern political, and particularly democratic, institutions developed under many of its impulses.

---

[22] Reijer Hooykaas, *Religion and the Rise of Modern Science* (Edinburgh: Scottish Academic Press, 1972); see also John Dillenberger, *Protestant Thought and Natural Science: A Historical Interpretation* (London: Collins, 1961) and T.F. Torrance's various contributions on the subject.

[23] pp. 844–5.

III Why did things go wrong, for surely they did?

1. The easy answer, containing many elements of truth, is that the re-divinisation of the human mind in the Renaissance and Enlightenment proved too strong for the essentially biblical celebration of culture in the Reformers. For some good reasons, Christianity seemed, and was made out by secular propaganda to be, hostile to science and culture generally, at least the culture of the time that wished to affirm 'the world' over against the 'other-worldliness' of medieval culture. That is the charge, endlessly repeated by Feuerbach and his heirs: that Christianity is idealistic – that is to say, 'spiritual' at the expense of the material, a Platonism for the masses – and must be overcome. The result is that there is no criterial control on culture, as is shown, for example, by the fact that science is widely believed to be right about everything, but, in the arts, matters of the truth and goodness of the created world are generally thought to be irrelevant. Culture which has consciously set itself free from any gospel vision is deeply problematic culture.

2. To venture a critique of the Reformers, we must say something like the following: Each of them, in their different ways, has a dialectical, rather than Trinitarian, theology of culture. In Luther, the dialectic is between old and new, the lost world of the fall and the renewed world of the gospel. There is much in what he says. Culture apart from Christ is finally unfulfilled, as a glance at the Manichaeism of some modern art makes only too clear. And yet – and I shall come to this – Christ is to be found not only where the gospel is consciously lived. In Calvin, over and above the pneumatological emphasis which we have met is a continuing dialectic of nature and grace, of such a kind that it is not surprising that the Reformed Dogmaticians so easily relapsed into the kind of Aristotelianism that Luther rightly saw was the antithesis of the gospel. That is to say, Calvin's attribution of efficacy to some residual natural righteousness runs the risk of suggesting that there is some human capacity that is not the gift of the Spirit; that, in this sphere, the Spirit's writ is not quite universal. Is that perhaps the loss of an eschatological, at the expense of a protological, conception of perfection? To follow that up in detail would take us too far from the topic of the paper, but it is important. If the creation was given its direction in the past, must it not also have its orientation and goal from its promised perfection and, therefore, from the Spirit alone? Perhaps more significant is the absence of any christological appeal in Calvin's chapters on the arts, science and politics. Does he have traces of a Spirit who is not the Spirit of Jesus, but rather a more generalised

divine force for good? That takes us to the heart of the question of the theology of culture.

It is at this place that the puritan dualism between the necessity for a simplicity of music for worship – with which I do not wish to quarrel; the gospel is not mainly for aesthetes and intellectuals – and the development of other criteria for secular music gives cause for reflection. It seems to come from Calvin's *duplex ordo cognitionis*, rather different though it is from that which has been institutionalised in modern Thomism:

> we must here set forth a distinction …: that there is one kind of under-standing of earthly things; another of heavenly. I call "earthly things" those which do not pertain to God or his Kingdom … but which have their significance and relationship with regard to the present life … I call "heavenly things" the pure knowledge of God, the nature of true righteousness, and the mysteries of the Heavenly Kingdom. The first class includes government, household management, all mechanical skills, and the liberal arts. In the second are the knowledge of God and of his will.[24]

Does that give rise to yet another version of the temporal and the spiritual, as distinct from a more pneumatological and eschatological set of criteria? Or rather, is its eschatology not dualistic, unlike a biblical eschatology which precisely does bear on the present life? That is simply a question which I wish to leave as a question. But where do we go from here for a theology of culture?

3.   The answer seems to me not to attempt to re-sacralise culture after the manner of the Milbankians, whose essentially reactionary view of culture has already been pointed out.[25] Bad dogmatics can be driven out only by good, otherwise a new devil takes over the house. Rather, we must go further than the Reformers in the attempt to develop a biblical and Trinitarian approach to culture, and especially in the matter of replacing the two-world ideology of platonised Christianity with the two era view of scripture. To say that the Spirit is the Spirit of truth is

---

24   Calvin, *Institutes*, II.2.13, 272, compare II.2.16: 'We ought to understand the statement that the Spirit dwells only in believers [Rom. 8:9] as referring to the Spirit of sanctification.... Nonetheless he fills, moves and quickens all things by the power of that same Spirit, and does so according to the character that he has bestowed upon each kind by the law of creation.'

25   Richard Roberts, 'Transcendental Sociology? A Critique of John Milbank's Theology and Social Theory beyond Secular Reason', *Scottish Journal of Theology* 46 (1993), 527–35.

to say that he is the Spirit of Jesus, and that means that a more firmly christological pneumatology is needed than is to be found even in Calvin. Who is this Jesus? He is the eternal Son of the Father, made man and seated at the right hand of the Father, *quodam modo praesens, quodam modo absens*, through whom the Father's Spirit offers all those things that *are being perfected* to the Father to his praise and glory. To be perfect is to praise or to be enabled to praise God, and here Calvin is right in saying that the work of the Spirit is not limited to the consciously Christian. But ought not our criteria be more explicitly christological if we are both to recognise what is true culture in a fallen world and to apply common criteria of truth, goodness and beauty to culture within and without the church? This is not to deny that worship may well require different forms from those used elsewhere; that goes without saying. But that should not be to put them into different worlds, like the clergy and laity of the culture Luther rejected. If the walls of the church are permeable, as they are, how are we therefore to conceive of the interaction of the gospel and culture in a world where we do not have the same prince worshipping with one kind of music in one place, another in another, but with many princes not worshipping at all? How is the one world held together in Christ, in whom all things, things in heaven and things on earth are to be summed up?

Perhaps assistance can be found in a doctrine of the image of God, christologically conceived, where it is conceived not to consist in reason but in a dignity and calling to be a person. That calling is perfected by one, but expected of all, and that returns us to Genesis 1:26–28. The cultural mandate involves two foci, human beings in relation to one another and in involvement in the material world in all its variety. They come together, above all, in the celebration of the Lord's Supper, that act of worship which so often appears to involve neither true human *koinōnia* nor real involvement with the material world. (When I made a similar point to this to the members of a theological society, one member of it pointed out that there is evidence that, in the early days of the church, the bread and wine left over from the Supper was distributed to the poor, an observation which throws much light on our present spiritualising of the rite.) But let me restrict the final remarks to points which emerge from the Reformers' theology of culture.

Two things have to be said. The first is that our assessment of culture needs to be somewhat broader than Luther's tendency to see it as the function of the fall, and Calvin's largely instrumental treatment, that pagan culture is good because it is useful to us. If pagan culture is, in part, the work of the Spirit – in a manner 'inspired' – then it needs to be conceived as in its own way praising God. This is where Barth's judgement on Mozart is worth repeating. Yet, second, at the same time the criteria by which we assess whether – or in which respects – a work of culture is the praise of God or some form of sin must be christological, because only in Jesus do we know what right culture is. Moving from a certain kind of life, death and resurrection to judgements on culture requires the wisdom that does not come easily, because there are immense complexities. For example, we know that the cross, the supreme blasphemy, is turned by the Spirit into the means of God's praise. This may mean that both tragedy and comedy can express the truth. Questions about the rightness of any work of art are to be asked across all the accepted genres. For example, we are not bound to buy into the aestheticising of the cross which sees it as a form of tragedy, but whether the same can be said of works of art which appear to glory in the ugly, and even evil, is less clear. The atheist critic Peter Fuller virtually rejected Francis Bacon's work as true art, on aesthetic and moral grounds and was dismissive of Gilbert and George, two other fashionable modern painters.[26] In a fallen world, there is no perfection without redemption, without labour to overcome the backwards direction taken by the whole created order, and restored only in Christ. We need, therefore, the representation of evil if we are to understand the plight of the world apart from redemption, but must ask when the representation of evil becomes Manichaean in denying the fundamental perfectibility of the creation.

In some way or other, therefore, we need to be able to develop a concept of *finite* perfection, eschatologically construed, in the light of which to assess the approximations to final perfection which are all that can be achieved this side of the end. The central criterion will be whether an action, event or thing praises the one who made it, and praises it in the way he was praised by his incarnate Son; but the nature of the perfection will be different according to the nature of that which is judged. This means that the humblest artefact can there succeed, the most beautiful act of worship fail.

---

[26] Peter Fuller, *Theoria: Art and the Absence of Grace* (London: Chatto & Windus, 1988).

6

Consuming the Body:
Contemporary Patterns of Drug Use
and Theological Anthropology

Luke Bretherton

Introduction

Why are contemporary patterns of drug use an important topic for theological reflection? At a basic level, use of drugs, legal or illegal, is a widespread and controversial social phenomenon. However, it is not simply the levels of drug use that makes it an appropriate topic for theological reflection, nor is it the debate that surrounds such use. In whatever way the term 'culture' is understood, patterns of drug use need to be considered as an aspect of it. Yet, trying to find theological reflection on drug use is like trying to find an unprofitable drug dealer. Such scarcity of reflection begins to look worryingly like myopia when we consider the prevalence and centrality of drug use in contemporary life.

This essay is an attempt to sketch out a theological response to the use of drugs in contemporary culture. My argument is that contemporary patterns of drug use, of whatever kind, firstly, are a paradigmatic instance of the modern, technocratic conception of the body as an object of manipulation, and subject to a regime of hyper-control; secondly, are the fruit of certain aspects of consumerism; and thirdly, contrast sharply with a theological account of the place of drugs in human life, in what they say about the human body and the way they shape human life together. It is important to note at the outset that an underlying assumption at work in this essay is that the use of drugs cannot be separated off as a realm removed from everyday life; rather, drug culture (insofar as such a thing can be identified) is a microcosm of, and intrinsically woven into, the mainstream of contemporary culture.

1. A problematic field of study

Before proceeding it is important to clarify what we are talking about when we talk about drugs. The World Health Organisation defines a 'drug' as 'any substance that, when taken into the living organism, may modify one or more of its functions'. This definition attempts to define the term 'drug' neutrally. A more colloquial usage is less broad than the WHO definition and tends to use the term 'drug' to refer to any non-medicinal, illicit chemicals such as cocaine. This colloquial usage points to only one negative aspect of drug use. However, in our understanding of the term 'drugs', we must take into account all aspects of the term. Yet this itself is problematic.

Derrida famously points to the ambiguity in the word *pharmakon* in his study of Plato's *Phaedrus*. He notes how the term *pharmakon* – meaning 'a drug' – can signify both a remedy and/or a poison. A *pharmakon* can be – alternately or simultaneously – beneficent and maleficent.[1] Without having to accept the literary theory Derrida stitches together out of the contradiction associated with the word *pharmakon*, we should take note of the ambiguity to which he alerts us.[2]

Derrida notes that Plato is suspicious of the *pharmakon* in general. Plato's suspicions extend even to instances of drugs being used exclusively for therapeutic ends and wielded with good intentions. Similarly, after scandals such as that caused by the use of the Thalidomide drug, we live in a society that is uncertain about its relationship to drugs, even those used for medicinal purposes. Derrida states that for Plato: 'There is no such thing as a harmless remedy. The *pharmakon* can never simply be beneficial'[3] Rather it is simultaneously pleasurable and painful, good and ill. Derrida states that the *pharmakon* always contains a mixture that is akin to 'relieving an itch by rubbing'. He notes that '[t]his type of painful pleasure, linked as much to the

---

[1] Jacques Derrida, *Dissemination* (trans. Barbara Johnson; London: Athlone, 1981), 70.

[2] The ambiguous nature of drugs is born out by much historical evidence. Rudi Matthee notes how the introduction of tobacco, coffee, cocoa, tea and distilled alcohol into Europe was accompanied by the same twofold reaction: these substances were viewed simultaneously as medicines and as a social menace. Rudi Matthee, 'Exotic Substances: the Introduction and Global Spread of Tobacco, Coffee, Cocoa, Tea, and Distilled Liquor, Sixteenth to Eighteenth Centuries', in *Drugs and Narcotics in History* (ed. Roy Porter and Mikuláš Teich; Cambridge: CUP, 1995), 24–51.

[3] Derrida, *Dissemination*, 99.

malady as to its treatment, is a *pharmakon* in itself. It partakes of both good and ill, of the agreeable and the disagreeable. Or rather, it is within its mass that these oppositions are able to sketch themselves out.'[4] Despite such contradictions, according to Derrida, Plato tries to master the 'ambiguity' of the word *pharmakon*, but his efforts prove futile.[5] Likewise, our efforts will prove futile if we try to resolve the ambiguity of the human relationship with drugs by either emphasising one aspect (they are bad or they are good) or by claiming they are neutral. Drugs are never neutral: they have concrete effects upon us, effects which may promote or diminish human flourishing, or do both simultaneously. Thus, we must heed the musings of the Friar in *Romeo and Juliet* (a play in which the dramatic device turns on the ambiguous nature of a drug) when he states:

> Within the infant rind of this weak flower
> Poison hath residence, and medicine power:
> For this, being smelt, with the part cheers each part;
> Being tasted, stays all senses with the heart.
> Two such opposed kings encamp them still
> In man as well as herbs – grace and rude will:
> And where the worser is predominate,
> Full soon the canker death eats up the plant.[6]

Before we leave Derrida's treatment of the word *pharmakon*, we must note one more problem that attends any analysis of drug use. Derrida believes, that to properly understand the term *pharmakon*, it must be related to the word *pharmakos* which means not only 'wizard' or 'magician' or 'poisoner', but also 'scapegoat'.[7] At the risk of a semantic

---

[4] Derrida, *Dissemination*, 99.
[5] Derrida, *Dissemination*, 102–3.
[6] *Romeo and Juliet*, II.iii.23–30. As Shakespeare well knew, the ambiguous nature of drugs is matched by an equally ambiguous human nature. A parallel literary use of the ambiguous nature of drugs mirroring the ambiguous nature of man is developed by Robert Louis Stevenson in *The Strange Case of Dr Jekyll and Mr. Hyde*. According to Lawrence Driscoll, Stevenson resists a simple binary opposition between Jekyll as the good/healthy man against Hyde as the evil/sick man under the influence of drugs. Instead, Driscoll argues that the characters of Jekyll and Hyde blur the boundaries between health and sickness, good and evil, so that one is healthily sick and the other has a sickly health, Jekyll commits suicide while Hyde has a 'love of life'. Lawrence Driscoll, *Reconsidering Drugs: Mapping Victorian and Modern Drug Discourses* (New York: Palgrave, 2000), 61.
[7] Derrida, *Dissemination*, 130.

sleight of hand, we should remember that not only are drugs highly ambiguous, but their use is also highly contentious; drugs and drug users have often served as *pharmakos*/scapegoats in contemporary culture.[8] In analysing drug use, we must beware of the moral panics and alarmist accounts that have attended most drugs, from coffee to crack cocaine.[9] We must also avoid the tendency to make drug users – or any particular section of society, including doctors, pharmaceutical companies or 'drug barons' – a scapegoat, likewise, for the problems drugs can cause. Likewise, we must not imbue drugs themselves with a malevolent agency. When 'drugs' become an omnipotent demon with the power to curtail freewill and drag the unsuspecting victim into addiction, crime and death, it becomes rational to 'wage war' on the demon. The metaphor of a 'war on drugs' in itself comes to justify the massive use of actual military force to combat the imagined threat to civilisation. Instead of resorting to making a scapegoat of drugs or any particular section of society, I will seek to analyse how and why contemporary patterns of drug use are a symptom of, rather than alien to, the shape of Western, late-modern society.

Bearing all this in mind, I will, for purposes of clarity, define the term 'drugs' heuristically, as referring to *chemical substances that, when taken into the human body through ingestion, injection or some other means, modify one or more of the capacities of the body for either ampliative or therapeutic purposes and not for feeding or nourishing the body.*[10] That is to say, drugs are distinguished from a warm bed in that the physiological changes effected in the body are accomplished through becoming part of the body's chemistry rather than external stimulation. For example, in contrast to the actions of a pumice stone, a non-cosmetic skin cream, such as an eczema cream, works through being absorbed into the body. They are to be distinguished from changes brought about by ascetic practices, for example, fasting, in that drugs are an external substance added to the body rather than simply a somatic exercise.

---

8   For example, Marek Kohn gives an account of how women and racial minorities who used drugs, notably cocaine and opium, became scapegoats for wider social anxieties in Britain in the early twentieth century. Marek Kohn, *Dope Girls: The Birth of the British Drug Underground* (London: Granta, 1992).

9   Coffee was controversial when it first appeared in the Muslim world in the sixteenth and seventeenth centuries. Also Charles II tried to suppress coffee houses which were viewed as 'nurseries of idleness' and hotbeds of sedition. Matthee, 'Exotic Substances', 36.

10   This definition excludes antibiotics, anti-virals and preventative medicines such as vaccines, since these act on parasites or 'alien' elements in the body as opposed to acting on the body as such.

Furthermore, although certain substances may also be used as food, such use is distinct from their use as drugs, although the use of a chemical substance as drugs and as physical nourishment may be simultaneous, for example, drinking beer.

The use of a substance as drugs is identified by particular kinds of usage. The first kind of use is what I call 'ampliative drug use'; that is, it is use that seeks to extend, augment, enhance or literally amplify an inherent capacity of the body for recreational or religious purposes (not primarily for medicinal purposes). *Ampliative* drug use ranges from steroids, to enhance muscle performance, to alcohol, to enhance conviviality. Such use might or might not be 'good' depending on the particular end such enhancement seeks and the vision of the human good such enhancement is being measured by.[11] The second kind of use is what I shall call 'therapeutic drug use', that is, it is drug use that seeks to cure, prevent or fix a real or perceived ailment of the body. *Therapeutic* drug use ranges from using antibiotics to prevent or heal an infection to using morphine as an analgesic. Again, there can be therapeutic use and misuse of drugs: for example, over-prescription of antibiotics leading to the development of iotragenic diseases.

I will focus on ampliative drug use because, generally, it is considered to be more problematic; moreover, I believe that ampliative drug use illustrates more starkly the nature and shape of contemporary patterns of drug use. I am not, however, claiming there is a clear distinction between one category of use and the other; rather, ampliative and therapeutic drug use are different aspects of the same phenomenon.

Before proceeding further and, in order to avoid confusion, the use of the term 'the body' within this essay needs to be situated within

---

[11] Most ampliative drug use draws on one or more of five types of drugs. It should be noted that the following descriptions are *extremely* simplified accounts of what are complex phenomena and many of these classes overlap. At the same time, variations between different drugs must be accounted for. A rough typology can be set out in the following way: there are *narcotics* (which relieve pain and induce feelings of euphoria: e.g. opium and its derivatives); *hypnotics* (which cause sleep and can reduce feelings of anxiety: e.g. sulphonal and barbiturates); *stimulants* (which cause feelings of excitement and increase mental and physical energy: e.g. caffeine, tobacco, betal, tea, coca and qat); *inebriants* (which induce drunkenness: e.g. alcohol, ether and solvents); and *hallucinogens* (which cause complex changes in visual, auditory and other perceptions, e.g. cannabis, LSD, mescaline and certain mushrooms). All of them may create dependency, while hallucinogens and stimulants may cause psychotic disturbances. Richard Davenport-Himes, *The Pursuit of Oblivion: A Social History of Drugs* (London: Phoenix Press, 2001), ix–x. Davenport-Himes fails to note quite how heuristic his classification is.

a theological anthropology. The Christian tradition presupposes an anthropology in which humans are conceived of as psychosomatic wholes. The body cannot be seen as distinct or separate from human capacities or attributes such as consciousness or autonomy as certain dualistic accounts suppose; for example, Ronald Dworkin argues for a separation between 'human life' and 'biological life'.[12] Augustine is representative of the Christian tradition when he states that: 'A man's body is no mere adornment, or external convenience; it belongs to his very nature as a man.'[13] Within a theologically-derived account of the body, embodiment is a central feature of being a person, and the body is seen as a good gift from God. Thus, for the Christian, our body is not a possession that we can dispose of as we see fit.[14] Alongside the affirmation of the human body as a part of God's good creation, human bodies are also affirmed as having a future in the in-breaking new creation. The eschatological affirmation of the human body in Jesus' acts of healing and, ultimately in the resurrection of his own body, underlines the value of human bodies in and of themselves. In addition, the eschatological future of humans as embodied beings emphasises the centrality of the body to the vocation of being a person in relation to God and others.

Taking this theological anthropology into account, in referring to the human body in this essay, I will be referring to that which is the psychosomatic entity in and through which a particular person comes to be present or personally available to others.

2. Modern drug use in historical perspective

Contemporary patterns of drug use cannot be understood outside their relationship to the processes of modernisation, notably, the development of technology (especially chemical technology), of global trade (initially through colonialism), of industrialisation and mass consumerism, and of bureaucratic control and the expansion of the nation-state.[15] For example, the introduction into early modern Europe of coffee and tea,

---

[12] Ronald Dworkin, *Life's Dominion: An Argument About Abortion and Euthanasia* (London: HarperCollins, 1993), 69.

[13] Augustine, *City of God*, I, 13.

[14] Cf. Barth, *Church Dogmatics* III/4, 404–5.

[15] For a broad-ranging discussion of the inter-relationship between all these elements, see David T. Courtwright, *Forces of Habit: Drugs and the making of the modern world* (Harvard University Press, 2001).

the most commonly used drugs, was inextricably bound up with the growth of colonialisation and the beginnings of mass consumption.[16] Likewise, cannabis, largely unknown in Europe before the eighteenth century, was introduced into Europe through colonial expansion into Algeria, Egypt and India.[17] Alongside the increasing range of plants available for use, from the early modern period onwards, was the application of the scientific method to medical practice and the study of plants. This application led to the isolation of alkaloids and the creation of synthetic and semi-synthetic drugs for medicinal use. Such developments were then combined with industrialised means of production. For example, cocaine, the psychoactive alkaloid in coca leaves, was identified in 1860 and its industrial production was begun in 1862.[18]

The introduction of cannabis into Europe provides a case study in the pattern of this expansion. The effects of cannabis were known about in Europe from the eighteenth century onwards, as a result of French and British colonial expansion and trade. Introduction was followed by a period of medical and recreational experimentation. Dr William Brooke O'Shaughnessy first began medical experiments with cannabis in the 1830s, while around the same time Parisian Bohemians, such as Flaubert, were experimenting with its more hedonistic potential. This experimentation led to its commercial exploitation. Under O'Shaughnessy's direction, a London pharmacist, Peter Squire, developed an extract and tincture of cannabis.[19] By 1887, cannabis cigarettes were sold by pharmacists for the 'immediate relief in all cases of Asthma, Nervous Coughs, Hoarseness, Loss of Voice, Facial Neuralgia and Sleeplessness'.[20] Inevitably, much of its use was not directly therapeutic. Concern about the effects of its use, both in Europe and its colonies, led to campaigns for greater restrictions on

---

[16] Rudi Matthee notes that tobacco, coffee, cocoa, tea and distilled alcohols were introduced at a remarkably similar time and in a uniform way. Tobacco began to be used in Europe from the 1500s onwards, the first distillery was established in 1575 in Holland, coffee was introduced in the early 1600s (the first European coffee house opened in Venice in 1645), as was tea. Matthee, 'Exotic Substances', 25–8.

[17] On this, see the extensive discussion of cannabis throughout Davenport-Himes, *Pursuit of Oblivion*.

[18] Davenport-Himes, *Pursuit of Oblivion*, 94–6.

[19] P. Matthews, *Cannabis Culture: A Journey Through Disputed Territory* (London: Bloomsbury, 1999), 172–3.

[20] Advertisement in the *Illustrated London News*, quoted in Matthews, *Cannabis Culture*, 173.

its use, and control over its production. Official investigations were established, in order to respond to the concerns being raised. For example, in 1893, the *Indian Hemp Drug Commission* was established to investigate the impact of the drug in India. From World War I onwards, a policy of prohibition and severely-restricted control was introduced. A similar sequence of introduction and experimentation, commercialisation, taxation and/or legal regulation can be traced for virtually all other drugs.

Attitudes towards psychotropic drugs such as cannabis or opium underwent a marked shift from the end of the nineteenth century onwards. In general terms, the shift was marked by a change from taxation to prohibition and the criminalisation of their use and distribution. This shift had a variety of causes, these included: geopolitical shifts, notably the rise of America as a world power and shifts in British Imperial policy;[21] economic developments, particularly what was needed from workers within industrial processes of production as against what was required of an agricultural labourer; social anxieties about how drug use sapped the fitness of a country for war – related to this were racist fears about 'foreigners' corrupting young people; greater understanding of the toxic and habit-forming properties of drugs resulting from scientific research; and the campaigns by Evangelicals, Socialists and other social reformers who were concerned about how drug use was morally corrosive and a pauperiser.

In many ways, the debate about drug use in Western societies has changed very little since the beginning of the twentieth century. A theological response to contemporary patterns of drug use needs to both understand the above historical background and also to stand back from it in order to develop critical theological perspectives on it.

3. Contemporary drug use as a symptom of, and gateway to, the technological society

In order to develop a critical theological perspective on drug use, it is necessary to discern how drug use conforms to central discourses within contemporary culture. My contention is that drugs are a form of technology and used as a means to 'progress' out of what is viewed as the tyrannous imposition of nature. As such, drugs are a symptom of modern, technocratic approaches to nature.

---

[21] America was very active and influential in promoting prohibitionist policies.

Oliver O'Donovan notes that what marks modernity from other moments of history is neither its instruments of making nor its technical achievements, but the way it thinks of everything it does as a form of instrumental making. Following Heidegger, and other critics of modernity, O'Donovan fears that practical reason and moral judgement have mutated into 'technique'. O'Donovan comments: 'Set free from obedience to comprehensible ends of action, confronting all reality as disposable material, [modern man's] primary imperative is manipulation.'[22] Thus, the human body ceases to have given ends which we may discern and judge how best to fulfil, but becomes an object for manipulation and shaping according to our will. O'Donovan states: 'The fate of a society which sees, wherever it looks, nothing but the products of the human will, is that it fails, when it does see some aspect of human activity which is not a matter of construction, to recognise the significance of what it sees and to think about it appropriately.'[23]

In practice, the implication is that there is an inability to discern whether technical intervention is appropriate or not, because everything is seen as raw material waiting to have something made out it. O'Donovan states: 'If there is no category in thought for an action which is not artefactual, then there is no restraint in action which can preserve phenomena which are not artificial.'[24] Everything from the environment to the human body becomes material for something to be made out of. However, unless we are attentive to creation and shape our own constructions in response to it, creation – whether it be the climate or our bodies – will break down, and with it, so will the products of our making and our laws imposed on creation. O'Donovan views this lack of attentiveness as a form of self-hatred: by asserting our freedom over and against creation, we end up hurting ourselves. In short, to set ourselves against the order of things is to be in self-contradiction. Yet this is precisely the 'modern' conception of freedom. O'Donovan states:

> Technology derives its social significance from the fact that by it man has discovered new freedoms from necessity. The technological transformation of the modern age has gone hand in hand with the social and political quest of Western man to free himself from the necessities imposed upon him by

---

[22] Oliver O'Donovan, *The Desire of the Nations: Rediscovering the Roots of Political Theory* (Cambridge: CUP, 1996), 274.

[23] Oliver O'Donovan, *Begotten or Made?* (Oxford: Clarendon, 1984), 2.

[24] O'Donovan, *Begotten or Made?*, 3.

religion, society and nature. Without this social quest the development of technology would have been unthinkable; without technology the liberal society as we know it would be unworkable.[25]

It is my contention that drugs – as a technology – are central to Western, liberal society, and the way we approach drugs is characterised by seeing them as a means by which to manipulate the body according to our will. This is not to say that drugs, of whatever kind, may not be used in ways that attend to the created nature of the body. Rather, it is to claim that drug use, under the mantle of a technological society such as ours, will only be correctly adopted either rarely or by accident.

That the use of drugs is determined by a technological rationality becomes especially apparent when we look at the anxieties surrounding the spectral figure of the 'addict'. The state of being an addict – whether of heroin, nicotine or caffeine – is feared and socially proscribed, because it is seen as being out of control, dependent on something, in a state wherein the body is not subject to the will. To be dependent on a drug is to deny the modern conception of freedom by making oneself subject to necessity. Such dependence constitutes a betrayal of the modern project and a retrenchment to barbarity. However, the fixation with a particular kind of dependence masks the ways in which society as a whole has become entirely dependent on drugs to maintain a particular conception and experience of normality or homeostasis characterised by comfort or *gemütlichkeit*. We deploy great vats of syrups, cartloads of pills and reservoirs of lotions in order to liberate ourselves from the everyday tyranny of the body's aches, pains, tiredness, allergies and the general effects of aging. And we are increasingly employing yet more kinds of drugs to tailor our personality and physical abilities to fulfil our desires or alleviate our anxieties about our sense of who we should be or what we should be able to achieve. One recent example of such tailoring is use of the drug Prozac. The psychologist Peter Kramer calls such tailoring 'cosmetic pharmacology'.[26] Yet, as with all human attempts at self-salvation from the effects of sin and death, the irony is that our liberation turns out to be bondage. We are, in effect, dependent on the technology of drugs to maintain our freedom from bodily necessity and constraint, but, by constantly manipulating our body

---

[25] O'Donovan, *Begotten or Made?*, 6.
[26] Peter Kramer, *Listening to Prozac* (London: Fourth Estate, 1994).

to maintain our cosiness or to fulfil our desire to be a different kind of person, we find ourselves in self-contradiction: we require ever higher doses to circumvent the diminishing returns of the potions we use, we then require more treatments to heal us from the sickness these drugs induce, and ultimately, despite all our best efforts and the strictness of our regimes, we can never win the battle against a body in which death is at work (2 Cor. 4:12). Ivan Illich identified the counterproductive dynamic at work in our technological, medicalised drug culture as clinical, social and cultural 'iatrogenesis': that is, drugs and medicine have themselves become a major threat to health.[27]

Central to the drive to maintain physical comfort – to be, in the words of Carl Elliot, 'better than well' – is the modern conception of suffering.[28] Within modernity, illness, pain and suffering are pointless: that is, they can play no role in helping us live our lives well. O'Donovan notes that suffering has become unintelligible in contemporary society, because it is a society orientated towards the individual and the exercise of the individual will. He states: 'The role society, on earth and in heaven, could play in justifying the individual's suffering is removed. The late-modern age, accordingly, is in perpetual rebellion against the "pointlessness", the "waste" of suffering.'[29] The replacement of wisdom by technique and the resort to technological means to 'solve' any perceived suffering exacerbates this rebellion. O'Donovan points out that, within the logic of modernity, suffering in any form must be eliminated through technical means.[30] Thus, when all else fails, we are given another pill – Valium or Prozac – to make us feel happy and calm, despite our condition. However, the drive to maintain physical comfort or, as is increasingly the case, to maintain a sense of self-fulfilment, ignores how physical or psychological pain is part of the way in which we may order our lives properly in response to the created order. For example, if I am tired and have a headache, the body does not need a coffee and an aspirin, but a rest. Yet, under the logic of contemporary modern life, bodily pain does not serve to alert me to my social, economic or political conditions (i.e. why am I having to work late); rather, bodily pain is a provocation to tighten up our regimes of control 'over' the

---

27 See Ivan Illich, *Limits to Medicine – Medical Nemesis: The Expropriation of Health* (Harmondsworth: Pelican, 1977).

28 Carl Elliott, *Better Than Well: American Medicine Meets the American Dream* (New York: Norton & Co., 2003).

29 O'Donovan, *Desire of the Nations*, 276.

30 O'Donovan, *Begotten or Made?*, 3–12.

body (I need to exercise more, eat better, buy a more comfortable chair, buy a stronger brand of headache pill, etc.), and thus treat the body as an object of manipulation. The same can be said of the use of enhancement technologies to address psychological or emotional pain. The quest to change my body, whether pharmacologically or through surgery, to make me feel better about myself, ignores the need to address a lack of virtue or character or the need for emotional healing. As Illich argues, within our technological civilisation, pain has become a demand 'for more drugs, hospitals, medical services, and other outputs of corporate impersonal care' and has become a source of 'political support for further corporate growth no matter what its human, social, or economic cost'.[31]

We see the same dynamic when it comes to recreational use of ampliative drugs such as LSD, cocaine, cannabis and ecstasy. Much of the rhetoric that surrounds use of these drugs is of liberation: 'free your mind'. Moreover, they are seen as ampoules of rebellion and social non-conformity: 'turn on, tune in, drop out'.[32] Yet, such use is in actuality conformity to the heart of the modern project. The ways in which drugs such as LSD and ecstasy are used reflects the desire to engineer an experience: more often than not, a 'high' or a good time. Why risk not enjoying yourself when you can chemically ensure that you will, like your friends, appreciate the music and won't get tired after a stressful week at work? Yet such engineering of experience imperils what it means to be human, for it deprives human existence itself of certain spontaneities of being and doing, which depend upon the reality of a world which we have not made or imagined, but which simply confronts us to evoke our fear, love and delight. A personal, spontaneous response to music and dancing is entirely different in kind from those resulting from a chemically manufactured response. Furthermore, drugs are used to manage the responses of the mind and body to maximise the enjoyment of a night out: ecstasy (to make you happy), amphetamines or cocaine (to keep you going), LSD (for its visual effect) and cannabis or temazepam (to 'chill out' and 'come down' at the end of it all). And drug dealers are just another service industry, responding to consumer demand.

---

[31] Illich, *Limits to Medicine*, 142.

[32] Reflecting on the reasons he used drugs, the writer Will Self articulates exactly these sentiments, stating: 'I revered drug-taking as a blow against conformity and a blow against the hierarchy and a blow against what was quite a privileged middle-class background.' Will Self and Steve Turner, 'Getting a Fix: Steve Turner talks to Will Self', *Third Way* 24.5 (2001), 18–21 (p. 20).

Far from freeing their minds, most clubbers and weekend party animals are bureaucrats of fun, administrating their enjoyment like a corporate manager organising her schedule. In doing so, they combine features of all the archetypes whom Alasdair MacIntyre identifies as the moral representatives of modernity. MacIntyre states that the values and morals of every culture assume embodied expression in the social world through certain archetypes or characters. He sees the primary moral representatives of contemporary culture as the aesthete, whose primary evaluative criterion is pleasure and the avoidance of boredom; the manager, whose key criterion for evaluation is effectiveness in matching means to predetermined ends; and the therapist, who, like the manager, seeks effectiveness, not of an organisation, but of the individual.[33] Thus, beyond the rhetoric, taking drugs is deeply conformist and conservative: drug taking conforms to the technocratic logic of modernity and conserves those patterns of life that are shaped by a modern vision of the good life (whether hedonistic or otherwise). Taking drugs is thus a moral imperative within the logic of modernity: they are a valuable technology through which we can manage and manufacture a better, more fulfilling life.

I am not saying that all use of drugs to manipulate the body is necessarily bad. There is a place for using chemical technology. The issue is whether using drugs in a manner determined by a technical rationality is a usage that enables human flourishing or not.

4. Contemporary patterns of drug use as a symptom of material conditions

Contemporary patterns of drug use are indicative of more than just a particular approach to suffering; they encapsulate the ways in which we discipline our bodies in our culture. The individual body is, to some extent, always interpreted and ordered to reflect social, political and economic relationships. The body is both a symbol of these relationships and a medium through which such relationships are realised, realigned or replaced.[34] In contemporary Western societies, one of the primary modes of involvement in society is as a consumer, rather than, say, an agriculturalist, warrior or hunter-gatherer. As Zygmunt Bauman puts

---

[33] Alasdair MacIntyre, *After Virtue: A Study in Moral Theory* (2nd edn; London: Duckworth, 1994), 24–30.

[34] On this, see, for example, Richard Sennett, *Flesh and Stone: the Body and the City in Western Civilization* (London: Faber & Faber, 1994).

it: 'The way present-day society shapes up its members is dictated first and foremost by the need to play the role of the consumer, and the norm our society holds up to its members is that of the ability and willingness to play it.'[35] Thus, we must attend to how contemporary patterns of consumption shape the relationship between the body and drugs, and encourage people to control their responses to life through adjusting their bodily chemistry. In short, we must answer the question: how does consumerism encourage drug use?

We must consume things in order to live; however, children are not born with a set of wishes to consume the goods on offer in late-modern, capitalist society. Rather, they are aroused into desiring them. Robert Bocock comments that:

> Consumption has emerged as a fundamental part of the process by which infants enter western capitalist cultures and their symbolic systems of meaning. Foods, drinks, toys, clothes and television are part of the early experiences of consumption of young children in western societies. Infants and children are being socialised into being consumers during the very early states of development.[36]

In his novel *Generation X*, Douglas Coupland has a poignant scene in which a group of twenty-somethings try to remember a precious moment from childhood that does not involve a commercialised, consumer experience.[37] They succeed, but only just. Whether future generations will be able to recall experiences that do not involve some kind of consumer exchange is an open question. The forming of children into consumers involves widespread drug use. Children

---

[35] Zygmunt Bauman, *Work, Consumerism and the New Poor* (Buckingham: Open University Press, 1998), 24. For a wide ranging theological critique of consumerism, see Vincent Miller, *Consuming Religion: Christian Faith and Practice in a Consumer Culture* (London: Continuum, 2004). It should not surprise us that in a society characterised by consumerism, the deregulation of drug use is called for. Bauman states: 'A society of consumers is resentful of all legal restrictions imposed on freedom of choice, [...], and manifests its resentment by widespread support willingly offered to most "deregulatory" measures.' Arguably, in contemporary debate, the real point at issue in calls for legalisation of drugs is not the morality or otherwise of taking drugs, nor is it making appropriate distinctions between different kinds of drugs and their effects, but the prohibition against using potential objects of consumption. Miller, *Consuming Religion*, 29.

[36] Robert Bocock, *Consumption* (London: Routledge, 1993), 85.

[37] Douglas Coupland, *Generation X: Tales for an Accelerated Culture* (New York: St Martin's, 1991), 87–96.

are fed caffeine in soft drinks; injections and medicines are a central feature of how children's bodies are managed and prepared to face the world; and pill shaped sweets and lozenges are standard fare.[38]

More significant than the link between drugs and the forming of children into consumers is the way in which the body itself has become commodified. Baudrillard argues that the body has become one more object to be consumed. He states:

> The body is [...] the finest of these psychically possessed, manipulated and consumed objects. [...] The body is not reappropriated for the autonomous ends of the subject, but in terms of a *normative* principle of enjoyment and hedonistic profitability, in terms of an enforced instrumentality that is indexed to the code and the norms of a society of production and managed consumption.[39]

It is my contention that our use of drugs is the paradigmatic way in which we consume, and literally devour, our bodies; that is to say, drug use encapsulates the primary way we manipulate and maximise the 'hedonistic profitability' of our bodies.

Drugs themselves – whether used for ampliative or therapeutic effect – are perhaps the ultimate consumer product. In a society in which, according to George Steiner's pithy aphorism, all cultural products are calculated for 'maximal impact and instant obsolescence',[40] drugs give an instant, maximally-intense hit and, unlike sunglasses or CD's, they are used up in one go.[41] In a society of experience collectors, ampliative drug use bypasses the equipment and preparation needed for a parachute jump or sailing trip and does not require the spatial and temporal investment of an adventure holiday or visit to Disneyland. Instead, they deliver a hit of pure experience without the need for training, travel or time. And apart from anything else, there is a huge

---

[38] Eric Schlosser sets out, for example, the ways in which soft drinks containing caffeine have been directly targeted at children and have replaced nutritious drinks like milk in the diet of American children. Eric Schlosser, *Fast Food Nation: What the All-American Meal is Doing to the World* (London: Penguin, 2001), 54–7.

[39] Jean Baudrillard, *The Consumer Society: Myths and Structures* (trans. Chris Turner; London: Sage, 1998), 131.

[40] Quoted from Bauman, *Work, Consumerism and the New Poor,* 28.

[41] Bauman states: 'Consumer goods are meant to be used up and to disappear; the idea of temporariness and transitoriness is intrinsic to their very denomination as objects of consumption; consumer goods have *memento mori* written all over them, even if with an invisible ink.' Bauman, *Work, Consumerism and the New Poor,* 28.

commercial investment in our continued use of drugs of all kinds.[42] In short, *in a consumer society, it is entirely rational to take drugs for ampliative purposes.* Drugs may poison and consume or use up our bodies, just as cars consume and use up our environment, but they powerfully satisfy the desires, albeit fleetingly, of persons whose hearts and minds are conditioned to consume, rather than seek first the kingdom of God.

Many critics of consumerism find fault with what they see as the scandalous waste generated by it. Such criticism, articulated, for example, by environmental groups calling for greater sustainability, is born out of a moral vision that sees the massive production of what is surplus to requirement as dysfunctional. However, as Baudrillard contends:

> All societies have always wasted, squandered, expended and consumed beyond what is strictly necessary for the simple reason that it is in the consumption of a surplus, of a superfluity that the individual – and society – feel not merely that they exist, but that they are alive.[43]

The movement beyond sheer necessity, so that a surplus, or more-than-is-strictly-necessary-to-survive, is produced, is the precondition of generating 'culture' in whatever way it is defined. Baudrillard states:

> The notion of utility, which has rationalistic, economistic origins, thus needs to be revised in light of a much more general social logic in which waste, far from being an irrational residue, takes on a positive function, taking over where rational utility leaves off to play its part in a higher social functionality – a social logic in which waste even appears ultimately as the essential function, the extra degree of expenditure, superfluity, the ritual uselessness of 'expenditure for nothing' becoming the site of production of values, differences and meanings on both the individual and the social level.[44]

But Baudrillard is wrong to think of this surplus as 'waste'; the issue is not waste or 'expenditure for nothing', but how a surplus is produced, used and to what end that surplus is directed. The movement beyond sheer necessity is what enables movement towards consummation or

---

[42] In 1999, the US Food and Drug Administration approved Paxil, which, like Prozac, is a serotonin reuptake inhibitor. Paxil is designed for use in relation to 'social phobia' or 'social anxiety disorder', which some suggest are simply technical sounding terms for shyness. GlaxoSmithKine who produce the drug spent $91.8 million advertising Paxil directly to consumers. Elliott, *Better Than Well*, 57–9.

[43] Baudrillard, *The Consumer Society*, 43.

[44] Baudrillard, *The Consumer Society*, 43.

fulfilment which is a movement beyond mere survival. However, the critical issue here is what kind of consummation is being aimed for in our society. The costly and extravagant expenditure of the woman who purchases a bottle of nard, in order to anoint Jesus before his crucifixion (Mark 14:3–10) signals something rather different from the women who, in the L'Oreal adverts, suggest you should buy L'Oreal perfume 'because you're worth it'. Instead of the sacrificing of a costly ointment on behalf of another – an act that foreshadows Christ's own death – the L'Oreal advert proposes that the pearl of great price is my own wellbeing, and that it is worth any sacrifice to ensure. The contrast between the kind of surplus generated from a social order organised around the economy of Christ's death and resurrection, in which the priority is to seek first the kingdom of God, and that of a social order structured around the satisfaction of my desires, begins to look like the contrast between the ecstatic communion of the messianic banquet and the anarchic tumult of a Saturnalia or Bacchanalia. However, before we launch into a jeremiad against the link between drugs and consumerism, we must address the following question: as a form of costly, often unnecessary expenditure, what kind of human consummation are contemporary patterns of drug use really enabling? And this question, perhaps surprisingly, maybe considered by reference to Marx's infamous maxim that religion is the opium of the people.[45]

If we are attempting to understand how the body is both a symbol of social, political and economic relationships, and a medium through which such relationships are realised, realigned or replaced, Marx's critique of religion is a helpful means to assess whether or not drug use is currently contributing to a Christian vision of human consumption. Whether religion is, or ever was, the opium of the people is open to question.[46] However, the functioning of opium in the way Marx envisaged (that is, the way that led him to use it as a metaphor for religion), is what I shall analyse now.[47] This

---

[45] For an account of the genealogy of the expression 'opium of the people' see Helmut Gollwitzer, *The Christian Faith and the Marxist Criticism of Religion* (Edinburgh: Saint Andrew Press, 1970), 15–23.

[46] For a critique of Marx's treatment of religion, see David McLellan, *Marxism and Religion: A Description and Assessment of the Marxist Critique of Christianity* (London: MacMillan, 1987), 7–32.

[47] For a pithy summary of Marx's critique of religion, see Alasdair MacIntyre, 'Marxism and Religion', in *Marxism and Christianity* (2nd edn; London: Duckworth, 1995), 103–16. See also Denys Turner, 'Religion: Illusions and Liberation', in *The Cambridge Companion to Marx* (ed. Terrell Carver; Cambridge: CUP, 1991), 320–37.

Marxist reading of drug use complexifies the previous point about contemporary patterns of drug use being a symptom of consumerism by identifying how drug use is simultaneously a protest against the dominant technocratic, capitalist, consumer hegemony and a means of conforming to it.

For Marx, religion was opium because, in a context of violent repression, or where the oppressed lack political and economic power, religion was simultaneously protest and consolation.[48] Marx states: 'Religion is the sigh of the oppressed creature, the heart of a heartless world, just as it is the spirit of a spiritless situation.'[49] In the same way, drug use of, for example, crack-cocaine or heroin, by the socially- and economically-marginalised, or even by those seeking to escape their privileged upbringing, serves as both a rejection of the status quo and as a relief or escape from their present condition.[50] Thus, drugs may play a revolutionary role by stimulating a thirst for a better social order; however, they become wholly reactionary when they distract humans from seeking to establish a good society. Furthermore, for Marx, religion had become a means to legitimise, to the power elite whose interests are served by the system, the deprivations of poverty and powerlessness.[51] Drugs function in a similar way. Their use by certain sections of the population serves to legitimise existing inequalities. Drug use is made a causal factor in crime rates and inner city deprivation, so that wider questions about contemporary economic and political conditions are glossed over. Marx believed that, in addition to acting as a narcotic, as a mask for, and legitimiser of, oppression, religion enabled the power elite to reconcile themselves to the system, which also inhibits them from being fully human. Similarly, drugs are the opiate of *all* the people, because they provide, to the weak an illusory satisfaction to an

---

[48] Engels clarifies what he and Marx see as the difference between Christianity and a true revolutionary consciousness when he states: 'Both Christianity and the workers' socialism preach forthcoming salvation from bondage and misery; Christianity places this salvation in a life beyond, after death, in heaven; socialism places it in this world, in a transformation of society.' Karl Marx and Friedrich Engels, 'On the History of Early Christianity', in *On Religion* (trans. not stated; Chico: Scholars Press, 1982), 316–47 (p. 316).

[49] Karl Marx, 'Contribution to the Critique of Hegel's "Philosophy of Right": Introduction', in *On Religion*, 41–58 (p. 42).

[50] The Exodus Collective based in Luton are a good example of how use of narcotics can become a focus for protest and a consolation. For an account for their activities and vision, see Matthews, *Cannabis Culture*, 35–43.

[51] See, for example, Karl Marx and Friedrich Engels, *The Communist Manifesto* (trans. Samuel Moore; London: Penguin, 1967), 92.

authentic demand, and they provide to the powerful a false justification for an oppressive system.

Marx held that to criticise religion was to direct people to their oppression, in order that they might transform it from an inhuman reality into a human one:

> Criticism has plucked the imaginary flowers from the chain not so that man will wear the chain without any fantasy or consolation but so that he will shake off the chain and cull the living flower. The criticism of religion disillusions man to make him think and act and shape his reality, so that he will revolve round himself and therefore round his true sun.[52]

What might have once been true for religion is now most certainly true for drugs. Criticism of contemporary patterns of drug use is a necessary part of any proper critique of our culture that seeks to alert humans to their own oppression. However, I do not criticise patterns of drug use so that others might think and act and shape their own reality, nor that they might be liberated through simply changing their material conditions. Rather, I criticise contemporary patterns of drug use in order to develop a clearer picture of where we are in relation to the pattern of life set out in the life, death and resurrection of Jesus Christ, who is the only means by which we might be liberated from the present conditions of sin and death, and might be conformed to reality as created and fulfilled by God.

The above critique of contemporary patterns of drug use is encapsulated in much of the literature and art associated with drug use. This literature is pervaded by a sorrowful despair and aching nihilism. It seems to centre on journeys to nowhere, trips that end in oblivion, movement that exhausts itself: for example, Tom Wolfe's *Electric Kool-Aid Acid Test*, Hunter S. Thompson's *Fear And Loathing in Las Vegas* (subtitled: 'A Savage Journey to the Heart of the American Dream'), Kurt Vonnegut's *Slaughterhouse 5*, Peter Fonda and Dennis Hopper's film *Easy Rider* and Irvine Welsh's *Trainspotting*. Here are, debunked, the dreams and aspirations of progress and a better life that modernity has so faithfully pursued.

Jack Kerouac's *On the Road* serves as a good example of the criticism of modernity implicit in much drug-related literature. After a dizzying number of road trips across 1950s America (an America notably unscathed by World War II) and extraordinary bursts of frenetic and chaotic idleness fuelled by Benzedrine, cannabis and alcohol, Kerouac's

---

[52] Marx, 'the Critique of Hegel's "Philosophy of Right"', 42.

On the Road reaches its culmination in a trip to Mexico. There, the main protagonists – Dean Moriarty and Sal Paradise – encounter what they take to be primal innocents or noble savages in the form of Mexican Indians. Kerouac writes:

> Strange crossroad towns on the top of the world rolled by, with shawled Indians watching us from under hatbrims and *rebozos*. Life was dense, dark and ancient. They watched Dean, serious and insane at his raving wheel, with eyes of hawks. All had their hands outstretched. They had come down from the back mountains and higher places to hold forth their hands for something they thought civilisation could offer, and they never dreamed the sadness and the poor broken delusion of it. They didn't know that a bomb had come that could crack all our bridges and roads and reduce them to jumbles, and we would be as poor as they someday, and stretching out our hands in the same, same way. Our broken Ford, old thirties upgoing America Ford, rattled through them and vanished in dust.[53]

The passage represents a sorrowful critique of modernity, found time and again in the literature associated with drugs. Kerouac originally conceived of the book as a quest novel like Bunyan's *Pilgrim's Progress*.[54] But *On the Road* contains no allegory of moral and spiritual growth, only a mournful travelogue of fruitless journeys already made by different roads.

Despite the hiatus of the 1960s, when many thought drugs presaged a new age – the Age of Aquarius – the nihilistic tone in drug-related literature soon returns.[55] In 1971, Hunter S. Thompson fictionalises an epic drug binge he embarked upon while making a trip to and from Las Vegas. He compares his drug-induced paranoia and nightmare visions with the fabricated lunacy of Las Vegas, and concludes that the American dream has become an inferno, and drugs, far from freeing the mind, are merely a way of coping with the political and social bedlam that surrounds him.[56] Thompson writes:

---

[53] Jack Kerouac, *On the Road* (London: Penguin, 1972; repr., 2000), 273

[54] Ann Charters, Introduction to *On the Road*, vii–xxxii (xiv).

[55] Even Tom Wolfe's paean to the LSD evangelist, Ken Kesey, closes with the rejection of Kesey's Nietzschian vision of a revaluation of values beyond morality and drugs, wherein everyone was to become a 'superhero', their life an act of artistic self-creation. Instead, the 'beautiful people' of Haight Ashbury took a solipsistic and passive turn to inner tranquillity that presages the *gemütlichkeit* culture of our age.

[56] For a more contemporary take on the lunacy of Las Vegas as the apogee of a consumer, technocratic culture, see Schlosser, *Fast Food Nation*, 234–9.

We are all wired into a *survival* trip now. No more of the speed that fuelled the Sixties. Uppers are going out of style. That was the fatal flaw in Tim Leary's trip. He crashed around America selling 'consciousness expansion' without ever giving a thought to the grim meat-hook realities that were lying in wait for all the people who took him seriously. [...] Not that they didn't deserve it: No doubt they all Got What Was Coming To Them. All those pathetically eager acid freaks who thought they could buy Peace and Understanding for three bucks a hit. But their loss and failure is ours, too. What Leary took down with him was the central illusion of a whole life-style that he helped to create [...] a generation of permanent cripples, failed seekers, who never understood the essential old-mystic fallacy of the Acid Culture: the desperate assumption that somebody – or at least some *force* – is tending that Light at the end of the tunnel.[57]

Thompson's metaphysical nihilism lies behind his criticism of the idealism of Leary and others. For Thompson, the central dynamic of 'Acid Culture' was not spiritual, but commercial, and far from bringing 'consciousness expansion', drugs created a generation of 'permanent cripples'. The work of authors like Thompson suggests that drug use habituates us to our material conditions, which are now the conditions of mass consumerism and a technocratic society. But, even if drugs do largely function in this way, we must ask whether they *necessarily* function in this way. It is important to analyse more fully contemporary attempts to use drugs in constructive ways. The primary form this shaping has taken is to try to conceive of, and structure, drug use as a mystical experience. I shall now assess whether Thompson is too quick to dismiss 'Tim Leary's trip'.

5. Drug use as a means to mystical experiences

There are those who would reject the account I have given of contemporary patterns of drug use as the fruit of the attempt to manipulate the body and reduce it to an object of consumption. Some have claimed that drugs, notably LSD, may be a source of transcendence to a higher consciousness, and many have noted a search for 'spirituality' among those who experiment with ampliative drug use.[58] This is a view that needs to be taken seriously. Drugs have always been associated with religious practices. There is a long and continuing history of

---

[57] Hunter S. Thompson, *Fear And Loathing in Las Vegas* (London: Flamingo, 1993), 178–9.

[58] For example, Kenneth Leech, *Drugs and Pastoral Care* (London: DLT, 1998), ch. 7.

the religious use of plants that contain psychedelic or mind-altering substances. Wine, central to the Christian Eucharist, is just such a mind-altering substance. However, more interesting than the fact that consciousness-changing devices have been linked with religious practice is the possibility that drugs actually initiated many of the religious perspectives which, taking root in a tradition, continued after their origins in psychoactive substances were forgotten. Gordon Wasson goes so far as to argue that most religions arose from such chemically-induced theophanies.[59]

What are we to make of these claims, and what do we make of the use of drugs as part of Christian worship? The first thing to be clear about is that there is inevitably some degree of correspondence between drug-induced experiences and religious or mystical experience. Even the Bible notes that chemically-induced psychic states bear some resemblance to religious ones. Peter had to appeal to a circumstantial criterion – the early hour of the day – to defend those who were caught up in the pentecostal experience against the charge that they were drunk: 'These men are not drunk, as you suppose. It's only nine in the morning!' (Acts 2:15). However, there is a critical difference between the mystical experiences born out of ascetic discipline and religious ritual, and the changed consciousness induced by drugs. The difference turns on the vision or *telos* of human consummation from which each is derived. It is my contention that the contemporary claims to mystical experience from drugs only emphasise the critique I have already given. The disciplining of the body, the socialisation of drug use and the education of desire within a religious framework and its particular vision of what human consummation involves is entirely different in kind to modern attempts to induce mystical experiences through chemical technology.

The interpretation of some contemporary drug experiences, notably those achieved through LSD, as equivalent to mystical experiences, have mostly been based on a conception of mysticism as a phenomenon common to all the major religious traditions and sharing certain generic characteristics. For example, Walter Pahnke argues that the experiences described by mystics are directly comparable to those facilitated by psychedelic drugs. He does not claim that drugs automatically lead to a mystical experience. He recognises that every experience is a mix of three ingredients: the drug itself, the psychological makeup of the

---

[59] Gordon Wasson, *Persephone's Quest: Entheogens and the Origins of Religion* (New Haven: Yale, 1986).

individual and the setting (the social and physical environment in which it is taken). Pahnke's argument is based on an experiment in which he administered psilocybin to ten Harvard theological students participating in a Good Friday service (ten other students received a placebo) and compared their experience to a ninefold typology of mystical experience.[60] His study was based on the presupposition that, while there may be some variation, all mystical experiences share certain fundamental characteristics that are universal and not restricted to any particular religion or culture.[61] William James gave the classic statement of this view in his 1902 Gifford lectures, 'The Varieties of Religious Experience'.[62] However, such a view is based on a modernist reading of religion that seeks to strip away the historical phenomena and doctrinal content of a particular religion and reveal the essence of any given faith tradition. Such an approach, as Schwöbel and others argue, fails to attend to the inherent particularity of each religious tradition, and constitutes a totalising discourse that erases the substantive differences between religions, in order that they either conform to a general abstract notion of religion, or are remoulded into instantiations of a general religious metaphysics.[63] Instead, all religious experience is tradition-situated and can only be interpreted in the light of a particular tradition.[64] The somatic phenomena may or may not be

---

[60] Walter Pahnke, 'Drugs and Mysticism', *The International Journal of Parapsychology* 8.2 (1966), 295–313.

[61] The characteristics were: unity, transcendence of time and space, a deeply-felt positive mood, a sense of sacredness, a sense of illumination felt at an intuitive level that was nevertheless felt to be authoritative in nature, paradoxicality, alleged ineffability, transiency, and lastly, persisting positive changes in attitude and behaviour.

[62] William James, *The Varieties of Religious Experience: A Study in Human Nature* (New York: Longmans Green, 1902). Even those who do not directly equate drug-induced experiences with mystical experiences still take an essentialist view of mystical experiences. For example, R.C. Zaehner, *Mysticism, Sacred and Profane* (Oxford: Clarendon, 1957).

[63] Christoph Schwöbel, 'Particularity, Universality, and the Religions: Towards a Christian Theology of Religions', in *Christian Uniqueness Reconsidered: The Myth of a Pluralistic Theology of Religions* (ed. Gavin D'Costa; New York: Orbis, 1996), 30–46.

[64] Constructivist accounts of mysticism recognise that there are substantive differences between particular kinds of mysticism. They argue that mystics do not have context-free, 'pure' experiences that they later interpret according to their own particular cultural and theological presuppositions. The very nature of the experience is itself socially constructed according to the culture, beliefs and expectations of the mystics having the experiences. For examples of such an

similar; however, the significance of what happens to the body can only by understood within a particular tradition and will be informed by the spirit of that tradition. Thus, the question we must ask is, what spirit informs the spirituality of those who use drugs to induce mystical experiences outside any formal religious tradition?

Perhaps the clearest Christian formulation of how to test what spirit informs a particular group of people or phenomenon is given by Christ when, after warning about false prophets who disguise their true identity, he states: 'By their fruit you will recognize them.'[65] The question then is, what constitutes good fruit? Within the Christian tradition the answer to this question is understood to be the fruits of the Holy Spirit: that is, love, joy, peace, patience, kindness, goodness, faithfulness, gentleness and self-control, all of which are given 'for the common good'.[66] Thus, a critical question to address to contemporary patterns of drug use is whether they produce the fruit of the Holy Spirit or some other crop. It is my contention, based on the analysis of contemporary patterns of drug use given above, that the spirit that informs the modern use of drugs for mystical ends is the spirit of a technocratic and consumer culture. The body is not trained and adapted to particular kinds of experience; rather, it is viewed as raw material for choice and intervention, and a technological solution is deployed to reach beyond the created and fallen limits of perception. I am not claiming that all drug use today for mystical ends is informed by such a spirit. I am simply saying that the foremost contemporary advocates of drugs as a means to a mystical or cosmic consciousness are situated within a particular discourse that is informed neither by a religious tradition (although it borrows from many traditions) nor inspired by the Holy Spirit. Instead, its context and inspiration is the *zeitgeist* of modernity.[67]

---

approach, see Steven Katz, ed., *Mysticism and Religious Traditions* (Oxford: OUP, 1983). However, constructivist theories have come under criticism for the way in which they fail to take sufficient account of the concerns of the mystics and literature they study. Furthermore, the whole study of mysticism, from James onwards, is now criticised for being located within a modernist and psychologised framework that inherently misreads the phenomenon of 'mysticism'. For example, see Richard King, *Orientalism and Religion: Postcolonial Theory, India, and 'The Mystic East'* (London: Routledge, 1999), chap. 8.

65 Matthew 7:15–20.

66 Galatians 5:22–23; 1 Corinthians 12:7.

67 One could, perhaps, read the use of drugs by Timothy Leary and others for mystical purposes as an extension of the attempt in Theosophy (and related late-nineteenth century movements) to reconcile religion and science through finding

Within the various strands of Christian mysticism, there is an emphasis on mystical experiences as part of an ongoing process of personal transformation, movement towards participation in God and care for the world and society around one.[68] However, drug use of itself usually, but not always, seems to militate against such personal transformation and movement towards loving relationship with God and neighbour. Aldous Huxley, one of the most prominent advocates of drug use for mystical ends, states: 'Mescalin opens the way of Mary, but shuts the door on that of Martha. It gives access to contemplation – but to a contemplation that is incompatible with action and even with the will to action, the very thought of action.'[69] The phenomenon of inaction is observed by Tom Wolfe in *The Electric Kool-Aid Acid Test*. He draws a contrast between Ken Kesey and the Merry Pranksters, who were actively trying to situate the taking of LSD within a philosophical and ritualised framework, and those who simply took LSD for its own sake. Wolfe gives the example of Paul Hawken, who, in 1965, was a political activist who risked his life for the civil rights movement, but a year later, as part of the Haight Ashbury psychedelic scene, is pouring scorn on his previous commitments while doing nothing in particular.[70] We can conclude that drugs by themselves cannot constitute a means to transcend oneself or become a better person. At best, they merely amplify what is already there; at worst they induce a kind of quietism about oneself and the plight of one's neighbour. In this respect, Baudelaire's analysis of his experiences of cannabis may be applied to all mind-altering drugs. He states:

> The idler has contrived to artificially introduce an element of the super-natural into his life and thoughts: but he is, after all, and in spite of the heightened intensity of his sensations, only the same man augmented, the same number elevated to a much higher power. [...] Thus let the sophisticates and novices who are curious to taste these exceptional delights take heed; they will find nothing miraculous in hashish, nothing but the excessively natural. The brain and body governed by hashish will

---

scientifically verifiable techniques for contacting a spiritual realm. For an account of Theosophy (and its influence upon American alternative culture), see Peter Washington, *Madame Blavatsky's Baboon: A History of the Mystics, Mediums, and Misfits Who Brought Spiritualism to America* (New York: Schocken Books, 1996).

[68] See Olivier Clément, *The Roots of Christian Mysticism: Text and Commentary* (4th edn; trans. Theodore Berkeley; London: New City, 1997), 263–9.

[69] Aldous Huxley, *The Doors of Perception and Heaven and Hell* (London: Flamingo, 1994), 26.

[70] Tom Wolfe, *The Electric Kool-Aid Acid Test* (London: Black Swan, 1989), 315–17.

yield nothing but their ordinary, individual phenomena, augmented it is true, in number and energy, but always faithful to their origins. Man will not escape the destiny of his physical and moral temperament: for man's impressions and intimate thoughts, hashish will act as a magnifying mirror, but a pure mirror none the less.[71]

Even when the emphasis given is to the nature of the experience itself and not to drug use as a means either to transform one's desire or to achieve a 'higher consciousness', there is no guarantee that drug-induced experiences resemble the somatic dimensions of a profound, personal encounter with God. Drug-induced experiences may well resemble something else entirely. Christian mystics caution us that not all of their striving leads to experiences that are mystical. For example, the writer of the *Cloud of Unknowing* warns of the dangers of turning from the true spiritual quest – the quest for God – and seeking 'empty, false physical comfort in so-called refreshment, in relaxation, of body and spirit!'[72] The writer goes on to say of those who are distracted from seeking God that, even if they escape the trap of seeking physical comfort, they might well fall into another trap, that of seeking:

> an unnatural glow and heat within, caused by the abuses of their bodies or their sham spirituality. Or again they feel a false heat brought about by the fiend, their spiritual enemy, because of their pride, materialism and human inquisitiveness. They thoroughly deserve all this, their spiritual blindness and physical discomfort is caused by their spiritual pretence and animal behaviour.[73]

In the light of these comments in the *Cloud of Unknowing*, we might want to go so far as to say that, when situated within the conditions of modernity, the claim to use drugs for mystical ends is nothing more than a kind of *ersatz* mystical practice.[74] But more probably, it is a form of magic that seeks to blur the line between God and creature in a human quest to reach beyond ourselves and make use of creation

---

[71] Charles Baudelaire, 'Artificial Paradises', in *Artificial Paradises: A Drugs Reader* (ed. Mike Jay; London: Penguin, 1999), 15–17 (p. 16).

[72] *The Cloud of Unknowing* (trans. Halcyon Backhouse; London: Hodder & Stoughton, 1985), chap. 45.

[73] *Cloud of Unknowing*, chap. 45.

[74] As is the attempt to use Christianity for mystical ends. The use of drugs for generating a mystical-like buzz is no more corrupt or corrupting than the attempt to use Christian spiritual disciplines and encounters with the Spirit for 'getting high'.

for self-consummation. However, while the immanent may provoke wonder and may even point beyond itself, it can neither initiate relationship with God nor can it directly reveal to us enlightenment about God. Therefore, we should be extremely suspicious of all claims to experience the numinous through contemporary patterns of drug use, and conclude that the ecstasies experienced under drugs are wholly different in kind from the pentecostal ecstasy that is a gift of the Holy Spirit.

Whether chemical substances can be helpful *adjuncts* to faith and traditioned forms of religious practice is another question. The peyote-using Native American church seems to indicate that they can be, as does the use of alcohol in more conventional Christian worship. There appears to be no reason to suppose that chemicals cannot aid the religious life, but the use of chemicals for religious purposes is always shaped and limited by a particular religious tradition that prohibits and excludes such religious use from being informed by a technical rationality, hedonistic gratification and consumerism. Within the Christian tradition, the use of drugs should always be determined by whether or not they contribute to human consummation in the body of Christ and not the consumption of the human body by man.

Aldous Huxley has given an eloquent and perceptive statement on the mind-expanding use of drugs. His essay 'The Doors of Perception' is perhaps one of the most widely referred-to statements on drug use ever written.[75] For a work of such renown, it is surprising that his conclusions about drug use and mystical experiences are not more adhered to. Huxley argues that ecstatic modes of expression are a proper part of Christian worship. However, there is a bifurcation in which God is acknowledged at a verbal and cognitive level, but excluded from how most people seek euphoria or ecstasy; namely in what Huxley calls 'religion's chemical surrogates' – alcohol, marijuana, coca and the like.[76] Drugs such as peyote, he argues, may be more compatible with Christian worship and could help overcome the false dualism between ecstatic euphoria and Christian worship that leads people to resort to 'religion's chemical surrogates'. He does not propose, however, that drugs can lead to Christian ecstasy. He states, 'I am not so foolish as to equate what happens under the influence of mescalin or of any other

---

[75] Allusions to Huxley's essay are a leitmotif of recent art and literature associated with drugs, from the cover of *The Beatles* 'Sergeant Pepper's Lonely Heart's Club Band' album to references in more contemporary films, for example, *The Matrix*.

[76] Huxley, *The Doors of Perception*, 47–8.

drug, prepared or in the future preparable, with the realisation of the end and ultimate purpose of human life: Enlightenment, the Beatific Vision'.[77] Rather, what he suggests is that 'the mescalin experience is what Catholic theologians call "a gratuitous grace," not necessary to salvation but potentially helpful and to be accepted thankfully, if made available'.[78] The question is whether drugs like LSD and mescalin should be used as a means of enabling or priming ecstatic experiences within the context of Christian worship. It is at this point that we must part ways with Huxley. Huxley, quite apart from his Jamesian conception of mysticism, believes that psychotropic drugs can cleanse the doors of perception and even enable us to see 'what Adam had seen on the morning of his creation – the miracle, moment by moment, of naked existence'.[79] In effect, Huxley supplants Christ, as the mediator and healer of true perception, with chemicals. However, there can be no return to Eden. Drugs cannot cause the cherubim's fiery swords to be drawn back. Neither can drugs enable us to see ourselves more clearly, 'For now we see in a mirror, dimly' (1 Cor. 13:12: NRSV). What clarity of vision we can receive is not given by chemicals but by the Holy Spirit, and is an eschatological vision, not a pharmacological one.

6. Drug use within the history of redemption

Having analysed how contemporary patterns of drug use manifest particular features of modernity, we shall now turn to how drugs can be understood within the history of redemption. We shall endeavour to understand how drugs should be used in the light of a theological anthropology.

6.1 'Natural Mystic'

As stated before, drugs are ambiguous. All drugs, whether generated within creation (for example, cannabis and opium) or fabricated from creation (for example, Paracetamol and MDMA), have the capacity to poison or heal, lead to human alienation or enable greater personal presence between humans. The location of drug use is, in the first place, the human body, and the body is, in itself, a created good, with its own

---

[77] Huxley, *The Doors of Perception*, 50–1.
[78] Huxley, *The Doors of Perception*, 51.
[79] Huxley, *The Doors of Perception*, 7.

limits and purposes. Drug use should not usurp or overstep the created boundaries of the body. The use of drugs should instead seek to work within and attempt to fulfil the created goodness of the body. Thus, for example, the use of drugs to deny (rather than heal or enhance) the physical limits of the body, such as using amphetamines or caffeine to completely deny physical tiredness, are prohibited, because such use constitutes the claiming of an illegitimate freedom that is inherently self-defeating. For example, one of the limits drugs like amphetamines seek to deny is the limit of time. Time and space are not constraints that we need liberation from, human existence in time and space is not to be circumvented or diminished through technologies of perception, but as Christ's incarnation affirms, creation is the proper location for humans to live and work and have their being. Thus, physical time limits on the duration we can work are good in that they set physical limits that help shape and properly order human relations.

Perhaps the most important limit to the human body is that life itself has an end or goal beyond itself. Karl Barth states: 'Life is no second God, and therefore the respect due to it cannot rival the reverence owed to God.'[80] Barth points out that the respect owed to life as a good in itself has as its limitation: 'the will of God the Creator Himself who commands it, and the horizon which is set for man by the same God with his determination for eternal life'.[81] What Barth says points also to how Christians understand the basis of their life: it is not their own but received as a gift and loan from God which can only be fulfilled in communion with God. Thus, Christians seek to live within these limits, recognising that between these limits lies the sphere of true freedom. They bear their life in trust for a certain time. In Christianity, life is a good, but it is not the greatest good. When drugs are used to prolong, protect or fulfil (whether hedonistically or medically) life at any cost, then such use indicates that life itself has come to rival God in human estimation, and the drugs themselves are being used illicitly; that is, they have become an adjunct to idolatry.

6.2 'Exodus'

That we live east of Eden, and in need of redemption from our condition of slavery to sin and death, has enormous ramifications for how drugs

---

[80]   Karl Barth, *Church Dogmatics* III:4 (trans. by A.T. Mackay and others; Edinburgh: T&T Clark, 1961), 342.

[81]   Barth, *Dogmatics* III:4, 342.

should be used. Firstly, the goodness of a particular drug cannot be ascertained with regard only to its properties or capacities, but will only become transparent in how it is used and to what end its use is directed. Secondly, we cannot eliminate what causes us to stumble by banning or abstaining from drugs. Drugs may open a door to the sin of gluttony (for example, drunkenness), but drugs themselves are not the cause of such sin. Even those drugs that can induce a physiological dependency, for example heroin, may be used with temperance over long periods of time.[82] What leads to gluttony is the character and circumstances of a person rather than the substance itself.[83] Christ's teaching on what defiles us is an important check on overinvesting drugs themselves with corrupting properties. Throughout the Gospels, Christ is portrayed as in conflict with many other programmes for the purification and holiness of Israel.[84] One of the central conflicts is with an approach to holiness that involves ritual purity, while ignoring character and intention. Mark 7:18–23 states:

> Jesus said to them, '[...] Do you not see that whatever goes into a person from outside cannot defile, since it enters, not the heart but the stomach, and goes out into the sewer?' (Thus he declared all foods clean.) And he said, 'It is what comes out of a person that defiles. For it is from within, from the human heart, that evil intentions come: fornication, theft, murder, adultery, avarice, wickedness, deceit, licentiousness, envy, slander, pride, folly. All these evil things come from within, and they defile a person.' (NRSV)

---

[82] Whether it is the chemical effect of a drug that induces a physiological dependency or whether dependency is caused by the fear and pain of withdrawal is a matter of much dispute. A related issue is the interaction between the user's expectation ('set') and their physical and social context ('setting') in determining the effects of drugs. Variables in either of these change the experienced impact of a drug upon the body.

[83] There is much debate between those who think drugs can artificially induce dependency in anyone (thus restricting exposure is key) and those who think that the chemicals themselves and their supply matters less than the personal and cultural values that modulate the demand for and use of any particular drug. Proponents of the former view point to the link between proximity and high rates of dependency. Proponents of the latter view point to examples such as the contrast between rates of alcoholism in Ireland and Italy or Spain: despite high levels of per capita consumption of alcohol in all these countries, alcoholism in Ireland is far more widespread. For an example of the second view, see Stanton Peele, 'A Moral Vision of Addiction: How People's Values Determine Whether They Become and Remain Addicts', *Journal of Drug Issues*, 17.2 (1987), 187–215.

[84] For an account of these conflicts, see Marcus Borg, *Conflict, Holiness and Politics in the Teachings of Jesus* (Lampeter: Edwin Mellen, 1972).

The use of drugs may greatly exacerbate our folly and licentiousness, but drugs do not cause them. The contrast between Dr William Stewart Halsted and Samuel Taylor Coleridge illustrates how it is not drugs *per se* that lead to drug binges and personal breakdown. Halsted (1852–1922), one of the four distinguished founders of the Johns Hopkins Medical School, sustained a dependency on morphine all his life while also being a practising surgeon of famed skill.[85] By comparison, Coleridge proved consistently unable to control his opium dependency, and the effects of his physiological and psychological dependency on the drug greatly compounded his personal, artistic and professional problems. However, the roots of Coleridge's problems lay not in his physiological dependency on opium, but in tragic flaws in his character, for example, his procrastination. Holmes notes that when, after 1814, Coleridge did finally confess to the full extent of his opium dependency, his admissions emphasise its moral as well as its physical dimensions. Holmes states that Coleridge's letters of confession 'reveal a strong philosophical or religious dimension, based on the notion of the corrupted human will – Coleridge's version of original sin ... Opium of course was his own particular sin, but it arose out of the fallen condition of mankind.'[86] If what causes problems with drugs is not initially or primarily the drugs themselves but our sinful characters, then we must learn how to manage our responses to drugs in the light of our fallen condition. Managing our responses to drugs means undertaking to school the flesh and avoid establishing patterns of life (either corporately or individually) that encourage dependency on drugs.

It is important, at this point, to make a distinction between temperance and abstinence. Temperance movements have generally confused one with the other, but temperance does not mean abstinence. Rather, it means 'the practice or habit of exercising self-control or moderation'.[87] Temperance is thus what Paul is referring to with regard to sexual relations in 1 Thessalonians when he calls for each one of us to know 'how to control [our] own body in holiness and honor, not with lustful passion, like the Gentiles who do not know God' (1 Thess. 4:4–5: NRSV).

---

85 Edward Brecher, *Licit and Illicit Drugs; the Consumers Union Report on Narcotics, Stimulants, Depressants, Inhalants, Hallucinogens, and Marijuana – Including Caffeine, Nicotine, and Alcohol* (Boston: Little, Brown, 1972), ch 5.

86 Richard Holmes, *Coleridge: Darker Reflections* (London: HarperCollins, 1998), p. 356.

87 'Temperance', *New Shorter Oxford English Dictionary* (CD-ROM ed.; Oxford: OUP, 1996).

John Paul II argues that the virtue of temperance is what Paul means when he calls for purity. In John Paul II's view, the virtue of temperance has a twofold aspect: it is both abstention from the passion of lust and, at the same time, control of one's own body in holiness and honour.[88] However, control and abstention from lust (rather than abstention from any particular created good) must be balanced with the need to avoid legalism. In Galatians 5, Paul talks of the mutual antipathy of Spirit and flesh (5:17); however, as O'Donovan notes, Paul's use of the term 'flesh' unites both flesh as 'desire' (*epithymia*) and flesh as 'law' (*nomos*).[89] In other words, legalism and licence are two sides of the same coin. Thus, legalistic abstention from, and prohibition of, drugs is as pernicious as the gluttonous or lawless use of drugs. Both constitute a false valorisation of one's own flesh and a denial of the work of the Spirit. Our proper response to drugs is one of temperate use; for it is through temperance that we properly respect the created goodness of the human body and grow in our detachment from what, in the human heart, is the fruit of the lusts of the flesh, rather than the fruit of the Holy Spirit.[90]

We must also avoid overinvesting any particular substance with demonic properties and denying the goodness of creation. Paul's teaching in 1 Corinthians 8 is particularly relevant here. N.T. Wright sees 1 Corinthians 8 as an attempt to fight a battle on two fronts: that is, against a gnostic-like dualism (which constitutes the rejection of the goodness of the created order) and against paganism (which constitutes the deification of the created order).[91] Drugs can become a form of idolatry or be used, like meat, as part of a wider system of idolatry. For example, we have already analysed the link between drugs and the idolatry of consumerism. However, for Paul, idols have no real existence (1 Cor. 8:4), and the things we consume do not, in and of themselves, establish our relationship with God or alienate us from God (1 Cor. 8:8). However, idols, and meat sacrificed to them, signal a real phenomenon that must be dealt with and not sidestepped. To place oneself in the sphere of idols is to be involved in demon worship. Wright states that for Paul:

---

[88] John Paul II, *The Theology of the Body: Human Love in the Divine Plan* (Boston: Pauline Books & Media, 1997), 200–1.

[89] Oliver O'Donovan, *Resurrection and Moral Order: An Outline for Evangelical Ethics* (Grand Rapids: Eerdmans, 1986), 12.

[90] John Paul II, *The Theology of the Body*, 205.

[91] N.T. Wright, 'Monotheism, Christology and Ethics: 1 Corinthians 8', in *The Climax of the Covenant: Christ and the Law in Pauline Theology* (Minneapolis: Fortress Press, 1992), 120–36 (p. 125).

To enter an idol's temple, and eat there alongside those who are actually intending to share fellowship with this non-god, this hand-made pseudo-god – this is to invite created powers to have an authority over one which they do not possess, a power which belongs only to the creator-God revealed in and through Jesus the Messiah.[92]

Therefore we may conclude that Paul is saying to avoid eating meat in temples of idolatry, but that the purchase and consumption of meat from the market is licit (for to say anything else would be to lapse into Manichaeism).

Our problem, of course, is that the marketplace has become the temple. In this situation, there must be an emphasis on creating mature habits of consumption, characterised by temperance, which are neither bound by the practices of the idolatry of consumerism, nor subject to the idolatry of technology, but directed to consummation in Christ. By saying that our primary concern is developing temperance in how we use drugs, am I saying that no drug is off limits? As with meat sacrificed to idols, so we must say of drugs: '"All things are lawful", but not all things are beneficial. "All things are lawful", but not all things build up' (1 Cor. 10:23: NRSV). There can be no drug that is not licit, although there may be many drugs of which we might say they are not recommended. Conversely, there can be no drug which we are commanded to consume, not even wine at the Eucharist. We cannot be commanded to consume a drug because, as Paul exhorts us, each should be concerned for the consciences of others in the community, and where patterns of consumption might cause a scandal to 'weaker' members, these substances should be avoided. Thus, for example, the practice of teetotalism by some Baptists in Russia may well be an appropriate response to extremely high rates of alcoholism in that country. But such abstention is a tactical measure, limited by particular circumstances. Nevertheless, our situation is a bit more complex than simply counselling moderation in all things and restraint where appropriate.

If the location of idolatry in a technocratic, consumer culture is the body itself, then there is a direct rivalry between the body as a temple of consumerism and the body as a temple of the Holy Spirit.[93] If drugs are a primary means of habituating ourselves to certain aspects of modernity, then all forms of drug use, therapeutic or otherwise, may be instances of what Paul calls 'sins against the body'; that is, drug

---

[92] Wright, 'Monotheism, Christology and Ethics', 134.
[93] 1 Corinthians 6:19.

use directly turns the body away from glorifying God and denies that our bodies were 'purchased at a price' through Christ's death and resurrection. Thus, within a technocratic and consumer society, drug use turns the body itself (as distinct from the act or substance) into a witness against God in a manner parallel to fornication.[94] Thus, while we may, in theory, moderately or occasionally consume drugs such as alcohol or tobacco in good conscience, when we recognise how consuming these drugs constitutes a way in which we participate in contemporary forms of idolatry, and how such use makes of our bodies objects of consumption by an all-pervasive system of domination, then temperance may, in practice, not always be enough. At the present time, abstinence may well be a necessary form of gospel witness.

6.3 'Redemption Song'

As well as being circumscribed by the conditions of witness, all use of drugs is relativised by the gift of the Holy Spirit and the fulfilment of time when there will be no more tears (and thus no more need for therapeutic drugs) and when we shall all be caught up in the euphoric ecstasy of the messianic banquet (and therefore, there will be no more unfulfilled desire for personal ecstasy that some drugs simulate and parody). All drug use is relativised as an activity limited to this age, with no significance in the age to come. Furthermore, we live between the times, betwixt this age and the age to come. Any attempt to falsely resolve that tension, either by engineering a permanent contentment now (through 'cosmetic pharmacology') or by chemically-induced attempts to experience God's kingdom come, are both ruled out, for they both seek to deny the *eschaton* as a gift given by God (which may, through the Spirit, be experienced now). In short, we cannot use drugs to create, what is in effect, an artificial paradise. The wine of the Eucharist is but a provisional supplement to the wine of the Spirit.[95]

---

[94] 1 Corinthians 6:18.

[95] Conversely, it is precisely the properties of wine which constitute part of its appropriateness for use at the Eucharist. The way in which wine acts as an inebriant is part of its theological symbolic value as a token of the *eschaton* and resurrection gladness. Thus, grape juice is not as good as wine. Moreover, the use of grape juice completely misses a central point of the use of bread and wine at the Eucharist; the pattern for the eschatological transfiguration of all creation is given at the Last Supper: Christ did not take pristine grain and grapes; instead, he took bread and wine, the products of human labour, creativity and culture (i.e. creation as priested by humans) and transformed them (not raw creation) into an anticipation of their eschatological fulfilment. Again, central to the appropriateness of bread and wine

Given that the wine of the Spirit is available now, there is no need to get drunk on wine.[96]

As a provisional supplement to the wine of the Spirit, drugs may be used both therapeutically and in an ampliative way to enable personal presence, either through healing the body or enhancing personal relations. For example, the use of alcohol to promote conviviality is good in the light of the *telos* of human being as communion with God and each other.[97] Indeed, the use of wine to foreshadow the messianic banquet lies at the heart of Jesus' actions at the wedding feast at Cana (John 2:1–11). Conversely, when drugs militate against greater personal presence and a deepening of communal relations, then a line has been crossed between proper use and abuse. The line between the use of alcohol (or cannabis) to enable conviviality and being drunk (or stoned) is drawn at the point at which alienation and the sundering of personal relations sets in. We must always ask, when someone is using alcohol (or cannabis) whether that person is more or less physically, spiritually, emotionally and rationally present to others and, if they are, at what point does the drug in use inhibit both an individual's present ability and their future capacity for personal presence to God and others.[98]

Drugs that create a false, chemically-induced sense of profound community (as distinct from a convivial or congenial one) are rendered illicit. While we may anticipate the messianic banquet in this age,

---

at the Eucharist is their intrinsic properties. Parallels may be drawn, for example, with the use of stained glass windows, the colour and light refracting properties of which are intrinsic to their use as icons.

[96] Or as the physician who treated Coleridge for his opium addiction, Dr Daniel, noted, after an evening with the poet, 'The Conversation was mantling like Champagne – & Laughter, as I have often observed, is the most potent Producer of Forgetfulness, of the whole Pharmacopeia, moral or medical.' Holmes, *Coleridge*, 360. On the theological significance of laughter, see Karl-Josef Kuschel, *Laughter: A Theological Essay* (trans. John Bowden; New York: Continuum, 1994).

[97] It is a false view of human relations to think it is possible to be wholly personally present to everyone all the time. Human relationships properly operate on a scale from casual exchanges in a bus queue to the profound conversations of deep friendship or the vulnerability of sexual intercourse. Conviviality lies somewhere between these two poles.

[98] This, of course, raises the huge question of what it means to be personally present to others. Two important and related questions are whether enhancement technologies like Prozac enable or disable authentic personal presence and how such technologies may function to enable the kinds of personal transformation that formation into the form of Christ entails. Discernment of how different drugs affect human relationships and personhood will become ever more pressing with increasing use of psychopharmacology. On this, see Elliott, *Better Than Well*.

such anticipations are shaped by Christ's crucifixion. Our joy in the communion presently available is found as, by the Spirit, we 'put to death the misdeeds of the body' (Rom. 8:13). The intrinsically strong effect of drugs like ecstasy short circuits the cruciform nature of personal relations, by attempting a technological solution to the painful, time-intensive dynamics of repentance, forgiveness, attentiveness to one's neighbour, sacrificial self-giving and all the other aspects of personal transformation that are required for profound community between humans.[99] The ecstatic joy of the Prodigal's embrace by his father is entirely different in kind to the unity enjoyed solely under the influence of drugs, the value of which is debased precisely because it is fabricated. One is an event of hard-won communion, the other is simply one more consumer event. Indeed, rather than bear witness to the life, death and resurrection of Jesus Christ in its life together, such drug-induced patterns of ecstasy and community constitute a parody of it.

The above theological deliberations can be summarised in terms of a series of questions that can be addressed to any drug. These are: Firstly, in the light of who we are as created beings, is a particular drug being used to manipulate or control the body in a way that denies the bodies created goodness and its created limits? Secondly, given our status as fallen beings, is the use of a particular drug idolatrous or not? And, furthermore, when we look at the context in which a particular drug is being used, is temperance or abstinence called for? Thirdly, as those who are redeemed through Jesus Christ and who may now enjoy communion with God, does using a drug make us more or less personally present to others and, if it does, at what point does the drug in use inhibit both an individual's immediate ability, and their future capacity, for personal presence to God and others? A related question to this last one is whether a particular drug being used allows for the cruciform shape of redeemed human relations before Christ's return, or does it seek to create an artificial paradise? The application of these questions to the drugs we use or proscribe should help in discerning the licitness or otherwise of any particular drug.

7. Conclusion

In conclusion, there is much more that could be said on the topic of drugs. However, I have sought to understand how, in the contemporary

---

[99] However, this is not to rule out the possibility that milder forms that have an effect analogous to small quantities of alcohol may be licit.

context, drugs are used and what, in the light of theological criteria of evaluation, they signify. I argued that contemporary patterns of drug use are: firstly, a paradigmatic instance of the modern, technocratic conception of the body as an object of manipulation; secondly, the fruit of contemporary patterns of certain dynamics within consumerism; and thirdly, that in what they say about the human body and the way it shapes human life together, contemporary patterns of drug use constitute a denial of the reality of the body as a gift of God, subject to sin, but redeemed through the life, death and resurrection of Jesus Christ and open to fulfilment through the perfecting and empowering presence of the Spirit as we await Christ's return.

7

Culture and the End of Religion

Colin J.D. Greene

Introduction

In this volume, the various contributors are endeavouring to face some of the difficult and complex issues involved in working out a coherent and constructive theology of culture. It goes without saying that all of us are daily involved in this task whether we recognise it or not. The reality of living in the modern world means we are immersed in a huge tidal flow of cultural artefacts, influences and consumer-driven flotsam that continually present us with theological, ethical and philosophical problems. However we choose to describe our present cultural situation – postmodern, post-secular, post-Christendom, post-industrial, post-Christian, post-ethical – the predominance of the prefix 'post' suggests that the changes we are presently experiencing in our cultural hinterland are so vast, so complex and potentially catastrophic that both the Christian church and the theological establishment are in danger of simply being left out of the equation altogether.

It is for this reason that I would like to concentrate on one particular aspect of our present cultural situation that has become so firmly situated in the cultural mores of contemporary society as to go virtually unchallenged. Moreover, I would suggest that this factor is the primary reason why Christians and theologians are not regarded as essential contributors to the discussions and debates that largely determine our future cultural horizons. I refer to what has become known as the privatisation of religion or the marginalisation of religion, from the public life of society and culture in general. This is a factor that signals for many the end of religion as a coherent system of beliefs and values that could unite a society or culture in a common sense of purpose and identity. This hugely debilitating factor, as far as the vigour and survival of the Christian church is concerned, is in fact rooted in the genesis of modernity and remains a deeply problematic aspect of our experience of the modern world.

In what follows, I would like firstly to argue that the demise of religion as a major contributor to social and political cohesion and cultural renewal was largely expedited, not through post-Enlightenment science or epistemology, nor through some insidious but inevitable process of secularisation that began in the eighteenth century, but via the ideological critique of religion that questioned the validity or legitimacy of religion in the modern world altogether.

Secondly, I want to argue that the ideological critique of religion, which inevitably found its way into theology as well, led, inexorably and unfortunately, to the transference of the religious question out of its natural context in terms of the genesis of modernity into the field of religious studies or comparative religion that, in turn, eventually produced a full-blown theology of the religions orientated around the inherently problematic schema of exclusivism, inclusivism and pluralism.

Finally, I would like to suggest that the cultural fissure we are presently experiencing, that which we refer to as postmodernity, has led to a splintering of the religious question, which means that any attempt to delineate a theology of culture must seek to rescue the category of religion from the ideological internment camp where it appears to be presently languishing in a state of turpitude and malnutrition.

How do we understand the Role of Religion?

Clearly, before proceeding any further, I need to be more specific about how I am using the term 'religion'. In a seminal and important book, Callum Brown has drawn attention to the way sociologists understand the nature of religion in the modern world.[1] He notes, quite rightly, that sociological studies tend to concentrate on the roles or functions religion exercises in a modern democratic society. In regard to Christianity, we can talk in terms of four central functions: *institutional Christianity* – measured in terms of the growth or decline of church attendance and religious practice; *intellectual Christianity* – understood as shared structures of belief or intellectual assent to

---

[1] C. Brown, *The Death of Christian Britain* (London: Routledge, 2000).

a particular religious worldview; *functional Christianity* – the role of religion in civil society, particularly government, education and welfare; and *diffusive Christianity* – measured in terms of the success or otherwise of evangelism and other mission-based activities. According to Brown, utilising insights from modern cultural theory, this analysis misses the crucial importance of a further factor, that which he refers to as *discursive Christianity*. By this he means the way personal identity and a sense of belonging are mediated to the population at large by certain key religious narratives and discourses. To measure the impact of this aspect of religion, one has to attend to the voices of the people articulated through the dominant media, such as books, magazines, television and film. Brown argues that it is in fact the discursive power of a religious narrative or system of beliefs that is the most decisive factor in guaranteeing the success or otherwise of a particular religion in a democratic society free from state coercion and control.

> For Christianity to have social significance – for it to achieve popular participation, support or even acquiescence – in a democratic society free from state regulation of religious habits, it must have a base of discursivity. Otherwise, it is inconceivable.[2]

Brown's central argument is that if one attends to the reality of discursive Christianity in the period from 1850 to 1950, one finds that it was the evangelical narrative, with its emphasis upon personal conversion and moral regeneration that fitted well with the cultural aspirations of many people brought up in what was, by and large, the last puritan age. Since the lifestyle and moral revolutions of the 1960s, this has changed dramatically, particularly in regard to the status and aspirations of women. It is this recent process of secularisation, or social distancing of the population at large from the Bible and the Christian church, that has led to the widespread collapse of Christianity in all its functions in modern British culture.

Brown's analysis has much to commend it, but for this writer at least it lacks a theological focus on what was taking place from the early eighteenth century onwards, which we refer to as the ideological critique of religion. A similar problem bedevils the usual theological account of the matter that tends to be expressed in the following terms.

---

2 Brown, *Christian Britain*, 13.

Modernity and the Religious Question

Theology, in the immediate aftermath of the Enlightenment, was dominated by repeated attempts to define the essence of religion; so, for instance, Schleiermacher's definition of religion as the sense and taste for the infinite, later to be superseded by the notion of religion as the feeling of absolute dependence, or indeed, Wilhelm Herrmann's equally arresting definition of religion as the expression of religious experience wholly without weapons, i.e. dependent on no *a priori* metaphysical or apologetic arguments, but based instead on the primordial experience of trust.[3] In the same idealist tradition, but much later of course, we have Paul Tillich's notion of religion as experience of the 'unconditioned', which defines the basis of our ultimate concern.[4] We are often reliably informed that the reasons for these diverse and varied attempts to define the essence of religion as that which is located in our common humanity were twofold:

1. The gradual secularisation of society brought about by the collapse of Christendom and the advent of the industrial revolution seemed to some to herald the end of religion. Many of the so-called free thinkers of the Enlightenment saw, in the rise of the natural sciences, the way to true knowledge of ourselves and the world which would expose the unwarranted superstition and priestcraft upon which religion was supposedly based. John Trenchard put forward such a view in his book *Natural History of Superstition* (1709). As late as 1928, at the International Missionary conference in Jerusalem, John Macmurray argued that religions would disappear as the scientific mode of thought continued to gain ascendancy. This form of hard-nosed scientific materialism has, of course, reappeared in our day amongst the socio-biologists like Richard Dawkins who are presently pushing back the scientific boundaries in the areas of molecular biology and genetics.[5]

2. Modern sociologists of religion, such as Peter Berger and Talcott Parsons, have taken a different tack. They have argued that the Enlightenment did not herald the end of religion, but simply

---

[3] See G. Dorrien, *Theology Without Weapons: the Barthian Revolt in Modern Theology* (Louisville: WJKP, 1999), 24.

[4] Tillich, 'On the Idea of a Theology of Culture', in *Paul Tillich: Theologian of the Boundaries* (ed. Taylor; Minneapolis: Augsburg Fortress, 1991), 40.

[5] See, for instance, the various writings of Richard Dawkins.

ushered in a radical change in its function. In a society becoming increasingly complex and differentiated, the old identification of church and state became inherently problematic and untenable. The inevitable separation that followed allowed both to carve out their respective spheres of influence within the context of the modern world. The problem with this analysis, however, as the late Lesslie Newbigin continually sought to argue, is that it overlooks the fact that the epistemological basis to this separation was located in the fateful Enlightenment distinction between knowledge and belief, or fact and value.

Science, it was argued, has to do with facts accessible to reason, which leads to the authority of public knowledge. Religion, on the other hand, like morality, the arts and just about everything else of interest, has to do with personal beliefs, or value systems, which, in the context of the secular society, are relegated to a wholly private realm.[6] It is also the case that this situation has bolstered the ideology of pluralism in our modern world. No longer is religious pluralism simply a reality we all experience, it has become an ideology we all cherish. The secular state tolerates religious diversity, indeed welcomes it as a potentially enriching aspect of modern life, provided the exponents of any particular belief system make no imperialistic claims for truth.

I want to argue, however, that the rise of the natural sciences and technology as the most effective way to understand the nature of the world around us, and therefore to render largely redundant theological or religious explanations of the same, or the success of Kantian epistemology in effectively reducing religion to practical morality, are not sufficient in themselves to explain the wholesale retreat of the Christian faith from the public life of society. Rather, it is precisely at this point that we must attend, yet again, to the pernicious effects of

---

6 As the authors of *The Mystery of Salvation* take note, such a view has serious consequences:

If society as a whole does not assent to a transcendent dimension to life, such assent becomes a matter not of public doctrine but of individual choice. Alternatively, a society fragments into smaller groupings each with its own frame of reference and religious outlook, and the individual chooses to which, if any, to belong. All religion therefore, even religion which claims universal truth or the capacity to offer universal salvation, comes to be seen in the society at large as a matter of personal choice, and therefore it becomes harder to treat universal truth claims as such.

The Mystery of Salvation, The Doctrine Commission of the Church of England, 7.

the ideological critique of religion. This fact has been recognised by Wolfhart Pannenberg:

> Radical criticism of religion stands or falls with the claim that religion is not a constitutive part of human nature, that in spite of its persistent influence on humanity and its history we must view it as an aberration, or at best as an immature form of the human understanding of reality which has been overcome in principle by the secular culture of the modern West, or by a new society that is still in the process of creation, so that it will finally wither away.[7]

Not surprisingly then, the ideological critique of religion took its initial stand on the already disputed territory of theological anthropology, claiming that religion was a perversion or distortion of our common humanity that should now be exposed as such within the context of a society let loose from its moorings in a particular religious belief system.

The Ideological Critique of Religion

The most notable attempt to define religion in terms of a fundamental distortion of our self-understanding was the infamous projection theory of Ludwig Feuerbach. Alister McGrath has pointed out, quite rightly, that the translation of the German word *Vergegenstandlichung* as 'projection' by the English translator George Eliot was in fact a mistake that obscured the Hegelian background to Feuerbach's thought.[8] Feuerbach was working from the Hegelian understanding of the relationship of consciousness to objective reality – the process whereby human beings objectivise their feelings of hate, love, fear or trust in relation to external agencies. This is an entirely legitimate exercise, except when one makes a category mistake and wrongly attributes these feelings to an inappropriate object. Feuerbach agreed with Schleiermacher that the essence of religion was located in the affective dimension of human personality. However, when these feelings are attributed to the outside agency of God, we are in fact confusing human self-feeling, or experience of ourselves, with experience of God.

---

[7] W. Pannenberg, *Systematic Theology* (2 vols; Edinburgh: T&T Clark, 1991), 1:155.
[8] A. McGrath, *The Making of Modern German Christology 1750–1990* (Oxford: Blackwells, 1986), 68.

In film — are we dealing with 'essences'? rel

The last refuge of theology therefore is feeling. God is renounced by the understanding; he has no longer the dignity of a real object, of a reality which imposed itself on the understanding; hence he is transferred to feeling; in feeling his existence is thought to be secure. And doubtless this is the safest refuge; for to make feeling the essence of religion is nothing else than to make feeling the essence of God. And as certainly as I exist, so certainly does my feeling exist; and as certainly as my feeling exists, so certainly does my God exist. The certainty of God is here nothing else than the self-certainty of human feeling; the yearning after God is the yearning after unlimited, uninterrupted, pure feeling.[9]

Schleiermacher's definition of the essence of religion in terms of *Gefühl* was always vulnerable to such a reductionist critique. All that Feuerbach does is claim that there is no outside referent to which such feelings can be attributed, and, at the same time, misrepresents the philosophical basis to Schleiermacher's theology of religion.

There is a direct line from Feuerbach's analysis of the essence of religion to that of Karl Marx. Both represent the left wing of Hegelianism. Marx claimed that religion is our own production and, as such, is the result of self-alienation. That alienation is caused by economic and social factors, such as the existence of private property and the division of labour. Religion is thus the opiate of the peoples, the way in which the masses inoculate themselves against the intolerable burden of economic alienation. Marxist materialism claimed that, given the amelioration of such alienating economic factors, religion would disappear. The revolutionary impulse of Marxism was, however, destined to produce its own alternative to traditional religious belief:

It is a paradox that a system which claimed that the beginning of all criticism was the criticism of religion should have ended up with a form of religion which was the end of all criticism.[10]

The psychoanalyst Sigmund Freud put forward a similar reductionist argument, but this time couched in psychological terms. This is the most commonly accepted form of the projection theory amongst modern atheists, namely, that religion is the regressive tendency in all of us to retreat to the security of our infant experience. Religion is, consequently, wish fulfilment, the desire to have some transcendent

---

[9] L. Feuerbach, *The Essence of Christianity* (New York: Harper, 1957), 283.

[10] O. Guiness, 'Mission Modernity: seven checkpoints on mission in the modern world', in *Faith and Modernity* (ed. P. Sampson, V. Samuel and C. Sugden; Oxford: Regnum Lynx, 1994), 349.

divine figure that is in control of our destiny and attends to our emotional and spiritual needs. In other words, God is a projection of our own need for security. Religion is, accordingly, an illusion that at times can degenerate into a pathological disorder.

A more nuanced treatment of the religious disposition is found in Freud's own account of the nature of modern civilisation, a book that first appeared in 1930, *Das Unbehagen in der Kultur*, translated into English eventually as *Civilisation and its Discontents*. Here Freud claimed that civilisation (translate modernity) has to do with the lure for beauty, purity and order. He also noted, however, that human beings are not naturally predisposed towards such civilising virtues or values. Their attainment is only realised by an exchange, a pay-off that is both costly and inherently insecure. Civilisation is, accordingly, constructed upon the renunciation of instinct, in particular, sexuality, aggressivity and the individual drive for freedom. Civilisation is the product of an unstable and negotiated compromise between instincts and virtues, individual wants and needs and societal restraints and responsibilities. Religion is clearly perceived as one way of keeping the lid on the potentially explosive conflict of interest that accompanies, interestingly enough, the maintenance of culture. Here Freud clearly moves close to Nietzsche's equally problematic view of the nature of religion.

Nietzsche and the Death of God

> Have you not heard of that madman who lit a lantern in the bright morning hours, ran to the market place and cried incessantly: 'I seek God! I seek God!' – As many of those who did not believe in God were standing around just then, he provoked much laughter. Has he got lost? asked one. Did he lose his way like a child? asked another. Or is he hiding? Is he afraid of us? Has he gone on a voyage? Emigrated? – Thus they yelled and laughed.

> The madman jumped into their midst and pierced them with his eyes. 'Whither is God?' he cried; I will tell you. *We have killed him* – you and I. All of us are his murderers. But how did we do this?[11]

In this famous passage from *The Gay Science*, the Madman announces what Nietzsche perceived to be the greatest event to overtake recent European civilisation. That event was quite simply the death of God,

---

[11]   F.W. Nietzsche, *The Gay Science*, part three, 'The Madman'.

in the sense that belief in such a God revealed in the Judeo-Christian tradition had become unsustainable. Nietzsche's critique of religion as the ideology of the weak, the insipid and the cowardly that refuse to accept that everything in life is driven by the will to power, is often regarded as the most trenchant form of modern atheism. There is, however, a more prophetic, disturbing, almost poignant note in Nietzsche's critical awareness of the significance of such widespread lack of belief. Both the Madman and the bystanders disdain belief in God, but only the Madman clearly perceives what has been lost, that the death of God in modern society, 'the god who dies in the event of his own incredibility',[12] leaves a yawning chasm in the modern psyche and, as yet, we do not know what will replace it.

> Are we not plunging continually? Backward, sideward, forward, in all directions? Is there still any up or down? Are we not straying as through an infinite nothing? Do we not feel the breath of empty space? Has it not become colder? Is not night continually closing in on us? Do we not need to light lanterns in the morning? Do we hear nothing as yet of the noise of the gravediggers who bury God? Do we smell nothing as yet of the divine decomposition? Gods too, decompose. God is dead. God remains dead. And we have killed him.[13]

At the end of the discourse, the Madman makes the further astonishing discovery that he has come too early, that no one is ready to accept the consequences of this momentous event, that, although churches throughout Europe have become the tombs and sepulchres of God, we will not accept our own responsibility and culpability for this irreversible situation. So just what was the nature of the apocalyptic event announced by the Madman? Was he referring to the apparent incommensurability of the Christian God with the exigencies of the modern world, or was he announcing the unbelievability of God given the failed reality of Christendom? Might it be that Nietzsche assumed that the existence of God was dependent upon our faithful belief and obedience to this higher reality? If this has been expunged from the heart of modern society, if we have chosen to eradicate this sacred covenant from our midst, then God is literally dead and a different history awaits us. We must become worthy of the new role that has befallen humanity. Nietzsche endeavoured to sketch out what this higher destiny might entail.

---

[12] Michael J. Buckley, *At the Origins of Modern Atheism* (New Haven: Yale, 1987), 29.
[13] Nietzsche, *Gay Science*, part three.

In *Thus Spoke Zarathustra*, the philosopher announces the relativity of all values and, therefore, the need to find just one goal to guide humankind. That goal is the emergence of the superman. 'What is great in man is that he is a bridge and not a goal: what can be loved in man is that he is an *Übergang* and an *Untergang*.'[14]

What must be despised and, therefore, sacrificed is the human – the all-too-human – in order that the superman may appear. The superman is the one who recognises the will to power and lives by it. 'Sultry heart and cold head: where these join together, there the roaring wind springs up, the "Saviour."'[15] The superman both grasps and masters his own destiny, and so transcends the slavish mediocrity of the herd instinct in all of us.

> On the other side, the herd man in Europe today gives himself the appearance of being the only permissible kind of man, and glorifies his attributes, which make him tame, easy to get along with, and useful to the herd, as if they were the truly human virtues: namely, public spirit, benevolence, consideration, industriousness, moderation, modesty, indulgence, and pity.[16]

It is doubtful that Nietzsche understood the arrival of the superman in terms of the evolution of humanity to a higher ideal, because of his cherished doctrine of the eternal recurrence. Again, this idea dispenses with the need for religion, because it offers another possibility in terms of the destiny both of the individual and of the history of humanity. Quite simply it is the notion that whatever happens does so an infinite number of times and will re-happen continuously in exactly the same way in which it happens now. Therefore, there is strictly speaking no single person, but an infinite number of recurring persons, and again it is Zarathustra who offers us this strange belief.

You would say 'Now I die and vanish.' And 'Now I am nothing.' Souls are mortal as bodies. But the knot of causes, in which I am tangled, returns again – and creates me again. I belong myself to the causes of eternal recurrence.[17]

It would seem that Nietzsche's faith lies in the power of human beings to untie themselves from the constraining bonds of religion

---

[14] F.W. Nietzsche, *Thus Spoke Zarathustra: A Book For All and None*.

[15] Ibid., I, "Von den Priestern".

[16] Nietzsche, 'The Natural History of Morals', quoted in Cahoone, *From Modernism to Postmodernism* (Oxford: Blackwell, 1996), 114.

[17] Nietzsche, *Zarathustra* III, 'Der Genesende'.

and acquiescence to the morality of the herd, and, in so doing, grasp the truth of our own eternal destiny. We live by the maxim that we should act in a way that we would be willing to act an infinite number of times. There is no other alternative life, be that heaven or hell, we can only 'stamp the form of eternity upon our lives'.[18] Authenticity assuages the guilt that leads to resentment or resignation, and *this* life becomes our eternal life. So what has Nietzsche achieved? A new form of philosophical vitalism, or has he merely espoused a renewed form of paganism? It is surely interesting that in terms of the postmodernists who take their cue from Nietzsche, Michel Foucault, Gilles Deleuze, Felix Guattari and Jean-Francois Lyotard, both possible interpretations are given equal weight.

Religion as the Idolatry of Unbelief

It is not surprising that the ideological critique of religion would find its way into theology, particularly in the midst of the extreme theological reaction that marked Karl Barth's break with his liberal protestant heritage. Barth set his face against the *cultural Protestantism* of his predecessors. His basic and fundamental theological criticism of the whole tradition of liberal Protestantism, from Schleiermacher to Adolf von Harnack and his erstwhile teacher, Wilhelm Herrmann, was that it represented the reduction of theology to anthropology. Barth opposed this notion of religion as the essence and highest achievement of our common humanity with the primacy of God's self-revelation in Jesus Christ. This was the introduction into the human sphere of a complete *novum*, a creation *ex nihilo*, the living Word of God that exposed and undermined all human attempts at self-justification. In this sense, religion was simply the idolatry of unbelief.

It was during the period, when Barth was writing the first edition of the *Römerbrief*, that both his radical break with his liberal theological heritage, combined with his strident criticism of religion, took theological shape and form. In an address given to a gathering of socialists at Baden on December 7, 1915, Barth took his definition of the essence of religion straight from Schleiermacher. "Religion" is a very weak and ambiguous word. Religion is pious feeling [*Gefühl*] in individual men and women, together with the particular morality

---

18 F. Nietzsche, *Werke in Drei Bänden* (ed. Karl Schlechta; München: Carl Hanser Verlag, 1954–6), 124.

and the particular worship which proceeds from it.'[19] This hopelessly ambiguous and illusory endeavour is contrasted with the *fact* of the kingdom of God, the rule and reality of the lordship of God forever outside history and, therefore, also beyond our grasp. This dialectic of God the 'wholly other' and the vanity of religion appears again in his lecture given in Aarau on January 16, 1916, entitled *The Righteousness of God*. Here, the radical separation is between two forms of will, the will or righteousness of God free from all 'caprice and vacillation', and the will of humankind supported by religion that is always 'grounded upon arbitrariness, whim and self-seeking'.[20] Accordingly, human religion is a tower of Babel, erected in defiance of God, and this time the definition of the essence of religion is derived from Hermann.

> It is a wonderful illusion if we are able to comfort ourselves with the thought that, in our Europe, next to capitalism, prostitution, housing speculation, alcoholism, tax fraud, and militarism, the Church's proclamation and ethics too, the 'religious life', go their uninterrupted way. We are still Christians! Our people are still a Christian people! A wonderful illusion, but still an illusion, a self-deception! ... What good is all the preaching, baptising, confirming, bell-ringing, and organ-playing? ... Will our relation to the righteousness of God be changed by all this? ... Is not our religious righteousness too a product of pride and our despair, a Tower of Babel, at which the Devil laughs more loudly than at all the others?[21]

Barth's acceptance of the Feuerbachian critique of religion was carried over into the initial volumes of the *Church Dogmatics*. He asserts that a fundamental distinction must be recognised between revelation, understood as 'God's self-offering and self-manifestation' and religion, understood as 'a human attempt to anticipate what God in His revelation wills to do and does do'. As such, 'It is the attempted replacement of the divine work by a human manufacture.' This in turn means that, 'The divine reality offered and manifested to us in revelation is replaced by a concept of God arbitrarily and wilfully evolved by man.' The result of this hopeless endeavour is equally clear.

---

[19] Barth, 'Religion und Sozialismus', quoted in B. McCormack, *Karl Barth's Critically Realistic Dialectical Theology: Its Genesis and Development, 1909–1936* (Oxford: Clarendon, 1995), 131.

[20] Barth, 'The Righteousness of God', quoted in McCormack, *Karl Barth's Critically Realistic Dialectical Theology*, 132.

[21] Barth, 'The Righteousness of God', quoted in McCormack, *Karl Barth's Critically Realistic Dialectical Theology*, 133.

> In religion man bolts and bars himself against revelation by providing a substitute … But what he achieves and acquires in virtue of this power is never the knowledge of God as Lord and God. It is never the truth. It is a complete fiction, which has not only little but no relation to God.[22]

The human being, claimed Barth, quoting Calvin, was an *idolorum fabrica*, an 'idol factory', and the idol so constructed was religion in whatever shape or form. In later years, Barth's attitude to religion softened and he came to accept it as an inevitable dimension of the fundamental human quest for God. Nevertheless, it still had to be distinguished from the initiative of grace that is God's self-disclosure in the person of Christ.

Pannenberg has been unswerving in his criticism of Barth's attitude to religion. He points out, to a certain extent quite rightly, that no theologian can appeal with impunity to the Feuerbachian critique of religion. If it is justified, then it applies to all religion, including that supposedly based on God's self-revelation. If no arguments are put forward to justify this distinction between revelation and religion, then it remains an arbitrary assertion. Pannenberg, utilising Gerardus Van der Leeuw's[23] research, subjects Feuerbach's analysis to critical scrutiny.

> In opposition to the view of religion as a purely anthropological phenomenon, as an expression and creation of human consciousness, modern religious studies rightly describe religion as a two-sided entity. It embraces deity and humanity, but in such a way that in the relation deity emerges as pre-eminent, awe-inspiring, absolutely valid, and inviolable.[24]

Religion as the Cultural Garment of Christendom

Dietrich Bonhoeffer's abiding legacy to modern theology was his awareness of the cultural situation that faced the Christian church between and after the two great Wars. Martyred by the Nazis for his part in the plot to overthrow Hitler, his *Letters and Papers from Prison* present a critique of religion that was substantially different from that of Barth.

---

22 Barth, *Church Dogmatics* 1:1, 301–3.
23 G. van der Leeuw, *Religion in Essence and Manifestation: A Study in Phenomenology* (London: Allen & Unwin, 1938).
24 Pannenberg, *Systematic Theology*, 1:142.

> What is bothering me incessantly is the question – what Christianity really is, or indeed who Christ really is, for us today? The time when people could be told everything by means of words, whether theological or pious, is over, and so is the time of inwardness and conscience – and that means the time of religion in general. We are moving towards a completely religionless time; people as they are now simply cannot be religious any more ... Our whole nineteen-hundred-year-old Christian proclamation and theology rests on the 'religious *a priori*' of mankind ... But if one day it becomes clear that this *a priori* does not exist at all, but was a historically conditioned and transient form of human self-expression, and if therefore man becomes radically religionless ... what does that mean for Christianity?[25]

So began Bonhoeffer's attempt to sketch out what he termed 'religionless Christianity', a radical re-presentation of the Christian faith that no longer depended on the religious a priori. The latter he understood as the culturally-relative religious garment of Christendom, into which Christianity was asserted as the quintessential expression of this supposedly universal religious disposition. For Bonhoeffer, the modern world was characterised by the rejection of this cultural garment. Modern people no longer needed such religious scaffolding in order to get on with their lives. He described the twin elements of religion as individualism and metaphysics.

> What does it mean to 'interpret in a religious sense'? I think it means to speak on the one hand metaphysically, and on the other individualistically. Neither of these is relevant to the Bible message or to the man of today.[26]

By individualism, Bonhoeffer meant the religion of personal salvation. Such a privatisation of the Christian faith, he argued, turned the church into a spiritual chemist shop, dispensing a variety of potions to meet the individual needs of its customers. In more modern parlance, we could say that Bonhoeffer was anticipating the commodification of the Christian faith, a problem that besets any church that conforms to the values of modern consumerist society. Such an individualised faith, he claims, has little to do with the Christ who was characterised as the man for others.

> For Bonhoeffer, belief in God is no hallucinatory anodyne which merely helps people to cope with discomforts, insecurities, or difficulties.

---

[25] Dietrich Bonhoeffer, *Letters and Papers* (London: SCM, 1981), 88–9.
[26] Bonhoeffer, *Letters and Papers*, 91–2.

Christian theology has nothing to do with the consumers' wishes to purchase power or comfort.[27]

By metaphysics, he meant recourse to the *deus ex machina*, the apologetic supernaturalism that pushes God to the boundaries of human knowledge and ability or, indeed, the God of theism who is so often metaphysically remote and distant from the real world of pain and struggle. So in the modern world, Christianity, if it is to survive, must distance itself from the apologetic paraphernalia of religion, where God is only assigned a place on the metaphysical boundaries of our existence or as the curator of the individual soul. Religionless Christianity, in a world come of age, would have to rediscover the theology of the cross, where Christ allows himself to be pushed out of the world in suffering and weakness.

> God lets himself be pushed out of the world on to the cross. He is weak and powerless in the world, and that is precisely the way, the only way, in which he is with us and helps us. Matthew 8:17 makes it clear that Christ helps us, not by virtue of his omnipotence, but by virtue of his weakness and suffering.[28]

It is clear that this negative assessment of religion by Bonhoeffer and Barth was not directed initially to the world of other religions, but to the general human religious disposition that was supposed to lie at the heart of our common humanity. Barth saw in this general tendency not a blessing but a curse that could easily disguise our true state of sinful enmity from a righteous and gracious God. Bonhoeffer saw it as a piece of cultural baggage that should be jettisoned in favour of a new christocentric theology that could address the radical nihilism of modern people. It is interesting that both theologians would appear to accept something at least of Nietzsche's critique of religion, namely, that religion is a deeply-flawed human endeavour and that atheism is a correct description of the autonomy of the world.

The Transference of the Religious Question into the field of Religious Studies

At the same time as the ideological critique of religion was being incorporated into theology in the name of the primacy of God's self-

---

[27] Anthony Thiselton, *Interpreting God and the Postmodern Self* (Edinburgh: T&T Clark, 1995), 22.
[28] Bonhoeffer, *Letters and Papers*, 360.

revelation, other theological influences were at work which would translate the question of the efficacy of religion in the modern world into a radically new context. Towards the end of his life, Paul Tillich began to take a deep interest in the history of religions.[29] His last public lecture delivered in Chicago in 1965 was entitled 'The Significance of the History of Religions for the Systematic Theologian'. Mircea Eliade, the renowned historian of religions with whom Tillich shared a seminar on the subject, remarked, 'Paul Tillich did not die at the end of his career … he died at the beginning of another renewal of his thought'.[30] In his study of the religions, Tillich developed what he referred to as a dynamic-typological approach to religious experience; an approach that was much influenced by Rudolf Otto's *The Idea of the Holy*. He discerned three interconnected elements found, to some degree, in all religions, which together constituted what he called the 'Religion of the Concrete Spirit'.[31] These foundational aspects of religion, he called the sacramental, the mystical and the prophetic, all of which form the parameters of our encounter with the Holy. The dynamic interaction of these three types of religious experience clearly represents the ideal form of religion for Tillich and here he connects with Schleiermacher.[32]

---

29 Hendrick Kraemer became the flag bearer of Barth's radical separation of religion and God's self-revelation in *The Christian Message in a Non-Christian World*, a book commissioned for the world missionary conference at Tambaram in 1938. Kraemer's work was in fact a response to the Laymen's Foreign Missionary Enquiry entitled *Re-Thinking Mission*, a book which bore the theological imprint of W.E. Hocking, a philosopher and lay-Christian, who advocated 'the way of reconception', which defined all religion as 'a passion for righteousness'. He believed that an ethical concern would lead to the convergence of all religions in a common inclusive form, with Christianity emerging as the universal world religion. W.E. Hocking, *Living Religions and a World Faith* (New York: Macmillan, 1940) and *The Coming World Civilisation* (New York: Harper & Brothers, 1956).

30 M. Eliade, 'Paul Tillich and the History of Religions', in *The Future of Religions* (ed. Jerald C. Brauer, New York: Harper & Row, 1966), 35–6.

31 Pan-Chiu-Lai in an interesting study *Towards a Trinitarian Theology of Religions: A Study of Paul Tillich's Thought* (Kampen: Kok Pharos, 1994), draws out the similarities between Tillich's proposals in regard to the religion of the Concrete Spirit and the more recent world theology of Cantwell Smith. Both develop a theology of the history of the religions which presupposes some unitive element which permits the possibility of inter-religious dialogue. See W.C. Smith, *Towards a World Theology: Faith and the Comparative History of Religion* (Philadelphia: Westminster Press, 1981).

32 So, for instance, G. Richards comments; 'His position in this respect is not far removed from that of Schleiermacher, for whom the essence of religion, the primordial form, pre-exists historical manifestation as a prior condition, and is

In many ways, Tillich was an early pioneer in the field of interreligious dialogue, and his book *Christianity and the Encounter of the World Religions* (1963) both reflected his personal engagement with the Buddhist and Shinto traditions he experienced in Japan, and demonstrated his affinity with the inclusivist position which has dominated much modern Roman Catholic thinking in the field of religious studies, and of course owes much to Karl Rahner's notion of anonymous Christianity. A common characteristic of the post-Enlightenment assessment of religion was the supposition that somehow all the religions represent derivations of the one common essence. It is assumed that religion can be shown to be either a universal human fallacy or a universal human disposition.

> Attention to 'religion' has led to viewing Christianity as one among many embodiments of a common essence or a priori, or else to the contrasting of a Christianity with all the others as a revelation or a movement of secularisation.[33]

This basic presupposition has received substantial criticism from a number of theologians. Cantwell Smith states that it is a typically Western approach to religion, which violates the cultural and historical pluralism of the diverse religious traditions. David Tracy states that there simply is no single essence or content of revelation and enlightenment, or a way of liberation and emancipation buried in the substructure of the enormous diversity of religious experience and description. Similarly, Hans Küng has argued that the notion that there is one distinct transcendental essence of religion, of which the particular religions are diverse historical forms, is as much a judgement of faith as Barth's assertion that God's self-revelation in Christ represents the end of religion.

Despite such objections, Tillich reflected the mood which was soon to engulf the whole field of religious studies, which was to transfer the religious question out of its setting in the evolution of modernity, to the dialogue with the other great religious traditions or world faiths, which had hitherto been relatively unexplored by mainstream Christian theologians. While this is clearly a laudable and genuine concern, it

---

comprehended in and through the language and traditions of particular, historical religions'. G. Richards *Towards a Theology of Religions* (London: Routledge, 1989), 67.

[33] J.B. Cobb, 'The Religions', in *Christian Theology: An Introduction to its Traditions and Tasks* (ed. Peter C. Hodgson and Robert H. King; Philadelphia: Fortress, 1985), 313.

left largely unanswered one of the most fundamental questions of the modern era, namely, how was it possible for a civilisation founded and nurtured on the Judeo-Christian faith to abandon its heritage in favour of a relatively new and attenuated religious judgement, i.e. that of modern practical atheism? How was it that over the period that Owen Chadwick has called 'the seminal years of modern intellectual history', one of the seeds that germinated and flourished was that of atheistic consciousness?[34] As Brian Ingraffia notes, Nietzsche offered his own answer to this question.

> According to Nietzsche, the reason that the rebound from Christianity was so great, the reason that one moves from complete faith to total despair, is the fact that Western society invested so much into this interpretation: 'the untenability of one interpretation of the world, upon which a tremendous amount of energy has been lavished awakens the suspicion that *all* interpretations of the world are false'. This is the negative response to the loss of faith in Christianity, to the death of the Christian God.[35]

The Splintering of the Religious Question in the Context of Postmodernity

One of the defining aspects of postmodernity is that the old hard-nosed scientific rationalism that previously undergirded the secular worldview is no longer believed to be the sole revered route to truth about ourselves and the wider world. Despite the modern advances in molecular biology and genetics, science and technology are no longer regarded as the harbingers of the new utopianian age. Similarly, there are those who argue that the advent of postmodern deconstructionalism has exposed a lacuna in the modernity project once occupied by the phenomenon of religion.

> Religion belongs to a family of curious and often embarrassing concepts which one perfectly understands until one wants to define them. The postmodern mind, for once, agrees to issue that family, maltreated or sentenced to deportation by modern scientific reason, with a permanent residence permit.[36]

---

[34] Cf. Buckley, *Modern Atheism*, 32.

[35] B. Ingraffia, *Postmodern Theory and Biblical Theology: Vanquishing God's Shadow* (Cambridge: CUP, 1995), 27.

[36] Z. Bauman, *Postmodernity and its Discontents* (Cambridge: Polity, 1997), 169.

Very important Q

Obviously then, the question still remains, what place has religion in the cultural landscape of the new postmodern world? It is our contention that the situation is complex and difficult to gauge, but that there are at least three interconnected strands of thought in regard to the efficacy of religion in the modern world that do not necessarily bode well for the Christian churches, but do, however, make the task of delineating a theology of culture all the more urgent.

Firstly, let me refer to the British Social Attitudes research undertaken by the National Centre for Social Research which, as Professor Robin Gill contends, is widely regarded as the Rolls Royce of questionnaire surveys, and is much used by government and university departments, if not by church leaders.[37] In 1983, in answer to the question 'Do you regard yourself as belonging to any particular religion?', 31 percent said they had no religion and 40 percent that they were Anglican. In 1998, it is now 45 percent who claim no religious affiliation and only 27 percent to be Anglican. Professor Gill, responding to these trends, comments; 'These two striking trends have been plotted by all the BSA surveys over the last fifteen years and do seem to be firmly established. People in Britain today, especially the young, are less inclined than before to claim nominal church membership, opting instead for no religion'.[38] What these trends disclose is that the church in Britain is still a privatised utility, dispensing a franchised commodity called religion which fewer and fewer people seem predisposed to purchase and enjoy. Similarly, it is my frequent experience in conversation with people that one of the most commonly-stated reasons for the rejection of religion is some variation of the ideological critique of religion first disseminated by Feuerbach, Marx, Freud and Neitzsche. This is not to claim that the population at large are avid readers of any of the aforementioned philosophers, but it is to assert that all of these thinkers were attending to atheistic critiques of institutionalised religion that were already apparent amongst the intelligentsia of their generation and which they believed would become more widespread amongst the population at large. In this respect, the judgement of history would appear to be firmly on their side.

Secondly, for those amongst the general population who take their stand on religion from within the parameters of the interreligious dialogue, it is the pluralist position espoused by people like John Hick,

---

[37] R. Gill, 'The Context of Mission in the 21st Century', *The Bible in Transmission* (Summer 2001), 4.

[38] Gill, 'The Context of Mission', 4.

Paul Knitter and Stanley Samartha, which has firmly won the day.[39] Again this trend is reflected in the BSA research, where two thirds of those questioned believed that there are basic truths common to all religions. In other words, to quote John Hick, God has many names and even in the churches fewer and fewer people are predisposed to argue for the unique and normative revelation of God in Jesus Christ, preferring instead some variation on the theme that all religions are of salvific significance, at least for their own adherents, if not for those of other cultural affiliations, a thesis at least as old as Ernst Troeltsch.[40] The pluralist position is often welcomed by those who prefer to embrace a non-tradition-specific viewpoint, advocating instead a non-judgemental openness to the salvific worth and integrity of other religions. As Alasdair MacIntyre has argued, however, the ideal that we can somehow abstract ourselves from specific traditions of rationality and belief is an Enlightenment myth that has produced the present impasse in moral and ethical theory.[41] Consequently, it should come as no surprise to us that the tradition the pluralists do in fact often unwittingly espouse is that of modern, democratic, liberal rationality. The fact is that we are all exclusivists, because we operate from within some already privileged tradition and, as Gavin D'Costa, has recently argued, judged against this criterion, the apparent plausibility of the exclusivist, inclusivist and pluralist schema simply melts away.[42]

While the continuing debate with the other great religious traditions is clearly a welcome sign both in religious studies and in the context of extensive religious pluralism, it remains itself a contested field of controversy and disputation. In the context of the cultural shift from modernity to postmodernity, there are ominous signs that the other faith traditions are already suffering the same fate as that of Christianity. On the other hand, there are those who take note of the recent rise in fundamentalism in the Jewish, Christian and Islamic traditions and argue that this is a concerted attempt from the young

---

[39] J. Hick, *God has Many Names, the Metaphor of God Incarnate* (London: Macmillan, 1980); P Knitter, *No Other Name* (London: SCM, 1985); S. Samartha, *One Christ, Many Religions: Towards a Revised Christology* (Maryknoll: Orbis, 1991).

[40] E. Troeltsch, *The Absoluteness of Christianity and the History of Religions* (London: SCM, 1972).

[41] A. MacIntyre, *After Virtue: A Study in Moral Theory* (London: Duckworth, 1981); also A. MacIntyre, *Whose Justice? Which Rationality?* (Notre Dame: University of Notre Dame, 1988).

[42] G. D'Costa, *The Meeting of the Religions and The Trinity* (Edinburgh: T&T Clark, 2000).

enthusiasts of all three world faiths to resist liberalism, individualism, the privatisation of religion and morality, and the ideology of democracy which, it is claimed, are the secularised values bequeathed to them from the Enlightenment.[43] The success of these attempts to resist the spirit of modernity does not, however, necessarily auger well either for the future of interfaith dialogue or, indeed, for the public credibility of religious faith and belief in general, because there is an inherent fanaticism and exclusivism about each attempt to rebuild society on a new religious foundation.

> Each of these religious cultures had developed specific truths which, insofar as they provide the basis for a strong reassertion of identity, are mutually exclusive. All they have in common is a rejection of secularism; beyond that point their plans for society diverge and then become deeply antagonistic, with a potential for bitter conflict in which none of these doctrines of truth can afford to compromise, on pain of losing followers.[44]

Conclusion

The future of religion in the context of the modern world clearly remains an open question. There are those, like Pannenberg, who remain convinced that the modern secular state merely represses the question in favour of the freedom of individual self-determination. Others would claim that the religious foundations to modern culture have now been replaced by a new metanarrative, namely, that of free-market capitialism with its secular religion of endless consumer satisfaction.[45] Clearly then, any theology of culture worth the name will have to attend to the claim first put forward by those who sponsored the ideological critique of religion that religion is now a redundant category in the modern psyche reflected in the continued decline of all forms of religious affiliation in modern Western societies, with the accompanying rejoinder that modernity and postmodernity represent the end of religion as the basis for widespread cultural renewal

---

[43] G. Kepel, *The Revenge of God: The Resurgence of Islam, Christianity, and Judaism in the Modern World* (Cambridge: Polity, 1994).

[44] Kepel, *The Revenge of God*, 192.

[45] In this regard, see Greene, 'Consumerism and the Spirit of the Age', in *Christ and Consumerism: Critical Reflections on the Spirit of our Age* (ed. Bartholomew & Moritz; Carlisle: Paternoster, 2000).

such as took place during the late medieval period and indeed the Reformation.

Increasing numbers of people who feel no allegiance to any form of religious affiliation, who regard all religions as either equally illusory or equally valid, who live their lives as if religion was simply an anachronism in today's consumer-driven society, suggests that some form of secularism is still deeply ingrained in the psyche of modern Western society. This is also reflected in the decline in significance of just about all of our public institutions. It is not just the churches, but government, the judiciary, the monarchy and the welfare system that have witnessed an increasing amount of cynicism and disbelief towards their continued relevance and public credibility. This, in turn, suggests to some that we in the West now live in a world that has been so radically disenchanted and dislocated from all transcendent sources of meaning that we are left simply amusing ourselves to death.[46] This is indeed a bleak scenario because without a renewal of the public significance of Christian faith, the very culture Christianity spawned will become unsustainable, and further cultural collapse and decay inevitable.

---

[46] N. Postman, *Amusing Ourselves to Death* (New York: Viking, 1985).

8

The Legacy of Romanticism:
On Not Confusing Art and Religion

Brian Horne

I

By the middle of the twentieth century, Dorothy L. Sayers was at the height of her fame as a novelist, playwright and Christian apologist; in February 1955, the Very Reverend Francis Sayre, Dean of Washington DC's Episcopal cathedral, aware of her reputation as an author of successful religious drama, wrote to her asking for advice about services for the celebration of the liturgy of Good Friday. She was, not unexpectedly, unwilling to offer any advice on liturgical matters, and replied, with her customary blend of courtesy and asperity,

> liturgies are one thing and dramatic performance another ... I am all for sacred drama, whether it is performed inside or outside the church building itself; but I am perfectly clear in my own mind that it can't be very well mixed up with the Liturgy, and ought not to be accepted as a substitute for it. Though it is, in a sense, an act of worship, it can't take the place of the Rite – and I don't think the great Holy Days of the Church are the proper place for it. I find by experience that it is all too easy for people to confuse these two things, and to suppose that hearing or taking part in religious drama is 'quite as good as' attendances at the Eucharist – better, in fact, because it works up their feelings more enjoyably. Sacred drama, and sacred art in general, can do a lot in the way of arousing interest and attention, but it cannot do much more.[1]

As this brief and entertaining exchange indicates, the relation between religion and art is often extremely complex, with a history that is so rich in incident, and fraught with paradox, that I shall not attempt to give

---

[1] Barbara Reynolds, ed., *The Letters of Dorothy L. Sayers* (Vol. IV; Cambridge: Dorothy L. Sayers Society, 2000), 4:211.

general of summaries of the main trends here. Suffice it
story of the relationship does not tell of an untroubled
ever necessary and inevitable the connection may be seen
valent, and sometimes problematic, relationship between
rts, between theology and beauty, between religious life
and about experience, is, in part, caused by the fact that while religion
and art may seem to differ in manner and method, they often also seem
to be confronting the same fundamental issues, and give the appearance
of dealing essentially with the same range of human experience – even
if they enter the human consciousness at different points. Consequently,
the risk of elision and confusion is always at hand, both on the part of
those whose primary concern is art and those whose primary concern
is religion. For example, when the new gallery devoted to modern art,
called Tate Modern, was opened in London in 2000, Sir Nicholas Serota,
the director of the gallery, was heard to remark, as he watched people
walking round the building, that what he observed was 'a sense of
exhilaration, delight, people finding things in themselves – moments
of self-recognition – or recognising something in the world that has
been presented in a new light'. In an earlier age, this kind of language
would have been thought appropriate for descriptions of religious
experience, and the journalist, Andrew Marr, was only one of a number
of commentators who could not resist the religious analogy: 'Serota is
the art bishop of Britain, whose brilliant mind, self-assuredness and
steely ascetic presence hangs over the galleries. The people who work
there, like members of some religious order, tend to dress in black and
grey.'[2] On the other hand, there are the voices of many of the modern
theologians who have proposed that the primary language of religion
is metaphorical and figurative, and that the specific insights of religion,
even the very content of faith, seem often to be most profoundly grasped
and articulated, not in theological language as it has traditionally been
perceived and understood, i.e. in dogmatic statement and rational
argument, but in a register that engages the imagination rather than
the intellect. Attention is thus directed, in the first instance, away from
conceptual reasoning and logical deduction to narrative patterns and
symbolic structures. If this is true, then we should have to conclude that
the language of religion and the language of art has, at the very least,
a close family resemblance.[3]

---

[2] *The Observer,* 9 April, 2001.

[3] For recent discussions of these and related arguments, see Aidan Nichols, *The Art of God Incarnate* (London: Darton, Longman & Todd, 1980); Richard Harries, *Art and the Beauty of God. A Christian Understanding* (London: Mowbray, 1993); George

It is doubtful whether either of these positions would have been assumed – at least not in this particular articulation – in any era before that change in western European sensibility to which we give the name 'Romanticism'. Since then, and with the secularisation of western European society and the 'disenchantment' of the world in our own age, there has been a kind of 'bouleversement' or a 'turning-inside-out' of the pre-Romantic understanding of the relationship between religion and art. The most obvious example is the secularisation of sacred art. We have become increasingly familiar with the deliberate displacement of religious objects: the removal of paintings, icons, sculptures and artefacts of all kinds from churches and chapels, and their relocation in art 'galleries'. Removed from their original context of worship, they are now on display as discrete objects requiring accompanying commentaries to explain their original purpose. Similarly, sacred music is severed from its liturgical setting and performed in concert halls: the kind of listening required for responding to a Mass by Haydn is, by implication, no different from that of listening to the *Five Pieces* by Schoenberg. This radical cultural re-contextualisation alters perceptions of the works. Sometimes this has been done without thinking; at other times, it is deliberate and been welcomed as an act of liberation. When it is deliberate, it is supposed to satisfy the desire, as one contemporary musicologist has, somewhat tetchily, put it, of 'enjoying the cultural content of sacred art without being pestered by the faith which ostensibly inspired the artist in the first place'. This unhistorical nature of this judgement is immediately exposed in the use of that word 'ostensibly'. The proposition of this highly questionable thesis is that contemporary society wants 'art ... as art' for what it tells us about ourselves and being human, rather than about the divine.[4] Since the latter half of the eighteenth century, the claims of art have been couched in remarkably grandiose terms, and what is apparent now is that, whereas in earlier centuries, the church had used artistic forms for the expression of its faith, it is art that is appropriating the forms of religion to identify and assert its own nature and purpose. A visit to an art gallery, a museum or theatre is compared to entry

---

Pattison, *Art, Modernity and Faith. Restoring the Image* (Basingstoke: Macmillan, 1991); Paul Avis, *God and the Creative Imagination. Metaphor, Symbol and Myth in Religion and Theology* (London: Routledge, 1999); Frank Burch Brown, *Good Taste, Bad Taste and Christian Taste. Aesthetics in Religious Life* (Oxford: OUP, 2000); Stephan van Erp, *The Art of Theology. Hans Urs von Balthasar's Theological Aesthetic* (Leuven: Peeters, 2004).

4   Peter Phillips, *Spectator*, 26 December 1998, 93.

into a sacred space.[5] Since the middle of the nineteenth century, there has been a growing conviction among many that religion being dead, art should move in to take the place it has vacated, and that aesthetic response should occupy the space that has been left empty by the disappearance of faith.

As I have said, much of this can be traced back to the beginnings of the Romantic movement in Europe in the latter part of the eighteenth century. Søren Kierkegaard, born in 1813 as the movement was gathering momentum in Western Europe, became intensely aware at an early age of both the problematic intertwining of religion and art, and the difficulties attendant upon determining the differences, between religious and aesthetic experience, if differences there were. By the time he came to write on these matters, Edmund Burke in *A Philosophical Enquiry into the Sublime and the Beautiful* (1757), and Immanuel Kant in both *Observations on the Feeling of the Beautiful and Sublime* (1764) and, especially, his *Critique of Judgement* (1790) had already produced their influential theories on aesthetics. Romanticism was at its flood when Kierkegaard wrote the book that was to be an assault on both the principles and practices of that movement.

In *Either/Or* (1843), he began to develop one of his most famous themes: that of the various 'stages' or 'spheres' of existence. In this work, only the 'aesthetic' and the 'ethical' are placed in positions of contrast, but by the time he reached the works of his maturity a third 'sphere' had been added: the 'religious'. Our concern is primarily with the aesthetic and with Kierkegaard's rejection of it as an authentic way of living. His target is neither art nor beauty as such; it is not, thus, to be read as a kind of simplistic, puritanical, iconoclastic manifesto – a direct attack on either beauty or images; it is rather the criticism of a particular approach to life, a manner of living that, in theory, might not *necessarily* involve either the appreciation of art or the enjoyment of beauty, but that would be most likely to occur in a life in which beautiful objects (whether natural or man-made) would be regarded as having determining significance. One cannot help but read in this rejection of the aesthetic an implicit acknowledgement of the seductive power of both beauty and art. Its attractiveness is suspected of being a lure away from seriousness; the aesthetic attitude is not exactly hedonistic, but is viewed as one that offers a means of self-forgetfulness, an avoiding of commitment, a refusal to make choices, an escape from engagement. The aesthetic disposition, which he sees embodied in many of the young

---

[5] See Peter Brook, *The Empty Space* (London: MacGibbon & Kee, 1968).

men and women who surround him, is, consequently characterised as amoral, lacking in stability and continuity and, in the end, deadly (pp. 240ff). This is contrasted with, and rejected, in favour of the ethical, and eventually, the religious, stages of existence which call for commitment, engagement, serious and life-determining sacrifices, existential choices. It is less a matter of sensual gratification (it is not the sheer pleasure of the senses that is the real danger) than a matter of uncommitted, unperturbed observation of life; a state of existential disinterestedness which would eventually become to be encapsulated, much later, in the phrase: 'Art for Art's sake'.

The Romantic sensibility is frequently characterised by expressions of the yearning to rise above mortality and finitude. Romantic art is replete with such imaginings, and Romantic theorising about the purpose of art is similarly full of discussions of these longings and desires: the defeat of mortality and finitude by the invention of worlds different from the ones we actually inhabit.[6] For Kierkegaard, the aesthetic condition can offer nothing but false hopes and escapist dreams. Aesthetic distance is the excuse for refusing to participate in the sordid and painful details, the mud and gore, of quotidian reality.

> ... in so far as art offers a plenitude of experience, a communion of ideas, it pre-empts the actual requirement laid on the self to pierce the mystery of nothingness in which the secret of human life lies hidden, and this act of pre-emption is scarcely innocent. Instead of embracing and living the vision of the void, art seeks to conceal and avoid that vision.[7]

Towards the end of the later work, *Practice in Christianity* (1850), he reflects harshly upon the artistic process itself. What, he asks, is going on in the mind and the imagination of an artist when he is depicting the figure of the crucified Lord? For Kierkegaard, Christ calls human beings to be imitators of him in his humiliation and obedience; their vocation is not to be detached, 'aesthetic' observers and 'artistic' interpreters of his suffering and death. So, for example, in painting this scene of the crucifixion '... the point of view of the religious is completely dislocated' and '... the beholder looks at the picture in the role of an art expert ... whether the play of colours is right, and the shadows, whether the blood looks like that, whether

---

6   See Monroe C. Beardsley, *Aesthetics from Classical Greece to the Present Time* (Tuscaloona: University of Alabama, 1975), 244ff.

7   George Pattison, *Kierkegaard: The Aesthetic and the Religious* (Basingstoke: Macmillan, 1992).

the suffering expression is artistically true.'[8] The actual suffering of the Holy One has become an object of detached admiration by the artist and, somehow, also been turned to pecuniary advantage. It is the art of the painter that, of course, is in question here, but Kierkegaard's criticism could apply with equal stringency to that of the poet, the musician or the dancer. (Doubtless it could also apply to the theologian who in discussing, say, the incarnation or atonement remained completely untouched by the subject matter and treated it as an interesting intellectual exercise.) And there is condemnation of the viewer too: the extraordinary act of condescension by God which is the incarnation and crucifixion of the Son, and which appears as a sign of contradiction in the world, is treated, by the viewer, as an object of beauty and rapture. We are to see the observer as complicit in an act, to use the phrase of later existentialists, of 'bad faith'. Even if one does not go so far as to postulate that '... Kierkegaard's view of religion is such as to demand the final sacrifice of poetry, art and imagination',[9] there arises a miasma of doubt about art as such, its status and function, and an uncertainty about whether it can have any connection with religion that does not involve faith in a fatal compromise.

Was Kierkegaard right? Is admiration of the artefact inimical to faith? What challenge to our own age does he offer? The contemporary challenge to this view of art came most strongly not from fellow-Christians, but from those whose relation to the church was ambiguous and tangential: people like Matthew Arnold in *Culture and Anarchy* (1869) and *Literature and Dogma* (1873), and John Ruskin in *Lectures on Art*, both of whom argued persuasively for the ethical content and moral seriousness of art, and its essential role in the formation of an ethically responsible society. But the challenge came, most powerfully of all, from one who was hostile to Christianity and scornful of the moralising of those who wanted to argue for ethically-uplifting power of art: Richard Wagner. Kierkegaard's exact contemporary. Wagner does something quite different from the later English critics of Kierkegaard's position, by defiantly rejecting what Kierkegaard would have understood as the ethical and religious spheres, and turning the posture of the Danish philosopher on its head. Instead of seeing the aesthetic as a stage of existence, a way of

---

8   Søren Kierkegaard, *The Practice of Christianity* (ed. and trans. Howard V. Hong and Edna H. Hong; Princeton: Princeton University Press, 2000), 254.

9   Pattison, *Kierkegaard*, ix.

progressing from art and beauty to ethics and religion, he collapsed
the two latter spheres into the former, maintaining that neither
morality nor faith could provide the authenticity that human beings
craved. Only art – and in his case particularly music – could do that.
Religion thus becomes art, and art, religion. If we reject Kierkegaard,
do we find ourselves in agreement with Arnold, Ruskin – or Wagner?
There is a serious question to be asked here: in our purportedly more
materialistic, postmodern age, Arnold and Ruskin seem to hold little
attraction, but Wagner continues to fascinate and to be influential. Is
he to be taken seriously?

If the literary scholar, Terry Eagleton, to is to be believed, it would
seem that we have to, because his philosophical position, even in our
post-Romantic era, is one which still attracts many propagators. In a
cogent review of Northrop Nye's late notebooks, published in 2000,
Eagleton attacks this notion by referring to T.E. Hulme's famous
description of Romanticism as 'spilt religion'[10] and comments: '… much
the same could be claimed of art in the post-Romantic epoch, an epoch
which is forever on the prowl for plausible secular versions of good
old-fashioned metaphysical values'.[11] Eagleton is himself sceptical of
this attempt and postulates that the effort to regard literature (and,
by implication, art of all kinds) as religion is doomed to failure'. 'For
another thing' he writes, 'art is too delicate, and too impalpable to be
bent to such ideological ends. If you try, as has been tried so regularly
since the Romantics, to atone for the death of God by fashioning art
into a political programme, an ersatz theology, a body of mythology or
a philosophical anthropology, you will impose on it a social pressure
which it isn't really robust enough to take, and you end up producing
in it what Jurgen Habermas called "pathological symptoms"'. This is
not to imply, of course, that Eagleton is on the side of Kierkegaard any
more than he is on the side of Wagner.

A modern philosopher who is far from sceptical, and who has
argued the case of Wagner, is Roger Scruton who, if I am reading him
correctly, has advanced the proposition that art is able occupy the place
that was previously the domain of religion, and that aesthetic response
is the only possible alternative to faith, and is even, in a mysterious
way, a kind of faith and a reaching for transcendence. Some of these
questions were raised by him more than twenty years ago in the

---

[10] T.E. Hulme, *Speculations. Essays on Humanism and the Philosophy of Art* (ed. Herbert
Read; London: Routledge & Kegan Paul, 1960), 118.

[11] Terry Eagleton, 'Having one's Kant and eating it', *London Review of Books* 19 (April
2001), 9–10.

volume of essays *The Aesthetic Understanding*.[12] More recently, he has addressed them more directly in a book entitled *An Intelligent Person's Guide to Modern Culture*. Early in the latter book, he states that 'the core of "common culture" is religion'[13] and that 'when art and religion are healthy, they are inseparable'.[14] But what can this mean? It could be deduced that he is, here, proposing the embracing of the church's creed and worship. But it seems not, for later on he writes in the following way: 'Religion may wither and festivals decline without destroying high culture, which creates its own "imagined community"' and asserts that 'our lives are transfigured by art, and redeemed of their arbitrariness, their contingency and littleness. This redemption occurs with no leap into the transcendental, no summoning of the god of the shrine'.[15] That may be so, but what then is meant by maintaining that 'art has grown from the sacred view of life'? What content can we give to the word 'sacred'? Does he mean that religion was a kind of staging-post and that we have now outgrown this once-necessary view? Perhaps this is what is intended, for he pursues his argument by saying, 'And this is why art suddenly leapt into prominence at the Enlightenment, with the eclipse of sacred things. Thereafter, art became a redeeming enterprise and the artist stepped into the place vacated by the prophet and the priest.' Redemption? The word is used with some frequency as though its meaning was self-evident. But we would want to ask: redemption from what to what? Hints have been given: 'arbitrariness', 'contingency', 'littleness'. What reality do these possess? And can the opposite of these states of being: non-arbitrariness, non-contingency, greatness, ever be permanent, or do they last only as long as the work is being perceived or remembered? If they are only temporarily imagined, giving us a sense of lost paradise, perhaps our state is ontologically tragic and we should accept it as such. Scruton senses this, but argues that the purpose of high art – and here Wagner's *Parsifal* is held by him to be the finest representation – is to maintain us in our enchantment 'as if' our lives in the world were not arbitrary, contingent, little, not ontologically tragic. 'We believe that gods are our invention, and that death is exactly what it seems. Our world has been disenchanted and our illusions destroyed. At the

---

[12] Roger Scruton, *The Aesthetic Understanding. Essays in the Philosophy of Art and Culture* (London: Methuen, 1983).

[13] Roger Scruton, *An Intelligent Person's Guide to Modern Culture* (London: Duckworth, 1998), 5.

[14] Scruton, *An Intelligent Person's Guide*, 17.

[15] Scruton, *An Intelligent Person's Guide*, 36–7.

same time we cannot live as though that were the whole truth of our condition.'[16] To which the simple riposte might be *why not*? Would it not show greater integrity to accept the absurdity of our existence and refuse any art which offered consolation? Macbeth sounds not only more realistic, but braver:

> Tomorrow, and tomorrow, and tomorrow
> Creeps in this petty pace from day to day.
> To the last syllable of recorded time;
> And all our yesterdays have lighted fools
> The way to dusty death.[17]

But Scruton will not have it so and invokes *Parsifal*: 'The Wagnerian drama creates its own religious background, its own awareness of a more than human cosmic order.'[18]

II

In our day, while places of worship are turned into concert halls, theatres assume the role of sacred spaces. Examples abound; two will suffice. In 2000, the English National Opera put on two productions that were mirror images of one another and admirably demonstrate the point I am trying to make. The first was a performance of J.S. Bach's *St John Passion*. Bach composed the *Passion* to be sung as an act of worship – at the very least to be framed by an act of worship, i.e. the Vespers of Good Friday in St Thomas's Church in Leipzig in 1723. When it was performed theatrically in London in 2000, it was not only cut off from its original liturgical context (modern audiences have become used to hearing sacred choral works as concert pieces, severed from their original settings), but was relocated behind a proscenium arch and presented as drama. The line between art and religion was deliberately blurred and left one with the question of whether this was intended to be a religious, as well as a theatrical, experience. Or was the intention to show that these experiences were actually identical? The audience was invited to join in the singing of the chorales, suggesting, inevitably, that this was, in some way, a participation in an act of worship. Was this indeed an invitation to faith? If so, faith in what? The Lutheran

---

16　Scruton, *An Intelligent Person's Guide*, 68.
17　William Shakespeare, *Macbeth*, Act V. Scene V.
18　Scruton, *An Intelligent Person's Guide*, 69.

theology of Bach? The action on the stage did not overtly seek to convey a Christian message, whatever the words of the text contained.

The mirror image of the *St. John Passion* was, and is, Richard Wagner's *Parsifal*. In the performance of the *Passion*, we witnessed a liturgical act being turned into theatrical spectacle, whereas in *Parsifal* the reverse occurred – and occurs: a theatrical form assumes the shape of the liturgy. (Modern producers are often embarrassed by, and uncomfortable with, the flagrantly religiosity of the work and flout the composer's intentions). This, the last of Wagner's operas, was performed for the first time on 26 July 1882. It is significant that he called it 'ein Buhnenweihfestspiel' a 'sacred festival drama', not an opera or even a music drama, a term he had begun to use when referring to his stage works instead of the more usual term 'opera'. He knew he had gone beyond that; something more portentous and solemn than either opera or music drama was now presented to the public. By this time, he had managed to complete the building of a theatre at Bayreuth, designed specifically as a kind of temple for his art. There was also, originally, a provision that this 'opera' could only be performed there in Bayreuth in that sacred space – a provision that was only broken after a court case in the USA in 1903. It was, until recently, listened to in reverent silence without applause, either during or after the performance had ended. In his earlier operatic cycle, *Der Ring des Nibelungen,* Wagner had plundered the Nordic sagas for his libretti; for *Parsifal* he turned to a medieval tale, *Parzifal,* by Wolfram von Eschenbach. This work forms part of the vast body of popular medieval narrative literature, dealing with stories of knightly prowess and the quest for the Holy Grail, narratives of chivalry, heroism and courtesy, stories in which Christian motifs are interwoven with pagan legends in a bewildering profusion of incident and commentary. It is still a matter of debate as to how far Wolfram von Eschenbach's account of the quest for the Grail, and his use of the stories that surround this central theme, can be called distinctly Christian, but there are clear Christian spiritual and moral preoccupations: love, humility, self-sacrifice, and the whole work is imbued with the sense of a Christian ethic. Even when there is an admixture of non-Christian, pagan elements that sit uneasily with the Christian gospel, the whole is, nonetheless, shot through with the language of Christian soteriology.[19] However, it is not *Parzifal* that is

---

[19] Brian Murdoch has recently not only demonstrated the Christian content of the epic, but drawn attention to the connection between *Parzifal* and Anselm's *Proslogion*. See Brian Murdoch, *Adam's Grace. Fall and Redemption in Medieval Literature* (Cambridge: Brewer, 2000), 92ff.

our prime consideration here, it is what Wagner does with the story in *Parsifal* that is.

The opera is performed, ideally for Wagnerites, on Good Friday and, given its German genesis, in such a way that would seem to supplant the *Passions* of the Lutheran liturgy. It is saturated with Christian references and symbols. The Grail, a miraculous stone in the *Parzifal* saga, is changed by Wagner into the cup that was used by Christ and his disciples at the Last Supper. (This is not peculiar to Wagner, of course: the Grail had already been transformed into the chalice in a number of later medieval texts) There are vigils and prayers, the sign of the Cross and innumerable Eucharistic allusions. The *mise-en-scene* is the castle of the wounded king, the guardian of the Grail, and is called Monsalvat. Themes of healing and redemption are central. There can be little doubt that, during the years in which the opera has been performed, it has, for many, supplanted the liturgy of Good Friday, has actually taken on the form of liturgy, has become an act of worship. So powerful has this sense of its being a sacred rite been that, when modern directors of the work have tried to rid it of its religious dimension, storms of execration have broken out as though blasphemers had forced their way into the sanctuary and were desecrating the holy places. Michael Tanner, for example, in criticising the attempted 'domestication' of Wagner, has particularly objected to the efforts of producers and directors to bring the operas down from their exalted sphere to make political statements. Roger Scruton has characterised these attempts as 'the ruination of the sacred in its last imagined form'. The vocabulary of these critics is of particular interest: 'Exaltation', 'Transcendent', 'Sublime', words frequently on the lips of audiences and critics alike when discussing *Parsifal*. They were, of course, part of the vocabulary of religious discourse until the eighteenth century, at which point they were appropriated by poets and philosophers to constitute the vocabulary of Romantic theories of aesthetics. That is the phenomenon we are dealing with here: an extreme form of Romanticism: art as religion.[20]

However, it could be argued that these modern producers and directors in our own post-Romantic era are perceiving, however inchoately, a truth that the worshippers at Wagner's shrine have failed to notice: that the religion on offer is hollow, that it is actually only

---

[20] Roger Scruton has described these attempts of modern directors of the opera as 'the ruination of the sacred in its last imagined form'. *An Intelligent Person's Guide*, 64.

religious posturing and, as such, bogus. It is, perhaps, only religiosity and not religion at all: it encourages the experience of feelings – exaltation, sorrow, self-forgetfulness – that are thought to be religious (as Dorothy L. Sayers noted), because they are powerfully evoked, but which are, in fact, unrelated to any object worthy of adoration, and lead, in the end, to an even more pernicious version of that aesthetic mode of existence condemned by Kierkegaard. For all its symbolism, it seems to lack intellectual content, by which I mean that who or what is being worshipped remains cloudy, obscure, vague. Such religious import as there is lacks specificity and intellectual clarity. Cut adrift from the community of understanding in which these Christian symbols are rooted and grounded in daily worship and shared action, the symbols themselves become meaningless. Or rather, as they float free from their Christian mooring, they encourage audiences – if they ponder the meaning of the work at all – to invest them with their own private, subjective significance. This is where Wagner's *Parsifal* differs so obviously from Wolfram von Eschenbach's *Parzifal*. I am not claiming for the huge, untidy, medieval saga the kind of Christian orthodoxy that is part of the fabric of the work like Dante's *Divine Comedy*, I am simply drawing attention to the context of the Catholic medieval society within which the saga would have been received and understood; a society in which Christian symbolism was apparent on every street corner and was the background for every social and political exchange; and the Eucharistic rite was everywhere to be observed. Wagner's opera has become the rite itself and he intended it to be so. Consequently, if this is the case, I suggest that it is spurious, because the object of worship remains undefined; unless it is the music itself which would be, strictly, idolatrous, but which is, at least, intelligible, and acceptable to those who are prepared to make a god of an art form.

It may seem that I am judging Wagner harshly, perhaps a little unfairly, and I must justify my position before I take the argument further. In his most recent book on Wagner, *Wagner and Philosophy*, the philosopher Bryan Magee spends some time discussing various misinterpretations of *Parsifal*. (Perhaps it is not insignificant that, of all Wagner's operas, *Parsifal* is the one which most frequently opens itself to unsettling interpretations). In particular, he draws attention to the persistent and long-lived interpretation of the work as a Christian myth. 'The commonest and most intellectually respectable misunderstanding has been to take *Parsifal* to be a Christian work.'[21] This may be incorrect,

---

[21] Bryan Magee, *Wagner and Philosophy* (London: Penguin, 2000), 278.

but it is, he maintains, more respectable to read the opera in this way than to harness it to a political ideology. 'Denial of the will and rejection of the world are incontestably among the things that *Parsifal* is "about", and whereas at least these, at any rate, might be made compatible with an interpretation in terms of Christian mysticism they are wholly incompatible with politico-social programmes of any kind.'[22] The burden of Magee's book is to show how Wagner developed as a philosopher out of an interest in the writings of Ludwig Feuerbach into an ardent disciple of Arthur Schopenhauer. 'It is not possible', he writes, 'to be a Schopenhauerian and a Christian.' This is, indeed, the case; and, if *Parsifal* is truly Wagner's crowning achievement, it cannot be a Christian work whatever symbols it tries to appropriate. Thus, to try to see in it an acceptable substitute for an act of Christian worship is simply a mistake; a serious mistake on two counts, for it misunderstands both the nature of the Christian religion and the intentions of the composer. It seems to me that Magee's presentation of Wagner is incontrovertible. There can be no doubt that his entire worldview was dominated by the philosophy of Schopenhauer by the time he came to write *Parsifal*: the documentary evidence is plain and abundant. Whether the composer succeeded in translating this worldview into dramatic form is altogether another matter and depends, among other things, upon the subtleties of aesthetic discrimination. Magee maintains that he did; I am less sure and believe that this possible failure of Wagner to realise his artistic ambitions may be related to the question of why the interpretation of *Parsifal* as a work of Christian sensibility has been so pervasive and persistent. If Wagner is the great artist his admirers claim and really did intend to dramatise the view of existence that he found in Schopenhauer, why have audiences been so reluctant to embrace it? It cannot be conscious resistance to the philosophy of Schopenhauer for, unless I am much mistaken, I doubt that many in the audiences for Wagner's operas would have even a nodding acquaintance with *Die Welt als Wille und Vorstellung* and recognise the operas as musical and dramatic renderings of its thought. The answer to the puzzle may be twofold. The first strand lies in the nature of Wagner's achievement itself, the second lies in the disposition of the audiences who willingly, but perhaps unconsciously, confuse art and religion.

Wagner had actually addressed the question of the relation between religion and art directly, in quasi-philosophical terms, while he was composing *Parsifal*. His essay *Religion and Art* was the last theoretical

---

[22] Magee, *Wagner*, 279.

work that he wrote and, in it, he made his position clear; a position he would try to embody in his last opera.

One could say that when religion becomes artificial it is for art to salvage the essence of religion by constructing mythical symbols which religion wants us to believe to be the literal truth in terms of their figurative value, so as to let us see their profound hidden truth through idealised representation. Whereas the priest is concerned only that the religious allegories should be regarded as factual truths, this is of no concern to the artist, since he presents the work frankly and openly as his own invention.[23]

Apart from the crude oversimplification of what 'the priest' – to use Wagner's own term – actually does with the language of faith, we have here an oversimplified understanding of the way symbols come to be constructed and the numerous and subtle ways in which they interpret the lives of both the individual and the community of which the individual is a part. But, for Wagner, it is as though beneath or behind the symbol, and essentially separable from the symbol, there is a truth that can be apprehended and appropriated, and that the artist is free and able to convey that truth by the genius of his (or her) own invention. Of course, Wagner was writing at a time before the research of social anthropologists revealed the complex genesis of symbols in society; and I have little doubt that his belief that symbols could be treated in this way was reinforced by his immersion in the philosophy of Schopenhauer who believed that the world of appearances was essentially illusory and that one had to pass beyond that world to a transcendent reality beyond. That seems to be at the heart of what is meant by redemption in *Parsifal*. As I said earlier, I am sure that Bryan Magee is correct in his fundamentally Schopenhauerian reading of the opera and that Roger Scruton is wrong in speaking of it as though it revealed 'a more than human cosmic order'. But one can understand why Scruton makes this mistake: the symbolism of the opera is not wholly under the composer's control; it invites the observer to enter a world that is the one he intended, and it is the Christian universe. However, in Christianity, the symbolic structures do not exist in a kind of parallel universe, a universe that runs alongside the historical narrative as though it were some form of decorative embellishment; each discrete symbol is related organically in some way or other both to the life of the community and to the particulars of certain historical events. The attempted dissociation of the symbolical order

---

23 Magee, *Wagner*, 281.

from the historical order is an attempt to turn Christianity into a purely mythological system and results in confusion in those who are not aware of what is happening.

III

This is not a new phenomenon in the history of Christianity: the genesis of this tendency can be found in patterns of gnostic belief as early as the first centuries of the Christian era. Certain forms of Gnosticism can, in fact, best be understood as attempts at, if the anachronistic term be allowed, a kind of aestheticisation of religion. The theology of Irenaeus, from whom we learn so much about the forms and intentions of contemporary gnostic teachers, was, among other things, precisely an attempt at preventing the Christian faith from becoming aesthetic appreciation, a mythological construction. We can say, to put it in modern terms, that what was being mounted by him was a strong argument against the confusion of art and religion. This tendency has always been present, but the specific contours of our own, contemporary predicament began to take shape in the age of, and under the influence of, the Romantic movement, with its remarkable power to commandeer the language of religious experience as a defence against the rationalism of the Enlightenment. The appeal of beauty was something that not even the most sceptical of the philosophers of the Enlightenment seemed able to resist. Roger Scruton's analysis of what occurred – that 'art became a redeeming enterprise and that the artist stepped into the role vacated by the prophet and priest' may well be true, but I have the gravest doubts about the ability of art to retain a power to keep the sense of the sacred alive, when actual belief in the existence of the sacred, and the worshipping community which lives to translate that belief into action, has disappeared. Terry Eagleton has expressed these doubts more colloquially, and with more pungency, than I.

> Religion is a symbolic form of ritual and practice, sometimes of a highly arcane kind, which nevertheless engages countless of millions of men and women in the course of their sublunary lives, and which connects their beliefs about when the universe was created with their beliefs about when it is permissible to fib or fornicate.[24]

---

[24] *London Review of Books,* 19 April 2004.

Dorothy L. Sayers, possibly sensing that the Dean of Washington Cathedral was in danger of confusing aesthetics and faith, wrote as she did in response to his request. Feelings without dogma were of little use as far as she was concerned. Christianity spoke of things that were objectively true, and could be expressed in rational propositions and ethical demands as well as signs and symbols. It demanded intellectual assent, and no amount of oceanic experience could replace that objectivity of those commands. If one wanted merely to experience such feelings, one was perfectly at liberty to do so, but one should not imagine one was a Christian simply because one had experienced such feelings. She returned to the fray in a letter to C.S. Lewis later that year, 1955, in which she complained to him about the failure of people to distinguish between, what she called, 'imaginative belief' in which there is a willing suspension of disbelief, the kind of activity in which one is involved in the theatre or when one is reading fiction, and 'factual belief': the kind of activity in which one is involved when one is reciting the Creed.[25]

Having said this, and having recognised with Kierkegaard the dangers inherent in a purely aesthetic approach to life and religion, I must disagree with what seems to be his considered position, and I am unwilling to relinquish my conviction that, whether we are aware of the dangers or not, art and religion are inextricably and intimately related. In one of his own attempts to delineate the relationship between religion and art, Hans-Georg Gadamer has claimed: 'In all cases, it would be quite meaningless to construct an opposition between art and religion, or even between religious and poetic speech, or attempt to deny any claim to truth in what art says to us.' But he also issues a warning, indicating the boundaries of the relationship: 'At the same time the claim of the Christian message transcends this and points in the opposite direction; it shows us what we cannot achieve.'[26] Nonetheless, I am in agreement with the contention of Stephan van Erp that it is 'a theological miscalculation that verbal theology stands on its own in explaining what faith is' and that 'art and beauty are appropriate concepts to describe the communication of faith.'[27] It is, of course, necessary that we take into account the inherent frailty and brokenness of humanity: a condition in which perception of the truth

---

[25] *The Letters of Dorothy L. Sayers,* 4:261.
[26] Hans-Georg Gadamer, *The Relevance of the Beautiful and Other Essays* (ed. Robert Bernasconi; trans. Nicholas Walker; Cambridge: CUP, 1986), 153.
[27] Van Erp, *The Art of Theology,* 37.

is obscured and the will is weak, a condition that makes the perils of both idolatry and frivolity ever present, but there is no sound reason for setting the love of art and love of God in opposition to one another. The rapture of beauty need not necessarily result in the kind of life which Kierkegaard believed was inimical to true Christianity. No one argued more passionately than Dorothy L. Sayers for the absolute necessity of recognising beauty in the world, the power of art to reveal and communicate that beauty, and the obligation on the part of the church to salute that power. At the same time, no one would have argued more passionately that, however closely related to true religion would be the understanding and appreciation of art, the two were not to be confused.

9

Valuing the Nation:
Nationalism and Cosmopolitanism
in Theological Perspective[1]

Luke Bretherton

We are the Church; Christ bids us show
That in his Church all nations find
Their hearth and home, where Christ restores
True peace, True love, to all mankind.

(James Quinn, S.J. b.1919)[2]

Introduction

In recent years, the impetus for trying to make sense of national identity and nationalism has come from the civil wars, nationalist movements and the political turbulence since 1989 when the Cold War lost momentum and the Soviet Union sunk, leaving, amidst its debris, the flotsam of fragile successor states which are interspersed by violent whirlpools of conflict. As John Hutchinson and Anthony Smith comment:

---

[1] I am very grateful to Joan Lockwood O'Donovan for her extensive response to an earlier version of this essay. The result is that the essay presented here differs considerably from the one she kindly references under the same title in her own essay 'Nation, State and Civil Society in the Western Biblical Tradition', in *Bonds of Imperfection: Christian Politics, Past and Present* (ed. Oliver O'Donovan and Joan Lockwood O'Donovan; Grand Rapids: Eerdmans, 2004), 276–95. It should also be noted that there is overlap in some of the arguments developed in the essay here and a previously published piece that relates these arguments to debates about refugees and asylum. See Luke Bretherton, 'The Duty of Care to Refugees, Christian Cosmopolitanism, and the Hallowing of Bare Life', *Studies in Christian Ethics* 19:1 (2006): 39–61.

[2] *The New English Hymnal*, No. 361, pp. 526–7.

In a multipolar world following the end of the Cold War, the trans-
formations, instability, and populist nationalism within Russia, the
long-standing conflicts in the Middle East, the renewed ethno-religious
violence in the Indian subcontinent, the risings of indigenous peoples,
from the Aborigines and Mohawks to the Chiapas Zapatistas, and the
deep antagonisms in East and Southern Africa, have placed 'the national
question' once again firmly at the centre of world affairs.[3]

Since September 11, 2001, there has been a tendency, at a popular level
at least, to occlude the relationship between nationalism and conflict
behind an emphasis on what Samuel Huntingdon calls a 'clash of
civilizations'. Yet even where religious factors are central to a violent
conflict, for example, in the Palestinian/Israeli conflict or the Iraqi
insurgency, national identity and the struggle for national autonomy
are still key dynamics. Indeed, a central, though often unacknowledged,
feature of the 'war on terror' is 'ethno-religious nationalism'. In Western
Europe and North America the question of national identity is at the
centre of debates about asylum and immigration and the political
re-emergence of the far right. Even if economic globalisation, the
increase in supra-national political structures and the homogeneity of
global consumer culture is accounted for, the nation-state is still the
primary point of political identity and an international order is still
the predominant way of structuring world politics. In short, while the
status and centrality of the nation-state has been eroded from above
and below, it is not about to disappear. Therefore, the questions of
how and why, theologically, we should value nationhood and national
identity are as pressing today as they ever were. At the same time, the
question of how to value national identity cannot be divorced from the
greater interrelationship and interdependence of different nation-states
under conditions of economic, technological and cultural globalisation,
and debates about the proper role and form of both regional political
institutions, for example, the European Union, and global ones, most
obviously, the United Nations. Thus the issue is not only how to
value national identity, but also how to do so in relation to a global or
cosmopolitan horizon of human relationships.

   This essay seeks to spell out the scriptural and theological grammar
of the universal and particular aspects of political identity that are
central to a Christian evaluation of nationhood. The theological account
developed here is, I contend, a normative one found consistently

---

[3] John Hutchinson and Anthony Smith, 'Introduction', in *Nationalism* (ed. John
Hutchinson and Anthony Smith; Oxford: OUP, 1994), 11.

across the Christian tradition, and constitutes a constructive theology of patriotism. I will suggest that it was precisely the cutting loose of the concept of nationhood and cosmopolitanism from their theological moorings that led, ineluctably, to the related problems of the undervaluing of the nation in cosmopolitism and its overvaluation in various forms of nationalism. Central to the essay is the contention that there is a proper theological affirmation of the socio-cultural and political reality that is 'the nation'. The form this argument will take is an analysis of how the term 'nation' and the notion of a universal humanity governed by a single law are theological categories. It is then the corruption of the theological conception of nationhood that forms the basis of modern forms of both nationalism and cosmopolitanism.

A Scriptural vision of nationhood

In order to make sense of the term 'nation' and thence, how to value national identity, it must be situated within a theological frame of reference. To do this we must begin with the notion of *pietas,* that is, the reverential submission to and concern for that to which one owes the possibility of one's own development, be it one's family, city or *patria.* Thus 'patriotism' may be broadly equated with the notion that there is a duty or *pietas* owed by each person to gods, parents, the civic community, the land and the cultural environment to which one owes the possibility of one's own development. Patriots value their national or ethnic identity, but that identity is not determinative of all their relations; for example, one's familial identity may stand over and against one's national identity.[4] Theologically, the issue is how to order and relate that to which one owes *pietas.* In classical political thought, land and kinship played a significant role in identity formation. However, it was not to the fatherland or ethnicity that the Roman or Greek citizen primarily owed *pietas,* but to the *res publica,* the political commonwealth, the *polis,* the common interests of the people.[5] Thus, to take a New Testament example, Paul, an ethnic Jew born several hundred miles away from Rome, could still be considered a Roman citizen capable of owing *pietas* to Rome. This vision of Roman

---

[4] This view of patriotism is the 'classical' view found in the likes of Cicero and Aquinas.

[5] Heinrich Schneider, 'Patriotism, Nationalism and the Duties of Citizens', in *Religion and Nationalism* (ed. John Coleman and Miklós Tomka; London: Concilium/SCM, 1995), 34.

patriotism, exemplified by Virgil in both the fourth *Eclogue* and the *Aeneid*, was carried over into Christianity.[6] However, it was not appropriated uncritically. Thus, for example, Augustine contrasts two cities and the kinds of devotion that characterise each of them. The 'earthly city', while commanding a proper *pietas*, is at root in opposition to God and is made up of members whose wills are orientated toward self and away from God (Bk XV.7). The *City of God* consists of those whose primary *pietas* is toward God and whose wills are orientated away from themselves. Central to Augustine's theo-political vision is a Christian cosmopolitanism wherein humanity is one, but properly differentiated into particular polities that, while sinful and orientated in on themselves, find their fulfilment beyond themselves in a universal communion with God. Such a view is found consistently throughout the Christian tradition. What I hope to demonstrate is that such a view follows on from the deep logic of Scripture.[7]

Etymology of the term 'nation'

The term 'nation' relates to a number of terms in Hebrew and Greek. Most frequently the Hebrew term *'am* is translated as 'people' when used in the singular, and 'nations' when used in the plural. Daniel Block suggests that the term *'am* has a personal and relational connotation, reflected in the common use of pronominal suffixes in relation to the term ('my, his, your people'). This contrasts with the term *gôy*, also translated as 'nation', which is less personal and more political in connotation. The term *gôy* is applied to a variety of entities, including the pre-Israelite Canaanite tribes (Deut. 7:1), nomadic desert tribes (Isa. 60:5ff.), kingdoms, and empires (Egypt, Babylon; Jer. 25:17ff.).[8] In the Septuagint, the term *gôy* is translated as *ethnē*, notably when a contrast is drawn between the chosen *laos*/people of God and the Gentile/

---

[6] Conor Cruise O'Brien, *God Land: Reflections on Religion and Nationalism* (Cambridge: HUP, 1988), 12.

[7] For parallel and complimentary accounts, see Karl Barth, *Church Dogmatics: The Doctrine of Creation* III:4 (trans. A.T. Mackay *et al*; Edinburgh: T&T Clark, 1961), 309–23; Oliver O'Donovan, *The Desire of the Nations: Rediscovering the Roots of Political Theory* (Cambridge: CUP, 1996), 66–73; and Nigel Biggar, 'The Value of Limited Loyalty: Christianity, the Nation, and Territorial Boundaries', in *Boundaries and Justice: Diverse Ethics Perspectives* (ed. David Millar and Sohail Hashimi; Princeton: Princeton University Press, 2001), 38–54; and Joan Lockwood O'Donovan, 'Nation, State and Civil Society', 276–95.

[8] D.I. Block, 'Nations', *The International Standard Bible Encyclopedia*, 492.

non-Israelite *ethnē*/nations. Thus, in the Septuagint, true peoplehood or nationhood involves a particular kind of relation to God and each other, in contrast to other patterns of political community. In the New Testament, it is the church that becomes the *laos theou*/people of God. However, the contrast is not so much with other *ethnē* as with other kinds of congregation, notably, a *demos* (a public assembly of people), an *ochlos* (a crowd, mass or populace) and a *polis* (a city-state or, more broadly, a political community).[9] As the people of God, the church does not wholly replace Israel (this is the conclusion of Paul's wrestling in Romans)[10] nor is it simply a new political community. Rather, a new pattern of relating together and to God is established, a pattern which collapses previous political and social distinctions between *oikos* and *polis*, Gentile and Jew, native and stranger, and redefines them. The church is both a household and a *polis*, its members relating as citizens and a family.[11] Gentiles become grafted into Israel, yet, in other ways, they remain Gentiles. Christians are resident aliens, strangers in their own land, yet strangers to no land (Eph. 2:9).[12] In short, no fixed etymological definition of the term 'nation' can be given, for its use must always be set within a particular theological matrix of how God's elect are situated in relation to both God and various 'others'. Thus, it is to the theological readings of the term 'nation' within the Bible that I now turn.

Birth of the nations

The first thing to say about Israel in relation to Genesis is that it is a secondary category to that of humanity. God creates not one nation, but humanity. There is neither a primordial place nor original locality, nor a primordial nation or people identified. Jon Levenson contrasts the Genesis narrative with that of the *Enuma Elish* and notes: 'Like *'elohim*, Marduk is also a cosmic creator-god; his power is not limited to Babylon. But, as is emphatically not the case in Genesis 1:1–2:3, his

---

[9]   H. Bietenhard, 'People, Nation, Gentiles, Crowd, City', *New International Dictionary of New Testament Theology* (4 vols; ed. Colin Brown; Exeter: Paternoster Press, 1976), 2:788.

[10] It should be recognised that this point is much debated in New Testament scholarship and relates to the broader theological question of supercessionism.

[11] On this, see Bernd Wannenwetsch, 'The Political Worship of the Church: A Critical and Empowering Practice', *Modern Theology* 12.3 (1996): 269–99.

[12] On this, see Miroslav Volf, 'Soft Difference: Theological Reflections on the Relation Between Church and Culture in 1 Peter', *Ex Auditu* 10 (1994): 15–30.

special relationship to a particular community is embedded in the very structure of the cosmic order.'[13] Levenson goes on to point out that, in Genesis, 'it is humanity in general and not any people in particular that is created. Israel is not primordial.'[14] This universal horizon of humanity's relationship with God finds particular expression in the Noahide covenant. However, it would be a mistake to see humanity as the primary or definitive category for divine-human relations. Creation is not static, but ordered and mandated to develop in particular ways. Just as the beasts of the field and the birds of the air do not remain an undifferentiated mass, neither does humanity. There is a proper process of differentiation and naming. The dual character of this process is the focus of Genesis 10, which sets out the Table of Nations, and Genesis 11 which recounts the Tower of Babel story.

While no nation, not even Israel, is found in the original givenness of the cosmic order, the ensuing rise of nations is a providential, if post-lapsarian, development. The priesting of creation – a task given to Adam, renewed with Noah, maintained in the temple cult and fulfilled in Jesus – involves voicing creation's praise, of which human life together is a constitutive part. Voicing creation's praise is the human participation in the communion of gift and reception that David Ford and Daniel Hardy refer to as an 'ecology of blessing' that exists between God and creation.[15] However, priesting creation through voicing its praise is a task that takes place against the backdrop of the fall. This is the central theme of Genesis 10 and 11. The Table of Nations in Genesis 10 portrays a process of differentiation that involves taking up goods of creation – notably, kinship, land and language – and enabling them to be drawn into, ordered within, and serve ongoing patterns of personal relationship directed to communion with God. Claus Westermann postulates that this is because the history of the nations cannot be presented as family history, yet the form of the genealogy is retained in part because it does represent the nations as constituting one family.[16] Westermann goes on to note that the Table

---

[13] Jon D. Levenson, 'The Universal Horizon of Biblical Particularism', in *Ethnicity and the Bible* (ed. Mark Brett; Leiden: Brill, 1996), 146. Levenson notes that the only *particular* vestige of the act of creation is a cultic rite – the Sabbath – which is not spatial but temporal and hence may be universalised.

[14] Levenson, 'The Universal Horizon', 147. See also Claus Westermann, *Genesis 1 – 11: A Commentary* (trans. John J. Scullion, SJ; London: SPCK, 1984).

[15] David Ford and Daniel Hardy, *Praising and Knowing God* (Philadelphia: Westminster, 1984), 81–2.

[16] Westermann *Genesis*, 499.

is the most forceful and most heavily underscored statement in the Bible about the effect of God's blessing, which extends over the whole earth and the whole of human history whereas, his saving action is of necessity bound to a people that has been chosen. Only a family tree of the nations, beginning with the one rescued from the annihilation of humanity and conceived as a unity both in time and in space, could say so forcefully that God's blessing, bestowed on his human creature means in reality the history of the whole of humanity, means humanity stretched across the face of the earth 'as long as the earth lasts.'[17]

This is to say that, while salvation history might work through a particular people, its origin and horizon is universal. All humans and sodalities of humans – even those that are oppressive (such as those that follow the pattern of Nimrod)[18] – are human and part of humanity created by God. Thus, the Table constitutes a counter to the tendency to judge what is 'foreign' as not-human or barbarian. It counters any attempt to define what is human solely in terms related to one's own people and demarcate all other nations as subhuman.[19] As we shall see, even where the nations are portrayed as of lesser status than Israel in the most polemical of language, for example in Ezekiel, the basic premise that all nations are created by Yahweh who is their Lord is still maintained. The category of demarcation between Israel and the nations is righteousness and not humanness.[20]

The counterpoint to all nations being human is that no nation is coterminous with the cosmic order. Not even Israel is given special status in the Table; indeed, the history of Israel's beginning in Genesis 12 is envisaged as simply emerging out of the general history of the nations. Thus, as Walter Brueggemann notes, while differentiation is good and a providential fulfilment of the creation order, the nations are in no way portrayed as an intrinsic part of creation, they are

---

[17] Westermann *Genesis*, 528–9.

[18] On this. see Jacques Ellul, *The Meaning of the City* (Carlisle: Paternoster, 1997), 10–23.

[19] This is in stark contrast to other Near Eastern primeval histories. The cosmology of the ancient Egyptians, for example, envisaged that only Egyptians were really human, all others were 'barbarians'. Mario Liverani, 'Nationality and Political Identity', in *Anchor Bible Dictionary* (6 vols; ed. David N. Freedman New York: Doubleday, 1992), 4:1031.

[20] The claim that the category of demarcation between Israel and the nations is righteousness and not humanness is controversial given the plethora of texts that would seem to contradict it. Thus, it will be defended in due course.

rather a development of it.[21] For Brueggemann, the basic principle of organisation at work in the Table 'is not racial, ethnic, linguistic, or territorial, but *political*. It reflects networks of relations at a given time.'[22] Hence, the Table portrays nations as political communities involving a range of aspects of creation and human life. Brueggemann argues that the political nature of the map is a break from mythological readings of the world apparent in other Near East texts. Thus, instead of writing political realities into the cosmic order, the origin of the nations is demythologised: that is, they are not inevitable, but result from human decisions and the exercise of power. As a consequence, Brueggemann notes, these patterns of life and polity can be criticised and subject to change.[23] Thus, while part of God's providential ordering of creation, nations are not part of the cosmic structure in the same way as the changing of the seasons or the boundaries of the water and the land.

Within the context of Genesis 10, a nation may be read as a providential differentiation of creation that enables particular persons to flourish via concrete patterns of sociality that encompass the goods of creation. The importance of differentiation, however, has been marginalised in many doctrines of creation operative in the Christian tradition. A doctrine of creation influenced by either Plato or Gnosticism envisages some ideal or non-material paradise that must be returned to, such that Eden ceases to be a garden in need of cultivation: that is, a beginning point of a movement towards perfection through time and space.[24] Instead, Eden becomes a fixed point to return to. However, the *telos* of humanity is neither a return to an original state of blessing nor a movement beyond the materiality of creation, but it is the movement, via differentiation and development through history, to an eschatological fulfilment of creation. Unlike modern rationalist cosmopolitans whose platonic, protological teleology posits a return to an undifferentiated 'humanity', a properly theological cosmopolitanism must incorporate the fulfilment of humanity via differentiation into particular sodalities of persons that involve differences of language, kinship and territoriality, and a myriad of other aspects of creation. For without discrete identities that take up and play with creation in particular ways through history, there can be no communion of embodied persons, no interplay of concrete persons

---

21 Walter Brueggemann, *Genesis* (Atlanta: John Knox, 1982), 93. Cf. 2 Esdras 3:7, 12 where nations arise naturally, and not as a post-lapsarian development.

22 Brueggemann, *Genesis*, 91.

23 Brueggemann, *Genesis*, 93.

24 For example, see the contrast between Irenaeus and Clement cited in John Behr, *Asceticism and Anthropology in Irenaeus and Clement* (Oxford: Clarendon, 2000).

in relation with each other through time and space. However, this is not to say that all patterns of differentiation are good. There can be false and destructive patterns of binding and loosing creation; that is, humans can be set apart and bound together in ways that are orientated to chaos and nothingness, rather than to eschatological fulfilment.[25] If Genesis 10 represents a process of providential differentiation, Genesis 11 portrays a pattern of destructive exclusion.

Genesis 11 draws out and emphasises points already made in Genesis 10, constituting an elaboration on the proper nature of human unity and relationship with God. If, as Brueggemann argues, the differentiation of humanity into nations is when the mandate to multiply given in Genesis 1:28 comes to fulfilment, then the refusal of humans to 'scatter' or spread abroad (Gen. 11:4) constitutes a rebellion against God's purposes for creation.[26] Furthermore, the attempt to make a name for themselves through their own action, and on the basis of their homogeneity, is an attempt to secure a future for themselves divorced from God and God's purposes for creation. The action of God in scattering humanity and confusing language is a twofold 'liberating intervention'[27] that both restores the created limits (which includes preventing their absolute autonomy from relationship with God),[28] and enabling once more the whole creation, humans included, to be brought 'each in its kind' to full fruition. For, as Brueggemann notes, Genesis 11 does not:

> presume that different families, tongues, lands and nations are bad or disobedient. They are a part of [God's] will. And the reason God allows for that kind of differential is that all parts of humanity look to and respond to God in unity.... Here that unity is expressed as a *dispersion* all over the earth.[29]

But why is dispersion expressive of God's purpose for unity? Brueggemann's response is that 'The purpose of God is neither *self-securing homogeneity* as though God is not Lord, nor a *scattering of autonomous parts* as though the elements of humanity did not belong to each other'.[30] Thus, diversity in unity of relationship to God is the way

---

[25] On this, see Miroslav Volf, *Exclusion and Embrace: A Theological Exploration of Identity, Otherness, and Reconciliation* (Nashville: Abingdon, 1996).

[26] Brueggemann, *Genesis*, 98–9.

[27] Westermann, *Genesis*, 550.

[28] Westermann notes: 'Humanity exists only in its state as creature; so its continuation is endangered by the threat of autonomy.' Westermann, *Genesis*, 551.

[29] Brueggemann, *Genesis*, 99.

[30] Brueggemann, *Genesis*, 99.

in which creation is to be properly ordered, all other attempts at unity constitute a 'totalitarian project to centralize, homogenize and control.'[31] The narrative is a critique of every effort at oneness – whether imperialist, technological or religious – derived from human self-sufficiency and autonomy, for finally, all such efforts will be in vain.[32]

For the purposes of my argument, what is important is that Genesis 11 underscores the proper ordering of humanity to differentiation in nations, and thence, the ordering of a pluriformity of nations to fulfilment in communion with God and each other.[33]

The election of Israel

With the call of Abram, we move from primeval history to 'our' time, and the 'liberating intervention' that was initiated in Genesis 11 takes a concrete focus in the election of a particular people. This call to Abram establishes a dialectic between universal blessing and particular election that runs through the rest of the Bible and continues today.[34] However, according to Brueggemann, it is not so much a tension as two sides of the same coin. He states 'The call of Sarah and Abraham has to do not simply with the forming of Israel but with the re-forming of creation, the transforming of the nations. The stories of this family are not ends in themselves but point to God's larger purposes.'[35] This point is emphasised by the nature of Abraham's call. The appearance of Israel is significant: it is depicted as utterly dependent on a free act of God's grace. Without God's grace, its origin and composition is just like that of any other nation.[36] The barrenness of Sarah highlights the point about grace even more forcefully.[37]

---

[31] Volf, *Exclusion and Embrace*, 226.

[32] Brueggemann, *Genesis*, 100.

[33] See also O'Donovan, *The Desire of the Nations*, 72 and Bietenhard, 'People, Nation, Gentiles, Crowd, City', 2:791.

[34] As Brueggemann puts it: 'There is a tension between the universal sovereignty (and *providence)* of God, who cares for and presides over all nations (10:1–32) and the *election* of God, who focuses on this distinctive people (11:10–29).' Brueggemann *Genesis*, p. 94. It is important to notice that the canonical location of Abram's call serves to remind us that the particular call of Israel must never eclipse the call and rule of God over all nations.

[35] Brueggemann, *Genesis*, 105–6.

[36] This point is reiterated time and again in the Old Testament. For example, see Amos 9:7 and Ezekiel 16:3.

[37] On this, see Levenson, 'The Universal Horizon', 153.

On the above interpretation, nationhood as a theological category denotes a particular calling by God to a regime of life consonant with God's order and purposes for creation. The particular election of Israel is to be the means by which the nations would hear of God's rule and know what was required. Duane Christensen states that within the canonical process, 'the nations are the matrix of Israel's life, the raison d'être of her very existence'.[38] Or as N.T. Wright puts it, 'the call of Israel has as its fundamental objective the rescue and restoration of the entire creation. Not to see this connection is to fail to understand the meaning of Israel's fundamental doctrines of monotheism and election.'[39]

We can return now to the claim that the category of demarcation between Israel and the nations is righteousness and not humanness. There appear to be numerous passages that would contradict this claim. There is, for example, the common *topos* in which Israel's enemies are characterised as a dragon or sea monster that stands as a motif for chaos (Ps. 18; 46; Ezek. 32; Jer. 51:34, 44; Dan. 7).[40] Another text that seems to stand against what is being argued here is that of Daniel 4 wherein those who do not acknowledge Yahweh's rule become bestial (a theme picked up in later apocalyptic and rabbinic material). However, the imagery of a return to chaos or the movement from humanity to bestiality necessarily implies that the identification of the nations with chaos or the beasts is a later development, a fall from what they were originally or a failure to grow into what they may and should be. Isaiah represents this dynamic: the strong identification of foreign nations with the chaos monster in Isaiah 27:1 must be set against the way in which the 'defeat' of the nations results in them participating in the eschatological banquet and being subject to the rule of Yahweh (Isa. 25:6–9). Therefore, the premise that all nations are created by Yahweh who is their Lord can still be maintained. What passages that emphasise the at-times ontological separation between Israel and the nations bear witness to is that a pattern of life directed against Yahweh's rule and the failure to fulfil the vocation of being a nation has the consequence

---

[38] Duane Christensen 'Nations', *The Anchor Bible Dictionary* (6 vols; ed. David N. Freedman; New York: Doubleday, 1992), 4:1037.

[39] N.T. Wright, *The New Testament and the People of God* (London: SPCK, 1992), 268.

[40] See John Day, *God's Conflict and the Dragon and the Sea: Echoes of a Canaanite Myth in the Old Testament* (Cambridge: CUP, 1985). Day notes that the conflict with the nations and the notion of the inviolability of Zion to the attack of foreign nations (Pss. 46; 48; 76) represent a historicisation of the theme of the divine conflict with the chaos waters (a theme that Day argues is taken over from Canaanite mythology). Day, *God's Conflict*, 183.

of misdirecting human life to chaos or nothingness. It is at such points that the separation between Israel and the nations is demarcated with such vehemence.

It is in Exodus that we find the nature of Israel's uniqueness portrayed. Exodus 19:6 spells out the threefold character of Israel's particular election: it is to be a chosen people, a kingdom of priests and a holy nation. Brevard Childs states:

> Israel is God's own people, set apart from the rest of the nations. Israel as a people is also dedicated to God's service among the nations as a priest functions within a society. Finally, the life of Israel shall be commensurate with the holiness of the covenant of God. The covenant responsibility encompasses her whole life, defining her relation to God and to her neighbours, and the quality of her existence.[41]

If Israel is to be a light to the nations, then its special status lies not in any attribute it possesses in itself – neither land, kinship nor cult – rather, the nature of its difference or holiness lies in serving as a witness to and message about what all nations should be. Thus, it can be argued that the real contrast is not between Israel and the nations, but between godly patterns of life and idolatrous, dehumanising patterns.

Conversely, those nations that do not fear God and refuse to learn godly patterns of life from Israel come under judgement.[42] Yahweh's judgement against the nations in Ezekiel 25 – 32 is directed against those that have delighted in the downfall of Israel; thus instead of learning how to be a nation from Israel, they have set themselves against Israel, and thus against God. Yet the action Yahweh takes is not simply to condemn these nations; rather it is designed to bring these nations to a 'knowledge' of the Lord. This is especially apparent in the satirical tale of the magnificent cedar of Lebanon (Ezek. 31:15–18). Daniel Block writes that its implication is: 'Nations are not self-made; they draw their vitality from resources built into the universe and they derive their place by divine appointment. . . . When such gifts become occasions of pride, like a lumberjack [Yahweh] brings down the tree

---

[41] Brevard S. Childs, *Exodus: A Commentary* (London: SCM, 1974), 367.

[42] We see a similar dynamic at work in the prophecies of Jonah and Micah. The portrayal of Nineveh repenting from a regime of life directed towards dehumanising chaos holds open the possibility that all nations may turn to God. Conversely, Micah represents what happens when no repentance is forthcoming and God withdraws, letting a regime run its course and destroy itself. For, as already noted, life apart from God is no life; without God's providential and sustaining action, the nations implode.

and consigns it to the netherworld.'[43] Hence, for all its polemic against the nations, a universalist thrust remains: salvation is for all nations and thence, so is judgement. Nationhood, theologically understood, refers to a pattern of political community directed to the kingship of Yahweh, of which Israel is the paradigm and ensign for all other nations to follow.[44]

Redemption of the nations

The conception of the nations as under judgement in Jewish prophetic literature must be set within an overarching vision of eschatological hope for the nations. The oracles concerning foreign nations in First Isaiah (chapters 13 – 27) provide a good example of this. These oracles are not simply for or against particular nations.[45] As in Ezekiel, these oracles concerning the nations announce God's rule over the nations. Christopher Seitz comments that these oracles 'are concerned with establishing Israel's God as God of all peoples and as judge over all forms of human pride and idolatry'.[46] Just as God judged Israel for human pride and disregard for his presence (Ezek. 2–4), so God takes his indictment beyond Israel's borders to include all nations with a grandiose claim to independence and self-determination.[47] However, if God is Lord of all nations, then there must be the possibility of redemption. Hence, there are oracles that speak of the final worship of Yahweh by foreign nations. For example, after Egypt is judged (19:1–7), it is restored and its people offer sacrifice and worship to Yahweh (19:19–22), finally becoming God's own people together with Israel and Assyria. In Isaiah 25:6–9, all the nations are envisaged as participating in the messianic banquet. They do so without even bringing gifts to honour Yahweh: that is, they do so by God's grace, with no tribute

---

[43] Childs, *Exodus*, 205.

[44] Similarly, O'Donovan notes how, in the Psalms and Wisdom literature, all nations are depicted as having the same vocation to exercise just judgement as Israel, and the failure to do so brings them under the judgement of God. O'Donovan, *Desire of the Nations*, 68.

[45] On the case for why chapters 13–27 can appropriately be read as a unified trope, see Christopher Seitz, *Isaiah 1–39* (Louisville: John Knox, 1993), 116–19.

[46] Seitz, *Isaiah*, 126.

[47] Seitz, *Isaiah*, 122. Seitz locates the root of this theological conception in Isaiah's treatment of Assyria, which, like the portrayal of Babylon in chapters 13 – 14, is an agent of judgement judged.

being demanded.[48] Levenson observes that the fact that so much of late biblical eschatology envisions the reorientation of the nations to Yahweh is highly significant:

> It suggests something like a restoration of the situation of the primeval history (Genesis 1–11), in which humanity was united, monotheistic, and YHWHISTIC. History has come full circle, except that Israel does not disappear into an undifferentiated humanity. Rather, it and the nations survive, only now centred upon the service of YHWH, the universal creator, king and redeemer, in his cosmic capital, Jerusalem. Israelite particularism, in this vision of things, is not destined to disappear. It is destined to reach its universal horizon.[49]

From the above, we can summarise four thematic ways in which God's chosen people are envisaged relating to others regimes of life. First, Israel is not a primordial people, rather all nations are part of God's providential differentiation of creation (Gen. 10). Second, Israel is to be an ensign through whom all nations come to know God and are blessed (Gen. 12). Third, Israel is the holy and godly pattern of life that contrasts with all Gentile, impure patterns of life (Joshua/Ezekiel). Lastly, Israel is envisaged as the paradigm of a pattern of community that is consonant with the created order and fear of God (Exodus/Isaiah). The contrast for this last theme is not with other nations (which may or may not accord with the created order), but with 'empire': that is, a totalising regime opposed to God and characterised by injustice, with Egypt and Babylon serving as the paradigmatic instances of empire.

Each of these ways of relating Israel and its neighbours has a parallel in how the stranger/foreigner/Gentile within its midst is to be treated. First, there is participation: for example, Leviticus sees the foreigners as participants in the blessings of the covenant, and while not equal in status, they are fully protected. Second, there is exclusion: for example, Judges and Ezra/Nehemiah see the foreigner as a threat to be excluded or eliminated.[50] Third, there is inclusion: for example, Isaiah and Ruth

---

48 The text contrasts God who swallows up death with the participants, from all nations, who swallow rich food and rejoice. Cf. Isaiah 56:6–8 wherein God welcomes foreigners who comes bearing sacrifices and offering worship.

49 Levenson, 'The Universal Horizon', 164. A counter-vision is given in various texts from the Second Temple period wherein the nations are excluded from the messianic banquet.

50 Daniel Smith-Christopher, 'Between Ezra and Isaiah: Exclusion, Transformation, and Inclusion of the "Foreigner" in Post-Exilic Biblical Theology', in *Ethnicity and the Bible* (ed. Mark G. Brett, Leiden: Brill, 1996), 117–42.

envisage foreigners becoming included in the people of God.[51] Fourth, there is transformation: for example, Daniel, Jonah and Esther point to the transformation of foreigners so they cease to be a threat because they now conform to God's rule (but remain part of their own nations). Proverbs has a similar but different implication: wisdom holds open the possibility of both Israelite and stranger sharing a common fear of God that enables them to share an overlapping set of moral standards.[52]

What is striking is that, despite the different ways in which Israel is depicted as relating to nations, there is a consistent and overarching conception of nationhood that transpires. All nations are defined in relation to their Creator. None have an autonomous existence independent of relation to God who rules them. Nationhood envisaged as a theological category is a way of describing a status in relation to God and the final end of history. Understood theologically, nations should be a social, political and economic regime of life that is properly ordered to that time when all nations will find their fulfilment in communion with God. We might, therefore, legitimately abstract the following theological, cosmopolitan vision from one strand within the Old Testament: humanity is one, but properly differentiated into nations which are orientated to move beyond themselves to fulfilment in a universal communion with God. It is this vision that is taken up, affirmed and developed in the New Testament in the story of Jesus' life, death and resurrection.

Israel and the nations after Christ

In and through Jesus Christ the time when all nations will worship God is inaugurated. If, as has been argued, the difference between the status of Israel as an *'am, laos* or people in contrast to the *gôy, ethnē* or nations is not material but formal – Israel is also a nation, but one elected to live out a particular regime of life which it is incumbent upon all other nations to respond to in appropriate ways – then the people of God, which now includes representatives from among the nations, is to do the same. In effect, the eschatological vision presented in Isaiah

---

[51] In the Prophets, what is promised is not subjugation and rule over foreign peoples (as in Judges), but increase in numbers because distant and foreign people come to Israel and want to belong to her because of the God of Israel: Isaiah 14:1; Zecheriah 2:10–11; Esther 9:27.

[52] See David Novak, *Natural Law in Judaism* (Cambridge: CUP, 1998), 16–26; and Levenson, 'The Universal Horizon', 148–51.

is reaffirmed in the Gospels. It is explicitly reaffirmed in Luke 13 where Jesus declares, 'People will come from east and west and north and south, and will take their places at the feast in the kingdom of God. Indeed there are those who are last who will be first, and the first whom will be last' (Luke 13:29–30). Most significantly, Jesus enacted this eschatological vision in his hospitality of sinners and Gentiles, and he fulfilled it in his hospitality to the point of death on a cross so that all who are strangers may sit and eat with God.[53]

After Christ, neither the nations nor Israel are wholly superseded. The kingdom of God is only inaugurated, but it is not yet fulfilled. We await Jesus' return and the complete establishment of God's kingdom. Thus, the maintenance and restoration of the creation order is to be worked towards. This is the tenor of Paul's speech in the Areopagus where he states:

> From one ancestor he made all nations to inhabit the whole earth, and he allotted the times of their existence and the boundaries of the places where they would live, so that they would search for God and perhaps grope for him and find him – though indeed he is not far from each one of us. (Acts 17:26–27: NRSV)

Paul's speech goes on to say that the search for God is now fulfilled in Christ and we have entered a time when we await the day of judgement (17:31). These two strands of affirming God's providential order of the nations and the relativisation of national identity with the inauguration of the kingdom of God come together in New Testament apocalyptic, notably Revelation. Richard Bauckham argues that Revelation envisages a two-stage process of redemption: 'In the first stage of his work, the Lamb's bloody sacrifice redeemed a people for God. In the second stage, this people's participation in his sacrifice, through martyrdom, wins all the people for God. This is how God's universal kingdom comes.'[54] Parallel to the ways already outlined in relation to the Old Testament, Revelation envisages all nations as under God's Lordship. Similarly, the role of the church, like that of Israel, is not to be vindicated, but to be a witness that serves to bring the nations to the time of trial/the assembly of God so that they might be humbled. As Bauckham notes in relation to John's interpretation of the Song of Moses: the emphasis on

---

[53] On this, see Luke Bretherton, *Hospitality as Holiness: Christian Witness Amid Moral Diversity* (Aldershot: Ashgate, 2006).
[54] Richard Bauckham, *The Theology of the Book of Revelation* (Cambridge: CUP, 1993), 101.

the judgement of the nations is not on an event by which God delivers his people by judging their enemies, but on an event which brings the nations to acknowledge the true God. Consequently, the martyrs 'celebrate the victory God has won through their death and vindication, not by praising him for their own deliverance, but by celebrating its effect on the nations, in bringing them to worship God.'[55]

After Christ, the church is the place particular political sodalities of persons may now gather under the Lordship of Christ. The church is *the* paradigmatic nation: that is, it is that body – the people of God – which is to be the training ground for that time when creation is fulfilled. Yet, at the same time, the church is an ensign for the life of the nations, just as Israel was. Therefore, what we might call the 'Christendom paradigm', wherein polities sought a common good that had as its fulfilment communion with God and others, was not an aberration. However, where it goes wrong is in the failure to maintain the eschatological tension wherein the church is the holy nation in which the fulfilment of the still existing nations is being anticipated. One important aspect of maintaining this tension is that the pattern of life of the church can never be wholly identified with the pattern of life of any particular nation. The most problematic example of this followed on from the creation of autocephalous state churches. Yet this is a late development in Christian history, arising most commonly in particular strands of Protestantism and in the modern history of Eastern Orthodoxy. And even then, these tendencies have been actively countered: by Radical Reformation movements within Protestantism and the explicit recognition within Orthodoxy that the move beyond ecclesial autocephaly to national churches whereby national identity and religious identity become synonymous (such that to be Greek is to be Orthodox) is heretical. The name for this heresy is Phyletism, condemned at the Synod of Constantinople in 1872.[56] However, it was the failure to maintain this eschatological tension that prepared the way for the emergence of both nationalism and certain strands of cosmopolitanism.

---

[55] Bauckham, *Revelation*, 101.

[56] The Synod recognised an instance of Phyletism as occurring when the organisation and identification of the church is inseparable from ethnic or national identity such that the ultimate communion of all the faithful in Christ is subordinated to the penultimate reality of nationality or ethnicity. Vigen Guroian, 'Church and Armenian Nationhood: A Bonhoefferian Reflection on the National Church', in *Ethics After Christendom: Toward an Ecclesial Christian Ethics* (Grand Rapids: Eerdmans, 1994), 115.

Nationhood and modernity

What led to the emergence of nationalism in the modern period is a wide-ranging and contentious debate. Within this debate there is little agreement as to how best to understand either the historical or ideological basis of nationalism. It is important to situate the theological vision outlined above within this debate in order to demonstrate how this theological vision contests many assumptions about the roots of nationalism. There is not the space here for an in-depth review of the debate about the definition of basic terms.[57] Suffice to say that, in contrast to previous 'primordialist' conceptions of the nation, notably, by earlier theorists such as Herder, J.G. Fichte and Giuseppe Mazzini, who viewed the nation as a 'natural' phenomenon ordained by God,[58] contemporary conceptions of the 'nation' see the nation as a wholly contingent cultural artefact. However, there is no necessary opposition between the notion that the nation is a cultural artefact and the proposition that nations are natural communities. Within a Thomistic-Aristotelian framework, the nation may be a proper fulfilment of the *telos* of certain patterns of social life. Even if such a teleological view is not shared, it cannot be assumed, as theorists such as Benedict Anderson and Ernst Gellner seem to, that, if nations are imagined communities, they can be dismissed as somehow imaginary communities. As Anthony Smith notes:

> Constructing the nation away misses the central point about historical nations: their powerfully felt and willed presence, the feeling shared among so many people of belonging to a transgenerational community of history and destiny. We do not have to reify the nation by conceding the vivid tangibility and felt power of its presence, irrespective of the way in which the nation or any particular nations emerged.[59]

---

[57] See Anthony D. Smith, *The Nation in History: Historiographical Debates About Ethnicity and Nationalism* (Hanover: University Press of New England, 2000) for a review of the different approaches to understanding nations and nationalism. Smith outlines four main paradigms: primordialism, the perennialist, the modernist and the ethnosymbolist. His typology can only be heuristic (although Smith seems to indicate it is definitive), for the theological analysis as set out in this paper cannot be accommodated within any of the paradigms.

[58] Mary Anne Perkins, *Nation and Word, 1770–1850: Religious and Metaphysical Language in European National Consciousness* (Aldershot: Ashgate, 1999), 15.

[59] Smith, *The Nation in History*, 57.

For our purposes, the view that 'the nation' is a cultural artefact that constitutes a shared community of identity will be taken as normative.

While there might be a general consensus among recent scholars that the nation is in some sense an imagined or constructed community, rather than an inevitable outworking of historical processes or biological relations, there is little agreement as to what the constituent parts of a nation are. Some see the nation as only existing in the context of a state, others see it tied to territory, others as the accretion of a common culture and shared history and others prioritise a shared language as the determining factor in constructing a national consciousness. Anthony Giddens sees nations not as the creation of nationalism, but of state and administrative structures: thus, he describes the nation as a 'bordered power-container'.[60] On the other hand, rather than linking the construction of national identity to the consolidation of the modern state, Gellner and Hobsbawm view the construction of national identity as the inevitable consequence of capitalism and industrialisation. In contrast again, both Anderson and Breuilly see the rise of nationalism, and hence the construction of nations, in terms of the decline of both monarchical dynasties and of religion, and the growth of printed literature. As previously noted, the modernist view, following Kedorie, and shared by all of these authors, is that the rise of nations and nationalism is a post-Enlightenment phenomenon. However, while the modernist view that nationalism, as an ideology and social movement, is a distinctively modern phenomenon is right, its supposition that the construction of political identity in terms of the category of the nation only occurs in modernity is wrong.

To understand why the nation is a pre-modern category that comes to the fore in modernity, the theological basis of the nation as a political entity has to be taken account of. It is the lack of such an account that contributes, in part, to the inconclusiveness and, one might say, incoherence of much contemporary debate about the basis and emergence of the nation, national identity and nationalism.[61] This

---

[60] Anthony Giddens, *The Nation-State and Violence* (vol. 2 of *A Contemporary Critique of Historical Materialism*; Cambridge: Polity Press, 1985), 119.

[61] Smith notes the 'notorious terminological difficulties in the field, and the failure to reach even a preliminary agreement on the definitions of key concepts.' Anthony D. Smith, *Nationalism and Modernism: A Critical Survey of Recent Theories of Nation and Nationalism* (London: Routledge, 1998; repr. 2001), 221. He goes on to point out that this stems from the incommensurable nature of the basic paradigms at work in the field.

is not to say that religious factors have been wholly ignored. However, they are generally viewed through the distorting mirrors of the secularisation thesis.[62] The secularisation thesis assumes that religious affiliation and belief decline with the onset of a host of phenomena related to modernity, including urbanisation, industrialisation, rapid technological change and the increasing influence of the nation-state (and its bureaucracy).[63] Yet such an assumption masks the religious nature of nationalism. Earlier theorists made no such mistake. For example, Hans Kohn, writing in the 1940s, discerned that: 'in the age of nationalism some nations have proclaimed for themselves a "mission" here on earth: the divine right of kings was replaced by the divine right of nations. Messianic dreams with the nation at their centre put the nation into immediate and independent relations with the Absolute.'[64]

Yet modernists such as Elie Kedorie have likewise not been able wholly to ignore the relationship between religion and nationalism. Kedorie sees nationalism as a secular analogue of millennialism, a kind of political messianism with links to earlier medieval millennial movements.[65] However, as Smith points out, the connections Kedorie makes between millennialism and nationalism fail to take seriously fundamental differences of aim and outlook between the two, and rest on tenuous historical links.[66] Kedorie is on firmer ground when, to explain the problem of how intellectual elites managed to mobilise mass popular support for nationalist projects, he argues that elites self-consciously sought to harness the symbolic and emotional power of traditional religions. George Mosse[67] and Josep Llobera take a similar view. Thus, Llobera argues that:

---

[62] For example, see Benedict Anderson, *Imagined Communities: Reflections on the Origin and Spread of Nationalism* (rev. edn; London: Verso, 1991), 12–19.

[63] For a review of the current debate over the secularisation thesis, see Linda Woodhead, ed., *Peter Berger and the Study of Religion* (London: Routledge, 2001).

[64] Hans Kohn, *The Idea of Nationalism* (New York: MacMillan, 1944), 8. See also *Prophets and Peoples: Studies in Nineteenth Century Nationalism* (New York: MacMillan, 1942).

[65] See Elie Kedourie, *Nationalism in Asia and Africa* (London: Weidenfeld & Nicolson, 1971).

[66] Anthony D. Smith, *Nationalism and Modernism*, 109–12.

[67] See Mosse, *The Nationalization of the Masses: Political Symbolism and Mass Movements in Germany from the Napoleonic Wars through the Third Reich* (Ithaca: Cornell University, 1991), 2. Mosse sees nationalism as a popular civic religion with secular, political liturgies and rites of mass participation; for example, Remembrance Sunday at the Cenotaph in 1919, and the Nuremburg rallies.

It is not only that institutionalised religion (the church) often played an important role in the legitimisation of the state and in fostering nationalist values, but more importantly that nationalism tapped into the same reservoir of ideas and symbols and emotions as religion; in other words, that religion was metamorphosed into nationalism.[68]

While the likes of Kedorie and Llobera are probably right – nationalism may well constitute the 'transvaluation', politicisation and 'ethnicisation' of universalist, transhistorical religious beliefs and practices – the terminology is questionable. It was not the abstract category of religion that metamorphosed into nationalism, but, in Europe at least, specifically Christian categories of thought and practice that were transmogrified by nationalist ideology.

In more recent literature, the theological roots of the political category of the nation and the rise of European nationalism are increasingly recognised. The ethnosymbolist approach of Smith and others allows for religious factors to contribute to the formation of nations and national identities as part of 'myth-symbol complexes'. For Smith,

> Such symbolic clusters are both subjective, in their reference to individual perceptions and beliefs, and objective because their patterning produces a structure of social relations and cultural institutions that persist across the generations, independent of any individual beliefs and perceptions.[69]

For example, Smith notes that 'myths' of divine election provide 'powerful cultural resources for ethnic persistence and mobilization'.[70] However, theological and religious factors are subordinated to the category of ethnicity that is the substantive basis of identity, thus denying the possibility that religious identity might be prior to, and definitive of, ethnicity. And while the religious dimension of the 'national question' is now once again admitted to respectable discussion, the nature and extent of the religious roots of nationhood are still largely uncharted,[71] and the specifically Jewish and Christian

---

[68] Josep Llobera, *The God of Modernity: The Development of Nationalism in Western Europe* (Oxford: Berg, 1994), 146.

[69] Smith, *The Nation in History*, 66.

[70] Smith, *The Nation in History*, 67.

[71] Recent work by Adrian Hastings and Mary Anne Perkins being notable exceptions. Moreover, there is a growing body of literature that examines the rise of religion in international relations and the phenomenon of what is, in effect, reverse engineering, whereby instead of nationalism co-opting traditional religions, traditional religions, as part of a rejection of Western modernity (rather

roots of the political category of the 'nation' are marginalised. As is apparent from the above argument, where theology and cultic practice are examined, the indefinable and abstract term 'religion' tends to be used, in place of any attempt to situate the analysis within the contexts of the specific history, beliefs and practices of particular faith traditions.[72] In trying to take account of the emergence of nationalism and modern strains of cosmopolitanism, it is necessary to locate them within an account of how they constitute a deviance from the particularities of Christian belief and practice.

The deification of humanity

Historically, something like the above scriptural cosmopolitan vision did inform the emergence of different political communities from late antiquity onwards. As Peter Brown argues that a universal cosmopolitan vision – with a concomitant universal law – only gains momentum in the late Roman Empire, with the church conceived of as a universal community, transcending ethnicity, nation, family and local custom. Judith Herron notes that the universalist claims of Rome had always been challenged by the Persian Empire, yet, with the rise of Christianity, a genuinely universal community came into being.[73] As she puts it:

> There is a sense in which the Christian faith, rather than the barbarian kingdoms, constituted the successor of the Roman Empire in the West. As a universal and fundamentally extra-territorial system, it could and did unite the various imperial remnants and non-Roman governments of the mid-sixth century. It could also extend Christian control to areas beyond the old imperial orbit – southern India, the Persian Gulf, Ireland, and the remoter parts of the British Isles.[74]

---

than modernity *per se*), co-opt nationalism. On this, see Mark Juergensmeyer, *The New Cold War: Religious Nationalism Confronts the Secular State* (Berkley: University of California, 1993) and Scott Thomas, *The Global Resurgence of Religion and the Transformation of International Relations: The Struggle for the Soul of the Twenty-First Century* (New York: Palgrave Macmillan, 2005).

[72] For an account of how the category of 'religion' came to be constructed, see Talal Asad, 'The Construction of Religion as an Anthropological Category', in *Genealogies of Religion: Discipline and Reasons of Power in Christianity and Islam* (Baltimore: Johns Hopkins University Press, 1993), 27–54.

[73] Judith Herrin, *The Formation of Christendom* (London: Phoenix Press, 2001), 73.

[74] Herrin, *The Formation of Christendom*, 126.

Brown points out that while the Roman *ius gentium* – with its notion of a law common to all peoples – was antecedent to the rise of the universal church, actual reference to *ius gentium* was not common before the codification of Roman law by the Emperor Justinian in the sixth century, long after the church had become one of the primary institutions of the Roman Empire.

For Brown, the actions of Constantine in calling together the Council of Nicea pre-date, and are of greater significance than, natural law theory to the development of the notion of a universal human community subject to one law. Brown notes:

> In 323, Constantine gathered together all the Christian bishops of his empire at Nicea ... for an 'ecumenical' – that is, a 'world-wide' – council, that included, even, a token party of bishops from Persia [that is, from a different empire not under Constantine's jurisdiction]. In so doing, he allowed the Christian Church to see itself, face to face, for the first time, as the privileged bearer of a universal law.[75]

He goes on to argue that, in contrast to the plethora of local customs and deities that characterised the polytheistic Roman Empire, the church constituted a coherent, universal community with its own universal law – contained in the Bible, now collected in easy to transport and consult *codices* – that was exalted even above the emperor. What was remarkable about Christianity, given its cultural diversity and geographic spread, was its consistency across the empire.[76] In short, it was neither the previously polytheist empire, nor the legal notion of *ius gentium*, nor even the Stoics, that provided the impetus or catalyst for the widespread conception of a universal *cosmopolis*; rather, it was the church, both as institution and as an 'imagined community'.

From the Renaissance onwards, we see the eclipse of the theological vision of the church as the concrete embodiment of the universal commonwealth in which each particular nation or local polity moved beyond itself into divine and human communion. It is eclipsed by a rival vision of an autonomous, 'natural' universal human community. Both are deeply influenced by Aristotle and notions of the *ius gentium* and natural rights. However, in the former (as witnessed subsequently in the likes of Vitoria, Saurez and Grotius, and continued in certain strands of both Catholic and Protestant social thought), there is a

---

[75] Peter Brown, *The Rise of Western Christendom: Triumph and Diversity AD 200–1000* (Oxford: Blackwell, 1997), 22.

[76] Brown, *The Rise of Western Christendom*, 32.

commonwealth of nations – Christian or otherwise – that can seek a common good of nations that ultimately finds its *telos* beyond itself in the communion of all humans together with God. In the latter (as witnessed subsequently in the likes of Montaigne, Jean Bodin, Locke and Liebniz, and eventually coming to fulfilment in Bentham and Kant and the subsequent tradition of liberal internationalism), *pietas* owed to the nation is not teleologically ordered to the love of humanity, but is subsumed within it: that is to say, love for humanity precedes, and has priority over, love of one's particular neighbour. This latter view is best summarised by Liebniz's statement that: 'I am indifferent to that which constitutes a German or a Frenchman because I will only the good of all mankind.'[77] The concomitant of this rationalist cosmopolitanism was natural religion expressed in the genre of tracts known as the *Catéchèse de humanité*; for example, the encyclopaedist Saint-Lambert's *Catéchèse universelle*, that instructed the public in their rights and duties as a brotherhood of mankind, an allegiance that the Enlightenment philosophers believed preceded any other religious or national loyalty.[78] In short, *pietas* to humanity or human nature is understood as overriding *pietas* owed to one's particular community or to God. By contrast, Christian accounts of what *pietas* is owed to whom consistently envisage *pietas* to family and nation as being ordered to *pietas* for humanity which itself is ordered to the *pietas* we owe to God.

The deification of the nation

In a parallel but opposite move, it is from the Renaissance onwards that the ongoing problem of how loyalty to God and church is to be reconciled with loyalty to one's political master and ties of kinship is increasingly resolved, both ideologically and practically, in favour of political authority and kinship conceived of in terms of nationhood.[79] The rise of civic patriotism – notably in fifteenth and early sixteenth-century Florence, from Bruno Latini to Machiavelli – reverses the earlier

---

[77] Quoted from Thomas Schlereth, *The Cosmopolitan Ideal in Enlightenment Thought* (Notre Dame: University of Notre Dame, 1977), xxiv–xxv.

[78] Schlereth, *The Cosmopolitan Ideal*, 90. For a review of the different approaches to international relations and schemes to bring world peace set out by Enlightenment philosophers, see Schlereth, *The Cosmopolitan Ideal*, 90–125.

[79] It is a conflict that is exemplified in the medieval period by the Investiture Controversy and the practice of simony.

process whereby the New Jerusalem usurped Rome as the primary focus of *pietas*. In Smith and Hutchinsons' view:

> A strong and consciously classical emphasis on civic virtue and solidarity became an important component of later civic nationalism, duly transposed to larger territories and populations. This in turn drew on ancient Greek and Roman models, notably patriotism of the *polis* and its ideological contrast between Greek liberties and barbarian servitude.[80]

Thus, at the Renaissance begins the process, which comes to fruition in the American and French revolutions, whereby the New Jerusalem in subordinated to the earthly city: that is to say, the *polis* rather than the *ekklēsia* becomes the locus of human fulfilment. However, if one's earthly city increasingly became the dominant object of devotion, this did not mean that Christian categories of thought were abandoned. Rather, they were transposed on to the earthly city: what had previously been seen as the domain of the church became projected on to the nation.

The nation or fatherland came to be seen as the foundation of society. Such a view is anticipated by Baruch Spinoza, who, writing in 1670, states in chapter nineteen of his *Tractatus Theologico-Politicus*: 'There is no doubt that devotion to country is the highest form of piety a man can show; for once the state is destroyed nothing good can survive.'[81] However, it is at the French Revolution that such a view is popularised and disseminated, and it is in the work of Abbé Emmanuel Sieyès, one of the key polemicists of the French Revolution, that it is most clearly articulated. Sieyès in his pamphlet entitled: 'What is the Third Estate?' declares that the nation is the sovereign ground of politics: it 'exists before all else', it is the 'origin of all things', it is independent of all forms and conditions, and its law is always the supreme law. In other words, Sieyès the theologian gave the nation the traditional predicates of God.[82] The nation becomes the ground and embodiment of the will of the people. Similarly, Johann Gottfried Herder, another key thinker in the growth of nationalism, developed the idea of the 'spirit of the people'. He claims that historical reality brings to manifestation a metaphysical substance that binds the members of a people to national identity, meaning that national solidarity rests on the participation

---

[80]   Hutchinson and Smith, 'Introduction', 6.
[81]   Quoted from O'Brien, *God Land*, 49.
[82]   Schneider, 'Patriotism, Nationalism and the Duties of Citizens', 38.

of the people in this metaphysical substance – the nation.[83] If Sieyès replaces God the Father with the fatherland, Herder replaces God the Spirit with the spirit of the people. All that is needed is for messianic figures (such as Attaturk or Hitler) to step into the place of Christ as the embodiment or 'incarnation' of the nation. Thus, the shift from patriotism (understood as a love for one's nation that is ordered to a range of other loves) to nationalism (understood as the deification of the nation resulting in total devotion to the nation) can be seen as a response to the problem of political authority that so concerned early modern political thinkers such as Rousseau: that is, what constitutes the unity of the polity and the proper ground of political authority.

The deification of the nation must also be seen, as Gellner argues, as Romanticism's reaction against the rationalism of the Enlightenment.[84] Taking closer account of the theological dimension of this reaction than Gellner, O'Brien states:

> The Enlightenment removes a personal God, object of fear and love. It delegitimizes kingship, by desacralizing it. What is left? In theory, humanity is left. But humanity is at best a colorless abstraction. For most minds, and most nervous systems, penetrated by the Enlightenment, there was nothing left but the people – a particular people in a particular land, together with which it constituted the nation. The idea of a deified nation begins to beckon.[85]

Hence, as Alter summarises it: 'In nationalism, the religious is secularised, and the national sanctified.'[86] Thus, in many ways, nationalism constituted a religious surrogate. The response may be judged to be wrong, but the question of whether human personhood and social identity can be constituted in solely material and political terms remains.

---

[83] For an assessment of Herder's work in relation to the rise of nationalism see: Perkins, *Nation and Word*, 58–62. Perkins pays special attention to how Herder's theory of language related to his sacralisation of the nation.

[84] Ernest Gellner, *Nationalism* (London: Phoenix, 1997), 66–71. See also, Michael Howard, *The Invention of Peace: Reflections on War and International Order* (London: Profile Books, 2000), 36–40.

[85] O'Brien, *God Land*, 49. See also Perkins, *Nation and Word*, 35. In her study of the period 1770 to 1850, Perkins draws attention to the theological 'backdrop' of national self-consciousness.

[86] Peter Alter, *Nationalism* (trans. Stuart McKinnon-Evans; London: Edward Arnold, 1989), 10.

Conclusion

It is my contention that the development of the nation as a political category, and its mutation into nationalism, is first and foremost a theological and moral problem. It is a theological and moral problem before it is a political and historical problem, because the question of how to value the nation is first of all a question of how to order our love for our neighbours, both near and far.

The co-option of the category of 'nationhood' by various political communities over the course of European history (although not exclusive to European history) is a process whereby particular commonwealths have been shaped in response to a variety of missiological and ecclesial developments. In doing so, these political communities have appropriated a way in which they could conceive of themselves as at once a shared community of identity, one political community among others, and a community under the authority and judgement of God. This kind of relativised conception of nationhood has a deep scriptural and theological foundation. What do not are the various anthropocentric nationalist and cosmopolitan visions that either over- or undervalue particular national identities.

Metavista

Bible, Church and Mission in an Age of Imagination

Colin Green and Martin Robinson

The core narrative of the Christian faith, the book that conveys it (the Bible) and the institution of the church have all been marginalised by the development of modernity and post-modernity. Strangely, post-modernity has created an opportunity for religious thinking and experience to re-enter the lives of many. Yet, despite its astonishing assault on modernity, post-modernity is not itself an adequate framework for thinking about life. There is therefore a new opportunity for Christians to imagine what comes *after* post-modernity and to prepare the church, its book and its story for a new engagement of mission with western culture. The church on the margins, through a creative missionary imagination can audaciously re-define the centre of western cultural life. This book will attempt to sketch what such an approach might look like

> 'If you have a taste for the subversive, a passion for the church, a heart for biblical engagement, and an eye on the future; this book is a must-read.' – **Roy Searle**, Northumbria Community, former President of the Baptist Union of Great Britain

Colin Greene is Professor of Theological and Cultural Studies at Mars Hill Graduate School in Seattle. He is author of *Christology in Cultural Perspective*.
Martin Robinson is an international speaker, a writer, and Director of 'Together in Mission'.

978-1-84227-506-1

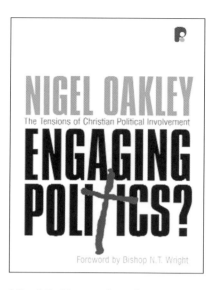

Engaging Politics?

The Tensions of Christian Political Involvement

Nigel Oakley

Nigel Oakley explores how Christians can, indeed must, engage with politics and with political debate. He shows, in chapters on Augustine, Liberation Theology, Dietrich Bonhoeffer and Stanley Hauerwas how certain tensions exist in every strand of Christian political thinking; and then he applies those tensions to case studies varying from today's highly charged debates on sexuality to the war on terrorism. This book is both an intelligent introduction to the difficult world of Christian political theology and to some of the key debates that are shaping our times.

'A constructive Christian position for the more difficult challenges facing us in our world today.' – **Stanley Hauerwas**, Professor of Theological Ethics, Duke Divinity School, North Carolina

'This book will be an important tool for individuals and churches.' – **N.T. Wright**, Bishop of Durham

'This hugely informative book will rescue Christians from simplistic or monochrome answers to the complexity of wrestling with political realities.' – **Christopher J.H. Wright**, International Director, Langham Partnership International

'A thought-provoking, stimulating and action-inducing read.' – **Steve Chalke MBE**, Founder of Oasis Global and Faithworks

978-1-84227-505-4